A

Home Life
In History

Pictorial Plan of a Feudal Manor.
(The perspective has been distorted to make the arrangement
and character of the various buildings clearer.)

Home Life in History

Social Life and Manners in Britain, 200 B.C. - A.D. 1926

by John Gloag *and*
C. Thompson Walker

Illustrated by
A. B. Read, A.R.C.A.

London
Ernest Benn Ltd
Bouverie House, Fleet Street
1927

Made and Printed in Great Britain
by H. & J. Pillans & Wilson, *Printers*, Edinburgh

To
John Metcalfe

CONTENTS

LIST OF ILLUSTRATIONS

INTRODUCTION

IT is the purpose of this book to show as clearly as possible representative examples of home life in Britain from the days of the pre-Roman British princes to the first quarter of the twentieth century. Our chapters are concerned with a broad outline of social conditions, also with meals, manners, and conversation ; so that each chapter tries to answer three questions about the people of the period with which it deals :—1. Where did they live ? 2. How did they live ? 3. What did they think and talk about ? No attempt is made to deal exhaustively with any one period—a task that would expand each chapter to a greater length than the entire book.

To help the lucid indication of links between times and changes and to illustrate the transitions from one phase of civilisation to another, progressive or retrogressive as the case may be, we have as a thread running through our chapters a more personal note in the history of a hypothetical family of Britons ; intelligent, hardy people of original Celtic stock, who assimilate, modify, and improve the influences that come with Romans, Saxons, and other invaders. As Mr G. G. Coulton has written : " It is very difficult to compare human lives at different times and in different places. Yet without such comparisons, explicit or implicit, social history can teach us nothing. . . ."

This is not a text-book in any academic sense. It is an endeavour to show something of the lives of our forerunners, avoiding as far as possible the misleading trick of perspective—tempting to the pens of those who write about the past—of giving to the centuries that are near to us a lion's share of consideration.

J. G.
C. T. W.

" Historians rarely descend to those details from which
alone the real state of a community
can be collected."
MACAULAY.

The ancient British home.

CHAPTER I

" BEFORE THE ROMAN CAME TO RYE . . ."

BRITAIN of the Druids and the native kings was
not a savage land of painted, uncouth warriors,
without art or ease or understanding of the mixed
blessings of commerce. The Celtic civilisation that
prepared the way for Roman conquerors and colonists
was by no means rudimentary; it encouraged the production of such decorative things as enamel, and the crafts
of the potter, weaver, and dyer flourished in pre-Roman
times.[1]

Britain was not devoid of cities, although architecture
was certainly undeveloped; but the picture so often
derived from a study of text-books on history, of hordes
of hairy, blue-painted savages rushing about the country
in wicker chariots with scythes affixed to the axles is
perhaps a little misleading. The Britons had chariots;
the more exalted classes fought in them, even as in
mediæval days the flower of chivalry and nobility was
mounted. The Britons also used woad,[2] but however

[1] Cf. Diodorus Siculus. See also collections in British and other museums.
[2] Julius Cæsar, and Pliny, *Nat. Hist.*, lib. XXII., cap. 2.

hardy and richly endowed with qualities of endurance, no people could long survive in Britain if coloured patterns on the skin formed their only clothing. The popular conception of nude Britons is presumably founded on the fact that the Britons wore little or no clothing in battle.

Our knowledge of ancient Britain is full of gaps. To reconstruct a convincing picture of life in that old, lost land is almost impossible. To make pictures of life in any period or place is difficult, even if the scenes to be drawn are contemporary. Suppose one wanted to write a description of a dinner party in Manchester in 1925, and had available as information street plans of Manchester, a complete knowledge of what sort of shops there were in those streets, and a fair idea of what was sold in them, the number of theatres in the city, the sort of clothes the various classes of people wore, the sort of things they had to eat and drink, and the type of people present at the dinner party in question ; although one would be in possession of more data than it is possible to obtain concerning any British, Romano-British, or Saxon city or settlement, it would be incredibly hard to write about that dinner party without the generous help of imagination. The setting of life in a period and place may be re-created, and our imagination stimulated to accept a possible picture, but the life itself is lost to us unless we can conceive the permanence of a national type.

Although Britain had certain arts and crafts and trade relations with the Continent, it was not possible for Celtic civilisation to flower fully because it lacked unity. There was wealth enough in the country, minerals of sufficient value and importance to bring those hardy Semites, the Phœnicians, to the coasts of Cornwall, and agriculture flourished in a few localities. The cultivated regions were chiefly districts near the Continent,[1] but they were not systematically extended because tribal war was a

[1] Cf. John Ward, *The Roman Era in Britain*, Chap. I., p. 3.

popular pastime, and the dense forest-belts kept the British tribes separate and suspicious. Not only was this intertribal suspicion an obstacle to a higher standard of life, but distrust, if not positive dislike, was extended to foreigners, and it is improbable that foreign traders ever established more than a coastal trade, at most penetrating to those queer, half-buried cities of earth and stone [1] that were fairly near the southern sea, and were reached by trackways through the grim forests. To visualise those dark forests with their bears, wolves, and wild cats is to gain a glimmer of understanding of the power possessed by the Druidical cults with their flavour of human sacrifice, their imposing ritual, and the mysteries they practised. The enclosing of wrongdoers in cages of wicker, half a dozen or so of poor wretches assembled in a vast structure that bore a rude likeness to a human figure, and their ceremonious roasting by a slow fire ; [2] the bearded Druids in their white robes assisted by the minor classes of priests in robes of sky blue and green,[3] all officiating at this happy blending of law, order, and entertainment for the spectators ; such scenes would be in keeping with the grim, perpetual twilight of the woods, and they may have burnt into the British character the sense of righteous enjoyment that made the survival of spectacular punishment possible until the nineteenth century.

An atmosphere more humid than we know, a heavier rainfall, choked rivers, marsh and morass, and stretch after stretch of woodland, damp and misty ; and running through it all the scarlet thread of tribal war, a vigorous colour in a sombre tapestry : that was ancient Britain. But there were clearings and settlements, streets of round

[1] Cf. Publications of Pitt-Rivers, and Robert Munro, *Pre-Historic Britain.*
[2] Cf. Cæsar, *de Bell. Gall.*, lib. VI.
[3] According to Dion Cassius there were three degrees of priesthood—Druids, who wore white robes ; Bards, who wore sky blue ; and Ovates, who wore green. The Ovates professed to a knowledge of astronomy and medicine.

huts of wood and stone, encircled by ditches and stock-ades,[1] and in those settlements life of a not very elegant sort imposed its duties and hardships upon people whose interests and activities were few but concentrated. The southern and eastern districts of Britain, partly by reason of their closer contact with the Continent, the coastal trade and the handling of imported goods, were higher in standards of civilisation, and we may go back to the second century before Christ and rebuild what we can of life in a Celtic settlement, the Cær Gwent of the south, a name that means White City, and which afterwards became a Romano-British city of some eminence, and centuries later an ecclesiastical centre and the capital of all England —Winchester. The Romans called the place Venta Belgarum, a name that aptly described its ancient British significance, for it was literally the outlet of the Belgic Tribe at the head of the Itchen valley which led down to the Solent ; a situation that made it accessible to the coastal trade and possibly a distributing centre for imports.

A citizen of this settlement might enjoy the highest standards that life could offer. To appreciate the limitations and possibilities and interests of that life, we must try to get a glimpse of the citizen, imagining him to be a man of wealth, courage, and ability ; perhaps a little faster in thought than his fellows. In appearance he would be broad shouldered, not very tall, with a dark skin, lightish brown hair, a face clean shaven, save for long, streaming moustaches—an immense, impressive, walrus-like growth. Around his neck a torque of spiral twisted gold would gleam, and on his head he would wear a cap, a long, inelegant helmet of woven material, not unlike a Balaclava helmet. His woad-tattooed body would be clad in a tunic of brightly coloured squares, a patchwork quilt effect, only with a very limited range of colours—red, green, and blue. Loose baggy trousers

---

[1] Cf. Munro, *opus cit.*, Chap. IX.

covered his legs, gathered in at the ankles and bound with strips of hide, and he would have a cloak, a plaid of coloured squares resembling his tunic, draped about his body with the ends passing through a ring on one shoulder. On his bare arms three or four gold bracelets would jingle, a gold brooch might keep his cloak in place, and for weapons, a bronze knife and dagger in his hide belt, and a small spear, which was probably used for a walking stick when out of doors as well as for protection, and a shield of ox-hide covered with a very brassy bronze, with a central boss ringed round with smaller bosses or studs to the edge. Perhaps he would carry an axe, and in winter an ox-hide or fur cloak would probably be added to his outdoor equipment.[1]

His wealth would be represented by goods, for although ancient Britain had a coinage—a primitive imitation of the coins of Philip of Macedon,[2] crude to a degree—it was in metals, pottery, fabrics, ornaments, brooches, torques, bracelets, cloak rings, safety pins (fibulæ), knives, spears, axes, and agricultural implements, sickles, hoes, and so forth,[3] and in accumulations of grain that riches were recognised. Land, except in the agricultural localities, would not have much importance for the individual tribesman. The wealth of our particular tribesman, Doli of the Belgæ, would be derived from trade. The Itchen valley might be a very important inlet for trade, not only with Phœnician merchants, but with Gaul. A little farther west towards Cornwall foreigners would come for tin and lead, and oysters from the south and east would be an additional inducement to enterprising traders. Doli, conducting his commercial operations from Cær

---

[1] This description is largely drawn from Munro, *opus cit.*, Dion Cassius, Diodorus Siculus, Julius Cæsar, and Herodian.

[2] See Bernard Roth, F.S.A., Vice-President, British Numismatic Society, in *A Literary and Historical Atlas of Europe* (Coinage Section).

[3] Examples of all these goods are to be seen in the British, Guildhall, York, Reading, and many other museums.

Gwent, would exchange skins of sheep, bear, badger, wolf, squirrel, fox, marten, and mole for fabrics, metals, and ornaments. Trade would be a vastly important consideration in his life.

The background of that life would be the smoke-grimed interior of a stone beehive hut, probably with a large chamber excavated below, roofed with timber, a store-house and perhaps a refuge should the settlement be raided and sacked in the course of a tribal war.[1] Without would be the narrow, dirty streets, unpaved, deep in mud, threading their way amid the humped shapes of other huts until the strong bordering walls of stone and earth marked the limit of this rudimentary city.[2] Day by day Doli would see a few men and women of the wealthier class clad like himself, the women, so far as clothes went, looking rather like the men, and the poorer tribesmen wearing sheepskin, cowhide, wolf, and bearskin garments instead of plaid cloaks and tunics.[3] His food would be monotonous, the raw materials of a meal changing but little from their original state when killed or gathered. During winter he would eat in the hut, in which there might be two rooms, if it was of the larger thatched variety, with a midden at the back. In the hut were rough tables of smoothed logs resting on stones or other logs, perhaps trestles ; stools, possibly of wicker, for people who could make coracles of wicker and dug-out canoes would conceivably apply their wood-working skill, such as it was, in other directions ; also a hide bed, or a wicker bed with hides on it. Hides hung on the stone walls, there were holes for windows covered at night, a stamped earth floor, and a gutter round the house to carry off water, leaving the interior passably dry : such was the setting of indoor life.

Set out on the rough tables at meals would be barley

---

[1] Munro, *opus cit.*, Chap. IX.   [2] *Ibid.*
[3] Cf. Dion Cassius, Pliny, and Julius Cæsar.

bread or bannocks, and although game and cattle, bear and wild boar would provide a variety of meats, cooking would be too primitive to provide anything except a wearying round of stew. Seething or boiling would be the usual treatment for meat, being more certain in results and also economical, for the meat would be eaten and the broth drunk. Rarely, very rarely, a roast would enliven the dullness of those meals, but such a departure would probably mark some special occasion, a feast, for instance, and it would be a spit roast, a spit of green wood being used. In extravagant outbursts of hospitality and feasting, a beast might be roasted whole. Grain soaked in sheep's milk, a sort of porridge or frumenty, might be another item of the ancient British menu. Although Doli and others of his kind and wealth probably experimented a little with spices brought by Phœnician traders, food would be nearly always unseasoned, half-cooked, and taste uncultivated, regard being given to quantity. This would suggest that table manners displayed voracity rather than elegant enjoyment; feeding was an orgy unqualified by any touch of art.

Bowls, spoons, and drinking vessels of alabaster, jade, and coarse earthenware, would grace the tables of the wealthy; humbler folk would be content with drinking horns, although a kind of pewter might be found in Doli's hut and in the homes of his poorer neighbours. He would accompany his gigantic meals with draughts of beer, possibly honey drinks, mead, sometimes milk, and imported wine, wine harsh and sweet, brought in skins from Greece and Spain, wine too common for any other market than Britain, where palates were easily pleased, and where men demanded of wine but two things, that it should be wet and potent.

Conditions were not favourable to sustained conversation, but the interests and manifold dangers of Doli's life provided three important topics round and about which

drifted the talk at meals and after.   First, for it touched
the life of every one very nearly, religion and the supply of
criminals.   The connexion seems strange, but it was very
real, for the Druidical mysteries which demanded periodic
human sacrifice had to be supplied with subjects, and if
there was a shortage of wrongdoers, innocent men were
condemned to those wicker cages of burning death.
Trade and the visits of traders from Gaul and the Medi-
terranean would come next in importance, and then war,
the red threat that always lurked beyond the immediate
forest-belt.

Discussed by a slow thinking and inarticulate people,
not unlike modern Britons, but very, very much slower
in their mental processes, these intensely dramatic topics
would be invested with a power, a grim significance that
would make boredom impossible.   Sport as such would
not be discussed ; wrestling, the use of weapons, hunting,
and all those things that gain a gallant importance in more
civilised countries would be everyday items of a hard-
working life.

Music might enter a little into the feasting that marked
some great event; mainly it would be employed in religion,
but an occasional story-teller, some bardic forerunner of
the novelist, might be tolerated in phases of security from
war and (by reason of abundant crime) the claims of
religion.   But picture the end of a meal in Doli's house in
midwinter in a period of general personal insecurity,
when men regard one another a little suspiciously, as
if fearing conspiracies that will accuse them of some
uncommitted crime to placate the forces of established
religion ; when the weather is damp and cold and a sea
mist drifts up the valley to the settlement.   The meal
has been without wine, the storms having set ships off
their track, and no trader has touched the coast for weeks.
A smoky fire is all that lights the dark, hide-hung walls.
The air is stifling, hot with the smell of stale food and

A Druid in white robes . . . stands before the feasters.

unwashed humanity. A few chiefs among the traders squat uneasily about the grease-coated table with its bones and crumbs.   Outside the rain sluices down, purring into the ditch around the house.   The next victim has been talked over and speculated upon until everybody's flesh creeps with apprehension, and then there is a long, low wailing of a horn [1] beyond the walls of the settlement, and presently the hissing and spluttering of rain against torches ; the stone is rolled from the door of the house, the hide curtain torn aside, and a Druid in white robes and a gleaming sun-disc [2] on his breast stands before the feasters.   Without are two Ovates in dark green holding aloft blazing torches which flicker in the wind and rain. The company is paralysed.   The Druid points first to Doli and then to three of his guests.   They rise and go after him as men already dead, casting off their torques and bracelets as they leave the house, and march in this ghastly torchlight procession to the inky forest, followed by the wailing of their wives. [3]

[1] A specimen of a Druidical horn or trumpet may be seen in the British Museum.
[2] Specimens may be seen in the British Museum.
[3] Women may have been associated in an official capacity with these Druidical ceremonies.   Tacitus, describing the attack of Suetonius upon the island of Mona (Anglesey, the stronghold of Druidism), says : " On the shore there were armed men in dense array, and women running amid them like furies, who, in gloomy attire, and with loose hair hanging down, carried torches before them." Describing another form of Druidical sacrifice, Diodorus says : " Pouring out a libation upon a man as a victim, they smite him with a sword upon the breast on the part near the diaphragm, and on his falling who has been thus smitten, both from the manner of his falling, and from the convulsions of his limbs, and still more from the manner of the flowing of his blood, they presage what will come to pass."

CHAPTER II

THE IMPERIAL SCHOOLMASTER

NEARLY three centuries have passed since certain painful rites were performed in some forest clearing on the person of Doli, a former citizen of Cær Gwent. But now, in A.D. 80, the smoke of the Druidical fires can only be seen by those who care to penetrate the forests that lie far from the arrow-straight roads that are beginning to form a network over Southern Britain, wooded retreats of the old, fierce but failing culture that even the most tolerant Roman official cannot brook. Britain has become an Imperial Province, and during two of the three centuries since Doli's death, his descendants have seen small progress in the art of living.

The Roman invasions and the settlement of numbers of officials and camp followers, made Britain for a time into a savage and resentful colony. The natives were misunderstood. The first Roman rulers, being generally of military training, could not always bring to bear the administrative subtlety that the character of the ancient Briton probably demanded. The colonists found the natives slow in thought, and impatient and uninterested they may have dismissed the British race briefly as brave but brainless. Consequently a certain tactlessness made their handling of the problems of government particularly unfortunate. There were risings, culminating in the fiery outburst of the Iceni under that inflamed amazon Boudicca.[1] On that occasion there were appalling atrocities. Camulodunum (Colchester) and Londinium (London) suffered horrible things before the Roman

---

[1] Generally, though inaccurately, known as Boadicea.

military machine could put matters right again, remove the rebels, and repair the wrecked cities. But afterwards the southern part of Britain gained freedom from disturbances and began to develop cities, traffic, and wealth. In the north, the Brigantes organised periodical rebellions, and in the far north, Rome did not make even a pretence at ruling apart from punitive expeditions when raids became too serious.

About A.D. 80, a descendant of Doli [1] lived within a few miles of Londinium, within easy reach of the smooth, straight road that led from the northern suburbs of the city to the old British settlement of Verulamium,[2] now in course of reconstruction as a Roman city. This Briton was, like his ancestor, a man of wealth according to the standards of his time, and he looked at the civilisation the Romans were introducing and found it good. He was impressed with its power, its perfection compared with the setting of his childhood and the surroundings his father had deemed desirable, and its innumerable gifts, material, sensual, and—although he would in no way have understood the meaning of the term—spiritual. Unlike his father he was bilingual, for he had learned Latin from the soldiers of a Roman detachment encamped near his home when he was a child ; learned it with all a child's aptitude for picking up knowledge forbidden by his parents ; acquired the words that would enable him to wheedle out of the rough, good-humoured men who wore hoopy bronze armour, tales of their adventures, and to understand those endless stories of marches, voyages, bitter campaigns in far lands, guards carried out in this or that governor's palace, in sun-bit Judea or Egypt, or in the city of cities, great Rome, where the Emperor lived. Those same good-natured story-tellers would give him

[1] See Appendix I. (page 265) for a list of the descendants of Doli, from 214 B.C. to A.D. 1926.
[2] The modern St Albans.

worn dice to play with, and sometimes a small share of their rations. There were other children who played about the camp, but it was this boy, Uassi, who became known to every man of the detachment. To the Romans he was Varasius, a name he finally adopted when his father died and he became head of his family and a man of some power and considerable wealth in his neighbourhood. Even as a child he saw the immense resources of power Rome commanded. He saw fresh faces come to the camp, and old friends go ; an ever-moving stream of traffic on the trackway that led through the camp, and, when he was eleven, a whole legion in all the pomp and glitter of military glory marched along that track on its way to relieve Londinium from the raid of the Iceni. And then there were engineers supervising the making of the track into something more than a track ; and after he had got used to seeing a smooth roadway of stone where once a worn earth footway ran, he saw more of Rome's power. That road was an endless story of the power that can secure wealth; along it streamed a pageant of commerce and enterprise, a procession of such vivid interest that Varasius suffered almost continual correction at home for haunting that road hour after hour. There would be hunters and trappers from the north, coming to Londinium with bears and wolves they had caught to be shipped to Rome for the theatres ; there were merchants setting out on trading expeditions with armed guards of Britons, equipped in somewhat clumsy imitation of the Roman legionary ; Roman officials with their guards, sometimes in litters carried by four slaves, and chariots accompanied by clattering horsemen ; trucks with pigs of lead from the north,[1] grain from the south on its way to Eboracum (York) or Deva (Chester), wine skins slung

[1] The lead mines in Nidderdale, Yorkshire, were being worked before A.D. 87. A pig of lead from these mines stamped with that date and the name of the Emperor Domitian may be seen in the British Museum.

on rough carts—an altogether wonderful road for a boy
who realised that his father and mother had known
nothing like it when they were young, for it was something new in the world, and he and this new thing were
growing up together and sharing a world that was very
exciting.[1]

Possessions and responsibility were to increase the
inclination of Varasius for things Roman and for the
wider wealth that Rome's guiding hand on Britain made
possible.   Varasius was born and reared in a stone hut,
and his business was mainly agricultural, raising grain and
sheep and supplying provisions to the Roman garrisons,
first to the road station, and, by dint of diplomacy and
well planned bribes, eventually to the garrisons of Londinium and Verulamium.   As a contractor he gained
wealth in forms distrusted by the older generation, but
believing as he did in the extreme desirability of all things
Roman, he acquired money and buried the coins in his
stone house until that same house began to fill him with
increasing distaste.   His business expanded as the building of Londinium and Verulamium and their suburbs went
forward, for he supplied timber and chalk.   There was
an enormous demand for raw materials, especially chalk,
in consequence of the proportions lime burning would
have assumed.[2]

We may figure him as a man of some importance, not
yet of middle age, conscious of his possessions and
anxious to gain full advantage of them.   Life in a stone
hut becomes absurd, and Roman architects are not above
accepting commissions for house building from wealthy

---

[1] Cf. W. St Clair Baddeley, *History of Cirencester*, Chap. IV., p. 51.

[2] Lethaby in *Londinium* referring to the Roman use of mortar and concrete,
says : " Roman builders early learnt how to make good mortar and concrete,
being careful to use clean coarse gravel and finely divided lime."   T. Wright
says : " Roman mortar was generally composed of lime, pounded tiles, sand, and
gravel, more or less coarse, and even small pebbles."   The Romans vastly
enlarged the existing British caves at Chislehurst, Kent, for instance, to obtain
chalk for lime burning.

natives. The Roman officials may smile at the spectacle of comfort and luxury taming a tribesman, but it is not a process they would ever discourage. Varasius builds his house, native workmen carrying out the instructions of an architect who is beginning to wonder whether the Britons are such fools as most Romans think — this interesting speculation having been started after the conclusion of a seemingly innocent bargain with Varasius regarding his maintenance during the supervision of building operations.

The house itself is a dream of wonder to Varasius and his wife. That lady would not be consulted regarding such important matters as building, but Varasius has indicated that her fashions in clothes, her ideas and behaviour, must be Roman and nothing else when they move into this palace of brick, cool concrete, and smooth plaster, with glowing floors of coloured stones (*tesseræ*) and walls patterned with stories of the Roman gods, designed by second-rate artists.[1] The house is of one storey, low, and shaped like an E without the middle member, a long arcaded front facing south, with a paved courtyard, flanked by the two wings of the building. The walls are of small red bricks, barred with courses of yellow tiles, sheltered by a tiled roof of red, the arches of the front springing from columns faced with plaster and painted in deep red and a corn coloured tone. The windows would be protected by iron, star-shaped guards. The house would be heated by a hypocaust, the flues going up from the hollow floors through the walls and provid-

[1] Fragments of a painted dado from a house at Caerwent have been described in *Archæologia*, LVIII., thus : " . . . there seems to have been an attempt to represent architecture in perspective, in far-away imitation of the later Pompeian styles of decoration ; but the colouring is crude in the extreme, and the intention of the artist by no means clear." Lethaby discussing Roman wall paintings in *Londinium* says : " Provincial Roman painting is not fine as compared with the great things in either Greek or Gothic art . . . it was the ordinary journeyman decorator's work of the time." Gordon Home, writing on the same subject in *Roman York*, says : " Taken as a whole, the designs were at about the same artistic level as that of the cheaper modern wallpapers."

Varasius inspects his future home.

ing a uniform temperature for each room. There would be a bath, one of the most important rooms of the house, for Varasius would not venture to expose ancient British traditions about washing to the ridicule of his architect, but it is possible that the bath would not be used with any frequency, at first. Lavatories, drainage, good water supply, all these things would raise the standard of life for Varasius so that his upbringing seemed horribly savage by comparison.[1] And then would come the difficulties of ignorance ; the task of living in this house when the architect had departed with his fees and the native workmen had been released from their obligatory labour.[2] It would be incredibly strange at first, but it increased his prestige with the Roman commanders in the two nearby cities, and even the Præfect of Britain, a most august gentleman in a white toga edged with purple, inspected this important tribute to Rome's civilising powers one flurried morning when Varasius was hunting in the woods to the west of the great North Road.

In appearance Varasius was entirely Romanised. His clothes of British-woven fabrics were cut in the Roman manner, and he sacrificed the check patterns of tradition for plain colours. Discarding his torque, he wore Roman ornaments such as fibulæ, ring brooches, bracelets, and one or more finger rings. The rough pieces of hide, laced together with sinews, that formed the clumsy footwear of his fathers were replaced by neat but heavy shoes. He was clean shaven, and his hair would have a barber's skill to change it from the matted mane his countrymen

[1] This description is largely drawn from details given by Lethaby in *Londinium*, John Ward in *Romano-British Buildings and Earthworks*, Gordon Home in *Roman York*, and from the published details and personal examination of many Romano-British sites.

[2] The tribal organisation with its family subdivisions obviously lent itself to serfdom. The strong man of the family or tribe was the natural chief who organised protection for his people in return for certain services of which free labour would assuredly be one. The natural development of this system led to the " villeinage " of a later period.

C

generally affected into the smoother and more ordered finish the Romans introduced.[1]

More and more did Varasius realise that his fortune and prosperity were bound up with Rome.   Everywhere he saw growing up about him convincing evidence of Roman accomplishment, and the ability of Roman-trained soldiers and officials to put the products of a country to strange and interesting uses.   Vast numbers of troops were now in Britain, and each Legion had its corps of craftsmen and artificers, skilled workmen who depended on British raw materials rather than on imported things, for the volume of shipping on the narrow seas was not sufficient to cope with the transport of a great bulk of cargo, being in the main devoted to the extensive troop and passenger-carrying traffic.

In the district over which he had tribal powers, a loose, adaptable, and ill-defined authority, he organised hunting, for the woodland was rich in game.   He began to regard his district as a means for producing wealth, and he felt his ignorance of governing in the easy, accomplished manner of Rome ; but he was not slow to borrow ideas. He was reasonably certain of support from the Roman officials in Verulamium and Londinium in all he did to further the cause of order and commerce.   Determined to win the best from his possessions, he grasped at power, magnifying traditional customs of service, both military and industrial, rendered by the rank and file of the tribe or settlement to its chief families.   His father had been a chief, and his family had ranked as gentry for generations ; but Varasius was the first chief of the new order, a master rather than a fatherly leader.   Being a far-seeing man, he was aware that his own people must be contented with his planning, and he suggested to his immediate neigh-

[1] Cf. J. R. Planché, *History of British Costume*. Throughout the chapters the descriptions of costumes are drawn, wherever possible, from contemporary descriptions, drawings, or sculpture, otherwise from the work referred to and *Costume in England*, by F. W. Fairholt, F.S.A.

bours, petty chiefs ruling certain areas, the benefits accruing from the adoption of such Roman customs as the provision of material for the slave markets of Londinium. The intertribal wars of Britain had provided a fairly steady flow of slaves to Rome before the settlement, and the rebellions from time to time brought fresh numbers of Britons into servitude in Italy or other parts of the Empire ; but it seldom occurred to British chiefs to dispose of their dependants and weaker tribesmen in this manner. By suggesting such a course to his fellow-chiefs, Varasius would strengthen his personal power in two ways : the number of his neighbour's followers would be depleted, and he would gain prestige among his own people for preserving them from actual slavery in far countries. He would be Roman enough to have slaves himself.

His whole domestic setting would be affected by his Roman proclivities. We have seen how his home was remodelled, and his wife, too, would reflect the vast strides made by her generation. She would be, if anything, more Romanised in her dress than Varasius himself. Clad in a long gown of coarse linen which was draped in folds, a strong coloured, not ungraceful garment, partially covered by a woollen robe with a fur cloak and hood, she would be a very different figure from her mother ; more dignified and more restrained in the matter of ornaments. Her hair would be dressed in the most ornate Roman style, agleam with decorative pins of bone, headed with gold and precious stones. Her personal possessions would include many things of bone, combs, pins, and so forth— for the Romans used bone for a number of objects which the Britons had never used—brooches of gold, bronze, and enamel, bracelets, rings, and necklaces of beads.[1]

His sons would do something unheard of, except in the case of one or two great chiefs in the past ; they would go

[1] Cf. Planché, *opus cit.*, and Home, *opus cit.*

to school, for the Governor-General of the Province, Gnæus Julius Agricola, established schools for the sons of British chiefs.[1]   This step opened the door to new codes, new manners, new modes of expression.   Of his three sons, the youngest desired of all things to be a soldier, and although rank and due honour awaited a chief's son in the British auxiliaries, a Roman Legion alone would content the youth.   Varasius used his influence with the Commandant of the Londinium garrison, an old, wise, and experienced soldier, a Spanish-born Roman, who had been a Tribune of Legio IX., Hispana, and whose long service had brought him the comfortable and honourable post he held in Britain's great port.   With all a soldier's enthusiasm for his old corps, he advocated the entry of Varasius's son, Varasius Brivinex, into Legio IX., which was then recovering and recruiting at Eboracum (York) after coping with a succession of revolts in the north.   A " crack " regiment with a great and splendid tradition behind it would not be unattractive to Varasius or his son, and through the old Tribune's recommendations and influence Varasius Brivinex was appointed Centurion to the tenth cohort of Legio IX., where he was to acquire a number of tastes, incur a variety of expenses, and bring home, during his occasional spells of leave, yet another supply of strange and foreign ideas.

The other sons of Varasius remained to help their father rule his district and develop its wealth.   A picture of their home life, a glance at one of their meals, would reveal a greater complexity in the business of living. Varasius, far removed from the " old man of the tribe " ideal of family life, would discuss over his abundant but inartistic meals the prospects of business.   He would sit down with his wife and children to food of much the same sort his father had known, though the cooking was better.   The introduction of spices was more general ;

[1] See Tacitus, *Agricola*, XXI.

wild vegetables such as boiled nettle would probably assist the meat courses, and after the Roman fashion there would be much wild fruit. The presence of the Ninth and Sixth Legions in Britain must have influenced and improved cooking, for both Legions had seen long service in Spain, and the wives of the legionaries, the countless camp followers, and the officers' cooks would certainly introduce fresh methods and influence taste in food. There were more wines, too, and certainly better manners. No longer would the dining table be a greasy and littered board ; the more elegant example of the Roman officials with whom Varasius had occasionally dined would leave its mark on meal times. Food would be eaten in a leisurely fashion ; fingers would seldom be pressed into service, knives and spoons being used chiefly for the various dishes. Possibly the diners would recline on couches ranged about a low table, but it is more probable that Varasius would not change his mode of eating so drastically, and would leave such ultra-Roman manners to his sons.

Brivinex, the young Centurion, would come home occasionally, whereupon the family would bestir them-selves in the matter of manners, and do their best to be up to date in behaviour under the eyes of this Roman-trained critic. Imagine the first meal he has with his family after a long absence, the first social rally after the passing of greetings and the exchange of news. Conversation naturally turns on the progress of the army in the north. Londinium was a clearing house for news from all over Britain, and all over the Empire for that matter, but in Brivinex they would have first-hand information from the raw, savage frontiers of the province. They would learn that the Brigantes, a most troublesome tribe, were well in hand for the moment.

Varasius would point out that the Legions did not have the monopoly of fighting.

" What fighting is there below Eboracum ? " asks Brivinex, tolerantly superior as befits a Roman officer who has survived two bloody campaigns in Northern Britain.

" None that the Legions have known since Boudicca's day," replies his father, " but we have had much trouble in getting our chalk of late."

It was true. The parties of chalk-cutters sent out to the spurs of the long hills to the west of the Verulamium road had been attacked by rival parties of labourers in the pay of a neighbouring chief, who denied the right of Varasius to monopolise the supply trade to the builders in the two adjacent cities.

" We have worked on that land season by season," said Varasius ; " it is *our* land, for chalk. It should be ours to hold."

" At least you can object," said Brivinex.

" We crucified ten thieves," said his eldest brother ; " the others ran. They should learn from that."

Varasius was doubtful regarding the wisdom of such strong action. His son had been too impetuous. It would cost him a heavy bribe to the magistrate of Verulamium to adjust matters. Suetonius, the magistrate in question, would insist that the crucifixion should have been done in the proper manner by legionaries delegated for civil executions. There would be endless difficulties and much expense. It would have been better, far better, to have killed the men and buried them quietly and without any needless fuss. He had sufficient claims upon his money for bribes in the ordinary way of business, and the money would have been better spent in getting all the orders from the Verulamium builders that were likely to be given during the next few moons.

The progress of Londinium and Verulamium building would occupy their talk for a time, business, prices, details of bribery and competition would be reviewed in turn. Religion as a subject fades into the background of life. It is no longer a menace : the easy nature-worship of the Romans had replaced the sanguinary Druidical cults, and Varasius and the tribesmen who worked for him violated the old beliefs by cutting down oaks and delivering the timber to the local builders. In ancient Britain the oak had been a sacred tree. In the Roman Province it was a business proposition. Nevertheless tradition could not be lost so quickly, and Varasius took no risks : he conformed with the official Roman religion, but he was also careful to erect a private altar near his house to the Genius Loci to meet the superstitions that lingered on in his mind.

A typical Romano-British house.

CHAPTER III

The Peaceful Province

VARASIUS prospered, and his sons after him continued the tradition of developing the possibilities of the flowering Romano-British civilisation, and extending their wealth thereby. Brivinex was killed during the destruction of his Legion, the Ninth, Hispana, at Eboracum in the second decade of the second century,[1] but his brothers, engaged in the safer and more comfortable courses of trade, made their families powerful in the south. With bigger lands beneath their control and a wider influence, warmed by the sunlight of official approval, these Romanised Britons were very different from their father, the earnest experimenter in new civilisation, and their sons, born in a more ordered and settled time, were different from them, but different only in degree of surface culture, education, and training. The seed of Varasius did not lose the hard-headed characteristics, the eye for the bargain, that their ancestors had developed in their long history of trafficking and trading with the adventurers of the earth.

So the main branch of the family progressed throughout the second century, until in the opening years of the third century Varies Claudius, a great-great-great-grandson of Varasius, was attracted to Eboracum by the vast promise of trade occasioned by the military operations of the Emperor Severus, who had made Eboracum his winter headquarters. Troops were pouring through the place, bound for the wild north, where the Caledonian savages

---

[1] Probably by the Brigantes. See Home, *Roman York*, and Oman, *England Before the Norman Conquest*, pp. 108 and 109.

were tricking the Roman officers and baffling the Legions who invaded their bleak country ; in the train of the Emperor had come a host of officials, hangers-on of the Court, lawyers, scribes, physicians, and a number of other professional men : and all these people had to be catered for by the scanty shops of the garrison city. Varies Claudius was the eldest son of his father, Julius Tertius, and he had seen the needs of Eboracum during a brief stay in one of the military hospitals there, for he had volunteered for service when the Southern Picts, or Meatæ, broke through Hadrian's Wall in 205, and had held a small command in some native British auxiliaries, and had been wounded badly in the foot and invalided home.

Settling in Eboracum shortly after Severus began his great northern campaign in 209, Varies Claudius proved that the special qualities of his family did not suffer from transplanting, and in the growing city it vied with the branch in the gentler south for power and possessions. It is with a descendant of this main line settled in the North that we are concerned, one Titus Paulinus, a Roman citizen, a member of the Ordo, or upper official class, a prosperous and cultivated gentleman who reaches his prime in the years immediately following the proclamation of Constantine I. as Cæsar at Eboracum in 306.

Eboracum in those days was attaining the zenith of its prosperity, and Titus Paulinus was intimately concerned with one of the great revenue-bearing assets of the locality, the lead mines and quarries that lay north of the road between Isurium (Ilkley) and Olicana (Aldboro'),[1] for he was general manager of the whole plant, a position of worth and dignity, and was, in addition, a Decurion, an ædile of Eboracum, or one of the superintendents of

[1] As noted on page 29, these ancient mines at Greenhow Hill, in Nidderdale, were being worked by the Romans as early as A.D. 87. Pigs of lead stamped with this date (Seventh of Domitian) have been unearthed there, and one of them is preserved in the British Museum,

public works, a municipal honour that enhanced his sense of importance very agreeably. The society in which he moved was essentially cultivated and wealthy, the official and military classes, British gentlemen with land and a pleasing, old-world flavour of hereditary titles, Roman citizens, of course, but apt to refer to the ancient glories of their stock—" our people were princes here before the Settlement " ; lawyers, distinguished visitors from more polished provinces who provoked imitation as to clothes and manners ; and on the more recreative side of life, philosophers, editors of games, and minor poets. His wealth was inherited rather than created by his own work, but it was maintained and enlarged during his lifetime. Lands had come to him from his father, rich lands where corn grew with prodigal abundance ;[1] and there were stretches of pasture-land also where slaves herded his cattle, and on the road from Eboracum to Calcaria (Tadcaster) his great house stood, a fine, dignified building. It was a well-planned, commodious place, easily gracious and toning with the landscape, unlike the first architectural essay in Romanisation attempted by his ancestor of seven generations before ; the house of Varasius in Agricola's time had looked what it was—a strange and foreign growth, pleasant enough, but of new things, very new. But about the home of Paulinus there was no suggestion of incongruity to mar its character. Built of millstone grit, weathered to a deep grey, it was a large corridor type of house, built round a spacious courtyard, roofed with limestone tiles, and heated like all the better class houses of Roman Britain with real skill, hypocausts warming floors and walls in the principal rooms, diffusing heat from several surfaces instead of radiating it from one spot in the manner of the coal or

[1] Corn from Britain was exported to the Rhine in considerable quantities, which proves that more was grown in England than was necessary for home consumption. Oman, *opus cit.*, pp. 154-155.

wood fire. The windows were glazed with small panes of fairly thin greenish-blue tinged glass set in lead or iron frames. The air of well-found comfort suggested by the outside of the house was amply confirmed by the interior. A British architect, trained in Rome and with experience in country house building in Gaul, had put his best into the place ; and apart from the conventional pillared entrance, the house was entirely British, representing a wise use of local materials and skilled labour. Its interior decoration naturally fell below the palace standard of Rome ; but in the triclinium (dining-room), for instance, a deep brown dado of coloured plaster was the base for a wall of golden yellow, laced over with diagonal patternings in pale blue, alternate diamond-shaped spaces of yellow being occupied by tiny painted figures of the Roman gods. A somewhat crudely designed mosaic floor reiterated browns and yellows, relieved with touches of vivid green and lightened by an ivory-hued background ; and the clumsy figures on the floor stared up at a plaster ceiling that was painted blue to match the diagonal lines on the plaster walls. The other apartments, sleeping and living rooms, would be treated in much the same way, and for furniture there would be chairs and low seats of cane-work, couches with wood frames carrying a load of rich fabrics, spread rug-like over their cushions, tables of various kinds, and in the library some form of rack for scrolls.[1]

We shall gain a clearer view of Titus Paulinus and the kind of life he lived if we record the events of a certain day of festivities in the year A.D. 306. It is a day full of significance for Paulinus, for Flavius Valerius Constan-

[1] This account is based on published descriptions and examination of Romano-British dwelling-houses found at Chedworth, Bignor, Silchester, Viroconium, and elsewhere, and from personal observation of typical Roman domestic architecture at Pompeii and furniture preserved in the Naples Museum. Cane-work furniture is shown on the sepulchral monument of a Romano-British lady, Julia Velva, discovered at York in 1922, and now housed in the Yorkshire Museum.

tinus has been proclaimed Cæsar at Eboracum.   The city
has been honoured, as indeed has all Britain, by the event,
and there are great celebrations in progress.   Special
performances at the theatre and three days' games in the
circus, form the introduction to the festivities that private
citizens prolonged and enlarged in their homes.   And
following the great procession through the city comes
the sudden wave of enthusiastic revelry, drunkenness,
and general excitement on the part of the legionaries of
the garrison, for the munificence of Cæsar had declared
that a week's extra pay to the troops was merited by the
great occasion.

The streets of the city are crowded day and night, and
the shops are conducting a roaring trade with the troops
freshly down from the Wall and the far north ;   worn
men with months of hardship and bitter British weather
to wash from their memories with sweet southern wine ;
officers eager for the clean and pleasant comforts of
civilisation after a long and grim campaign against the
Picts.   These war-weary soldiers are spending their
accumulated pay with the royal freedom of their kind ;
and, as we have seen, Cæsar has been generous.   The
shops that ease the troops of their coins are rich and
varied, and if you are so minded you can buy glass,
earthenware, bronze and silver goods, carpets, fabrics,
feathers, furniture, basketware, and clothes ;   there are
goldsmiths and jewellers, also dealers in horse furniture
and horses, farriers, shoemakers, boat-builders, and, on a
somewhat higher plane of professional activity, lawyers,
bankers, doctors, minstrels, actors, clerks, public letter-
writers, and the priests of half a score of the Empire's vast
collection of religions.[1]   The baths are crowded, so
crowded indeed that Paulinus is compelled to forego his
usual visit to the skilled attendant who understands so

---

[1] As a reaction from the persecution of the Christians under Diocletian, there
was great religious toleration under Constantine.   See Oman, *opus cit.*, Chapter X.

well his special needs in massage, shaving, and hair-dressing. Instead, he carries out the more ornate details of his careful toilet in the spacious bathroom of his house, with its sunk bath of warmly-veined marble and its golden plaster walls. A lithe young Nubian slave attends to his needs in the bath, and afterwards robes him as befits a Roman citizen of good estate.

His clothes are sober enough, but in excellent taste. There is no touch of provincial vulgarity for the young Roman-born officers and officials to snigger over with the furtive humour of the educated snob. He wears a tunica of russet brown, reaching to the knee, brown woollen stockings, a woollen undershirt, and stout leather boots, and over all a dark green toga fastened with a brooch of delicately wrought gold, spangled with jewel-like enamel. That is his outdoor dress, to which is added in the driving winter weather of Eboracum a hooded woollen cloak. Indoors he wears white stockings and light hide shoes, with an intricate pierced pattern in the uppers. A belt of gold with a jewelled clasp is worn on special occasions, supporting a short Roman sword. On the fingers of his well-kept hands he wears two or three fine rings, and possibly a brooch sparkles at the throat of his tunica.[1]

His appearance is dignified and commanding. A strongly featured face with a closely trimmed brown beard, close-growing thick brown hair, greying at the temples and by the ears, keen grey eyes, and a voice over which he has perfect and absolute command. Educated in the age-old Roman tradition, he has been taught to regard his voice as an instrument for oratory, his hands as assistants to the words he utters, so that his conversation is accompanied by a wealth of subtle and appropriate gesture. He is very

[1] See Home, *opus cit.*, for description of fully clothed body of Roman Briton discovered intact in a peat-bog on the Yorkshire moors. Also J. R. Planché, *opus cit.*, Tacitus, *Agricola*, and collections in various museums.

much a Roman citizen, and his culture is not a veneer applied in one lifetime : his education and upbringing have made him a very finished gentleman without softening or destroying the abilities of his race.

Fresh from the bath, he reviews the programme of the day and issues his orders. In his library, where his morning's work is to be done, he is met by his secretary with official papers for his seal and a rather disturbing message from the lead mines. The black forests that flank the road between Isurium and Olicana have a grim reputation, for in their depths lurk some untameable remnants of the old and ever-savage Brigantes. Although the final subjection of this tribe had taken place a century and a half ago, some of the survivors had retired to the forests and caves round about the rushing River Nidd that crossed the road from Olicana to Isurium and ran parallel with the branch road to the lead mines, flowing into the Ouse after a stormy, boiling progress through a sinuous valley. These savages seldom ventured on to the roads that penetrated their forest fastness, for the Roman engineer working in conjunction with the warrior saw to it that clearings, half a mile in depth, flanked the forest roads, so that ambushes were impossible and travellers placed beyond arrow-flight. Nobody went into the forests, and it was the sudden disregard of this customary prudence on the part of the under-manager of the lead mines controlled by Eboracum that Paulinus found so disturbing. Caius Annius, the under-manager, was the right hand of Paulinus in the organisation of this most important industry, and it was disturbing to be told that this promising young man of business should carry his celebration of Cæsar's office-taking to the lengths of irresponsible intoxication and a wild, hot-headed raid into the forest at the head of a mixed band of slaves, labourers, and legionaries on leave, all loud with wine and loyal excitement—a raid made with the avowed intention of putting a stop to the constant thieving of weapons, pigs of lead, and any things which might be easily removed from the settlement about the mines, thieving which was always credited to the natives of the inner forest.[1]

Paulinus saw his morning's work disappearing. His accounts must wait, and there were several things he must do very quickly if he was to receive his guests in the evening in comfort. First a letter to the military governor of the city requesting a cohort of the garrison to reinforce the camp guard at the lead mines in case of serious trouble, and another cohort to proceed in search of the reckless Annius. That search would, of course, be limited by the prudence of Paulinus, for he intended to head it himself.

Meanwhile he would ride to the mines with his own armed guard, for as a Decurion he kept a proper state, and four huge troopers from a British auxiliary legion were stationed at his house. Umbo, his Nubian slave, Lathius, his secretary, a reliable and brave man, a member of the Servii Augustales (non-official educated class), and half a dozen Saxon slaves (survivors from a Saxon raid that the Comes Littoris Saxonici had dealt with very thoroughly), armed with axes, would accompany him also. He told his wife, Agrippina, of the urgency of his mission. His eldest son, Paulinus Flavius, was to preside at the feast if he should be detained—an arrangement that effectually silenced the young man's suggestion that he should assist in the search for the forest raiders.

"You must represent me here," his father had told him curtly; "as for Annius—I don't know that Annius will be very glad to see me, if he should be alive." And then the ebony-skinned Umbo announced that his horse

[1] For details of Nidderdale and the Greenhow lead mines in Roman days see Grainge, *History of Harrogate and the Forest of Knaresborough* ; Grainge, *Nidderdale* ; and C. Thompson Walker, *History and Topography of Hampsthwaite in Nidderdale*.

was waiting, and the whole party mounted and rode off, Paulinus helmeted and armed in bronze and iron at the head of his little force. Followed in an hour or so a cohort of Legion VI. (" Gordiana "), swinging slowly along the grey road to Isurium, a hot-eyed young Centurion at the head on a shaggy pony, cursing the heaviness the previous night's dissipation had left, and feeling his plumed helmet like a burning weight on his brows. But the cohort had no work before it. At the point where the Isurium-Olicana road forded the Nidd, they met Paulinus returning with a litter in which lay Annius, now thoroughly sober and utterly unwarlike, as befits a man who has led some score of his fellows to unpleasant deaths and has himself suffered mutilation.

" This has been a little costly, this boyish amusement," Paulinus informed the Centurion. " I don't mind one or two slaves being lost ; one expects a few deaths in the ordinary way of hunting ; but to get twelve fine barbarians killed in such folly is expensive—too expensive." He sighed. " I bought them in competition with the Games Editor, too," he continued, " he wanted them for gladiators."

" And the legionaries who went, what of them ? " queried the officer.

" Old soldiers to a man," smiled Paulinus. " They all returned, and brought this silly boy back with them." And he nodded at the litter with its bandaged and silent occupant. " He has lost an ear," he explained, " and is fortunate in that he keeps his life, for had he lost it, he would have done so most uncomfortably, losing nearly everything it is possible to lose first."

His gesture indicated that the incident, so far as he was concerned, was closed. Nor did he make much of it that evening at the feast. Beyond saying that a more direct road was needed to serve the lead mines, and that the forest might well be burnt back a mile or even two on either side, not so much for the safety of travellers as for the discouragement of fools who were too venturesome, his guests learned little of his morning's work.

It was a pleasant meal, marred, perhaps, by the slightly dogmatic assertions of an old and valued friend of Paulinus, a gentleman who owned a neighbouring estate, one of the six Decurions of Eboracum, a magistrate named Vibius Gallienus. He deplored the tendencies of the times, the encouragement of an evil slave religion, the general lack of belief in the old gods. His son, it appeared, had advanced to a high degree in the religion of Mithras,[1] in fact he had got to the stage when he no longer wore garlands at feasts;[2] that was all right; quite a number of respectable people agreed that Mithras was inspiring, and so on; but now his son was talking about this new religion that had caused all the trouble down at Verulamium a few years ago.

" The affair of Albanus ? " said Paulinus. " I recall the incident well. But you must remember that it was after a lot of trouble. We were all cut off from Cæsar for so long that even a legionary thought for himself."

A laugh ran round the circle of couches on which the guests reclined. The meal had been rich and varied; fine cooking; subtle flavouring; and wines of rarity and worth had warmed the conversation to a confidential temperature. The British province had endured a decade of independent emperors, beginning with Carausius and ending, a little abruptly, with Allectus in 296, and the memory of restricted trade and the consequent discomfort of the wealthy Ordo was an unpleasant one; so, too, was the general unsettling of the soldier and slave by the thought of Rome too far removed to matter. The defeat

[1] Oman, *opus cit.*, in a note, p. 108, says : " Mithras got a wonderful popularity in the third century, and was worshipped not by Oriental immigrants only, but by many a western citizen and soldier."
[2] F. Legge, *Rivals and Forerunners of Christianity.*

D

of Allectus by Constantius was welcome news to every
official and landed proprietor.   The Emperor, Diocletian,
had shown admirable firmness in suppressing the propaganda about brotherhood and freedom which had come
in the name of some specious Eastern religion, called after
an obscure and long-dead criminal ; and had rightly enjoined the persecution of the Christian cult.   This was
the accepted and approved view of the whole company,
and when Gallienus referred to the Albanus incident, he
was recalling the starting point of a lot of troublesome
and subservient influences in the social structure of the
peaceful province.   Albanus had been an educated and
brilliant young officer who not only became a Christian,
but planned the conversion of his brother officers and the
legionaries under his charge.   He was executed, naturally,
but his fortitude and the easy grace with which he conducted himself in his deplorable situation converted even
his executioners.[1]

The religion of Paulinus was the official religion of the
Empire ; the worship of Jupiter and the deified Cæsars ;
and he had built beyond the Nympheum on the south side
of his house, a little altar to the Genius Loci.[2]   Actually
he counted himself too busy to bother much about the
forms of any religion, but his friend's words about that
slave religion, the followers of Christus, struck home
nearer than he would have cared to admit, for his own
daughter had recently confessed to her parents that she
had been visiting for instruction in this alien faith one,
Eborius, who had a tiny temple beyond the city, and who
bore the title of Bishop of Eboracum.[3]   The girl had
been punished and practically imprisoned in her room,
but the problem of her future and her faith remained
unsolved and troublesome.   No, religion was a distaste-

[1] These details of St Alban's life are drawn from the generally unreliable
Gildas.   There is no means of proving or disproving them.
[2] Such altars have been unearthed in many parts of the country.
[3] Eborius was present at the Council of Arles in 314.

ful subject to Paulinus, and he guided the conversation to simpler matters, and soon the programme of games at the circus was under discussion.

A slave brought in a finger bowl of clear crystal containing perfumed water, warmed and tinted a delicate rose hue. Each guest dipped his fingers therein, drying them on linen towels brought by another slave.

The games of the circus led the talk to chariot racing and bear baiting, until a young poet, bored by the interest of the company in muscular and bloody spectacles, described in a few vivid and pretty phrases a recent performance at the theatre in which some scenes from a supposed Christian service were amusingly parodied. Paulinus saw the threatened revival of the subject he disliked. So he asked the poet, with all the charm and courtesy of manner he commanded, to recite his latest composition. Upon the youth's assent, he clapped his hands, and to the crooning of soft strings and the gentle music of a lute, the poet gave to his hearers a song of love in the golden Latin tongue. It concerned a lady who was captured by a savage Saxon sailor, who ravished her from the fair coasts of the long Saxon shore, but in time she came to love the Saxon, who was a prince in his own land, and as his wife she became a great queen, and by her power added to Mother Rome's guardianship a new, rich province in the white lands of the north.

Although most of the gentlemen present considered it great nonsense, their criticism, softened by good wine, was not expressed, and they derived real pleasure from the rolling syllables, the soft harmonies of the unseen musicians, and the extreme comfort of Paulinus's dining-room furniture. Only Paulinus was startled into a strange line of thought by the poet's verses. Those white lands of the north from whence came the tall red and yellow-

The poet gave to his hearers a song of love in the golden Latin tongue.

haired Saxons ; what did Rome know of them ? He
remembered years ago, before Carausius made himself
Emperor, those fierce and persistent raids on their coasts
by Saxon ships ; those swift, sudden inroads into the
peaceful country by tall, fearless men, giants they were,
head and shoulders above the helmets of the legionaries
of the Sixth. And they fought like bears at bay, not
altogether, but separately, without order or military
formation, and with a ferocity that made them terrible
foes. What, indeed, did Rome know of the homes of
these people ? They made good slaves, when they had
overcome their first impulse to kill themselves rather than
endure captivity. But apart from the few they captured
in the now infrequent raids on the Saxon shore, they
knew nothing of these strange and strong barbarians. It
was a pretty fancy of a poet to suppose that a woman
could add the country of these savages to Rome's mighty
Empire. And then came a thought that Paulinus found
disturbing—a thought that had the quality of vision ;
what if the Saxons should add a Roman province to their
lands ?

He glanced at his guests, a little startled in spite of
himself. His thoughts had carried him away from the
conversation. They were speaking of the forthcoming
election of the Council of the Hundred in Eboracum. All
their words, the calm and ordered beauty of their surroundings, the essential security of that rich life with its
ease and its wealth, reassured him of Rome's eternal
triumph over all races. This could never end, he told
himself. What he had known, his sons and their sons
would know also, generation by generation : Rome
would remain and rule. And yet, upon the very floor of
that dining-room, upon the walls, were those slight indica-
tions of a growing feebleness, a slackness, a lack of
inspiration in the art that touched the floor and walls
with coloured figures. In the very stamping of the coins

that changed hands as the dice spun down in the guards'
quarters, there were those lines of weakness, the want
of finish that marked the decay of craftsmanship, the
beginning of decline. . . .[1]

[1] " From the time of Commodus there was a rapid decline. The age of
Diocletian and Constantine shows a well-meant but hopeless attempt at revival
of art."—*Encyclopædia Brittanica*, article on " Numismatics."

CHAPTER IV

Arthur—the Last of the Romans

THE life lived by Paulinus Flavius was much the same as his father had known, and, like Titus Paulinus, he came to the management of industry, the enjoyment of wealth, and the civic honours proper to a great landholder and Roman-British gentleman. And to his son in turn came the enjoyment of that finished, easily secure existence, the serenity of which was broken only by a northern war against the Scots. The savages did some damage, but in a brief winter campaign the Emperor, Constans I., defeated them, and the Province, once more at peace, continued its industry and the creation of wealth. There were small changes of fashion, crazes and modes that fluttered around the huge Empire, and there was open adhesion to the Christian cult by many of the official and educated classes, but many families retained the older forms of religion, and presently the views of the Emperor Julian [1] seemed to suggest that theological die-hards were more politic than their fellows.

The great-grandson of Titus Paulinus was named Aurelius Velva, and he was the first head of the family to become a Christian. In 364, when he was forty-three, he saw service against the Picts, and was destined to spend five years in a bitter war in which Scots, Saxons, and Atecotti swept southward into Britain. The trouble had been brewing for years, and there was a hint of it in Julian's brief rule : that Emperor had even sent the Magister Equitum, Lupicinus, to inspect the defences of Britain, recalling him fairly soon when the threat on the

[1] Julian the Apostate tried to overthrow Christianity and re-establish Paganism.

northern border had seemed slighter on investigation ; but three years later the storm burst. The country was overrun, and some very drastic changes came about in its standards of civilisation and its possibilities of comfort. The cities were in a state of siege, and the smoking ruins of opulent houses dotted about the land within a few days' march of the Wall testified to the mobility and the destructive ferocity of the invaders. The comfortable house that Aurelius Velva had known all his life as an exquisitely appointed home was burnt, its furniture smashed, and the bath filled with charred and mutilated bodies, and it was this deserted wreck he found upon his first homecoming after five years of campaigning. He had left home a careless, fashionable man, to help in the repulse of what had seemed to be a mere raid ; he returned a grim veteran, to find himself the head of his family and its sole survivor.

So disastrous had been this long invasion of the Province that many high officials had lost their lives, and the civil machinery of the country was badly deranged. Early in 369, Count Theodosius was appointed Governor-General with Civilis as Civil Governor. Theodosius was an able soldier, and under his generalship the country was cleared and then reorganised. But the easy life of the place, the cultured calm of the cities and great country houses, had been jarred and jolted too violently for immediate resumption, and although Aurelius Velva rebuilt the house of his fathers, restored his lands, and by selling part of his estate was enabled to buy sufficient slaves to work the remainder profitably, for many years his home lacked the luxuries and comforts that were lost when the Pictish war ruined the flourishing trade of the cities and stopped agriculture. For over ten years there was a steady recuperation ; and prosperity seemed once more to be the lot of Britain. Aurelius Velva had married and was a Decurion of Eboracum ; and then began the great, romantic adventure of Maximus, and the rising tide of prosperity ebbed.

Magnus Clemens Maximus, Comes Britannia, made himself master of Britain and Gaul, and in 383 became Emperor of the West. Again the threat of war beyond the Wall troubled Britain, and when in 388 Maximus was killed by the Emperor Theodosius, the Picts and other savages poured into the country. Aurelius Velva was killed in that war, and his eldest son, Velva, a man of thirty-one, was the last member of the family to benefit by the refinements and elegancies of a traditional Roman education. All his life he was doomed to see standards of living failing ; civilised advantage after civilised advantage slipping and sliding out of the general order of things. He was to live in an age of emergencies, of blatant military adventurers, of failing civil organisation, and his children learned but one art—that of the warrior.

His son, Velva Constantius, lived to be an old man, dying in 458, when he was seventy-two years old, a curious link with a great civilisation that was crumbling and melting year by year, like mud walls under rushing rain. Old men were rare when he died, for the wars of that century of blood and darkness swallowed up the youth of Britain, and the barbarians who drove their frontier further westward year by year were restless and reckless warriors who generally died as they lived—by the sword. He married in 407 at the age of twenty-one, during what seemed to be a period of promise. It was but a temporary lull. And presently the most disturbing news alarmed the Province. Great Rome itself was threatened, and troops were hurried over the narrow seas to Gaul. Legions that had been stationed in Britain since the first settlement went, from Eboracum, from Deva, and other military cities. Overseas trade had been dislocated for years, for the Saxons and other bold sea thieves were very active. Their black, dragon-prowed vessels sailed down from the north, swooping upon luckless merchantmen from Gaul or Hispana or Italy, raiding inland for half a day on some strip of coast far removed from one of the fortresses of the Saxon shore, killing, burning, women-stealing.[1]   The transport of troops from Britain to Gaul was another blow to trade, for every vessel was required, and there were civil and military disturbances in the Province itself, and then for one mad year a succession of petty emperors were set up by discontented soldiers, to be deposed and killed as the whim of the common man ordained, for it was beyond the comprehension of the rough legionaries or the British auxiliary troops that they were hurrying towards the end of their world of plenty and good organisation.   There is, for example, a coin shortage and consequent difficulties about pay. The mints of Londinium have been comparatively idle since Magnus Maximus strutted his little and lamentable strut.   Four or five years' work still awaits builders and woodworkers in effacing in many cities the damage of the last war—rebuilding and repairing.   In some of the cities are many empty shops, and luxuries are rare and impossible in price.   But there are still games in the circuses, fifth - rate touring companies of gladiators, although only the soldiers patronise these places.   Christianity has now an official standing, and condemns such spectacles.

By 460 the orderly life of the Romano-British gentleman is receding into the past ; it becomes a treasured memory of the last generation.   Constantius Valens, the son of Velva Constantius, lives on in the house his grandfather rebuilt, manages his estate, brings up his sons to be ready for every emergency, sees to their training in military matters, wears simple clothes of British-woven materials, but still of Roman cut, and lives a life of extreme simplicity, with cooking that would have disgusted his

[1] See Oman, *opus cit.*

great - great - great - great - grandfather, Titus Paulinus, although it was by no means crude or primitive; and his voice is not unimportant in the city of Eboracum.

Rome was weakening, and an order from the Emperor Honorius that the cities of the Province should plan and arrange their defences and raise troops independently and without the sanction of the Imperial City was a little startling. The order came after an attempt at invasion on the part of a horde of barbarians, and it produced much confusion. Hereditary British princes were remembering their titles, and civic rule tended to centre around an individual rather than a council.[1] Communication with Rome ceased abruptly, for Gaul was flooded with barbarians, and for some years the barrier remained. Those were years of great agricultural prosperity and internal disorder.[2] Coins now vanished, and clumsy barter hampered trade. Then came a vast invasion of Picts and Scots which was eventually smashed in 429 by Germanus, a talented soldier and also a Christian Bishop, who was visiting Britain in connexion with his Church and the extension of its work.[3]

Wars and raids followed one another, demanding all the energy of Britain's worried and divided rulers. The land was sinking back to a purely agricultural state, the cities, in ill repair and grimly fortified, sheltered a certain kind of life, but their trade had gone, their luxuriousness had vanished, particularly in the north and east. Eboracum was visited and burned by Anglian raiders when Constantius was already an old man,[4] and with his family he sought shelter in the dense forest, where, with his

[1] Local Kingships were beginning to spring up in the West and North, and that these were Celtic rather than Roman in character is suggested by the Celtic names of many of the princes. Oman, *opus cit.*

[2] See Bede, *Hist. Eccles.*, Book I., Chaps. XIV. and XXII.

[3] This was the so-called " Hallelujah Victory," described by Bede, *opus cit.*, Book I., Chap. XX.

[4] See Oman, *opus cit.*

armed slaves, he made a fastness away up the valley of the boiling Nidd, a wild district into which the invaders would be unlikely to penetrate.

Forest folk, as many of the chiefs and people of Eboracum had become, made common cause against a common enemy with the forest outlaws. There were collisions at first, but the fugitive city and house dwellers were organised and armed; moreover, they were still Roman citizens, and that gave them authority with their rougher neighbours, who presently intermarried with their slaves and servants, the latter taking more and more to the British tongue.

With age Velva Constantius became garrulous, and would talk for hours to his small grandson, Valens, of the vanished glories of Eboracum, whose blackened and noble ruins lay nearly thirty miles to the south-east of their forest home. He would, with senile love of unimportant detail, relate story after story about the city and its shops, its soldiers, its magistrates and their guards, the wonder of its theatre, its temples and churches, the school he had attended when a boy, the forum, where with other judges he had sat enthroned in the cool vastness of the basilica and executed justice, the baths and their skilled attendants, the wine and food of great feasts, and the glory of a legion on the march. . . .

The child would drink it in, half unbelieving, half regretful that these wonders could never be tested for their truth. "And has it all gone?" he would ask, a little dolefully.

"Calleva, Corinium, Aquæ Sulis, they still live," [1] his grandfather would tell him, pointing southwards, " or so they tell me. Londinium, perhaps. Who knows, the Præfect may still be there." And then he would mutter and smile to himself, and anon weep weak tears

---

[1] Oman, *opus cit.*, suggests that British states had by this time lost all traces of Roman culture save in the Severn Valley and thereabouts.

for the great and glorious thing that was no more—the might of Rome.

Valens remembered those talks. As a youth they haunted him long after his grandfather died and was utterly forgotten. As a young man he was always looking out for something that his neighbours and relations told him was not to be found in all the wide world, a Roman Legion bright with bronze and iron, its gilded eagles borne ahead by the standard-bearer, brave in his leopard skin garb. Soldiers he saw in plenty, for Britain was parcelled out into kingdoms and petty states, city states, aggressive states, treaty-making states, and bordered on the east by a long, savage barbarian state, full of Saxons waiting and resting, ready to burn and destroy their way westwards. Ruined Eboracum was in their hands, although they had but little use for cities. Londinium, still busy with trade, and passing rich, was almost surrounded by barbarians. The roads were dangerous, and the whole country suffered from violent crime, brigandage, and a complete cessation of arts and industries, except in the remoter western cities.[1] Valens became a soldier of fortune, living by his sword, and taking service with any prince who seemed likely to fight against the barbarians. Independent, although property-less, he had dreams of finding some one worth following, some leader who would end the rule of stupid princes, too stupid even to make war together against that ever-present eastern threat of the red barbarians.

Valens was twelve years old when his grandfather died, and nearly twenty years after that event he was to hear news which seemed to promise a fulfilment of his grandfather's hopes that Roman traditions would help British princes to realise that an orderly province is better than a number of insecure petty kingdoms. The country was split up into so many states that a big attack of barbarians

[1] See note on page 60.

could not be met.   The experiment of paying mercenaries had been tried, and it had only increased the number of savage enemies.[1]   Now, Valens learned, the kings and princes of south and west Britain had been wise enough to forget their little personal dignities and give power to a capable officer, Ambrosius Aurelianus, a Roman-British gentleman of a military family, trained and versed in the Roman tradition of warfare, an organiser and a military genius.   Aurelianus stood for many things that gave Valens a sudden flush of hope, suggesting the revival of all that power, peace, ease, and fine living his grandfather had pictured so well.   Even his title of *Dux Bellorum* [2] was a promise of Roman order and discipline.   Valens was bilingual, but as he grew older his Latin was seldom used, and when he married, British was the language of his rather primitive and uncomfortable home.

A forest clearing, a wooden hut, coarse food, unskilled slaves, ill-defined rights and property boundaries, hunting, constant alarms of raids, constant flights and reconnaissances, periods of service with this king and that fighting barbarians, and then back to the restless, half-savage home life ; such was the experience of Valens from boyhood until the great news of Britain's *Dux Bellorum* breaking the Saxon power in a vast battle at Mount Badon travelled north, and made the year 475 memorable to Valens.[3] That news sent him south.   He left his family of three sons, the eldest of whom was seven, his wife and her three slaves, and took with him, armed and equipped as well as his limited resources would allow, six strong slaves, British of tongue, though descended from Saxon forefathers captured three generations earlier.   They marched through the great forest away to the west and south to Deva, passing the fort of Mancunium (Manchester), where

---

[1] Bede, *opus cit.*, Book I., Chap. XV., and Oman, *opus cit.*
[2] Oman.
[3] Bede, *opus cit.*, Book I., Chap. XVI.   Mount Badon is generally thought to be Lansdown, Bath.

the army of the King of Elmet lay encamped, resting by night at deserted stations, following the smooth Roman road from dawn to sunset.   And all the land seemed forlorn, the houses mere shells of brick and stone, the roadside altars broken, uncared-for, creeper-grown ; a few slaves tending the fields, and here and there the clustering wood-built hovels of the rustics.   Wolves howled by night on the naked moors and hills, and the woods through which the road passed were dark and sinister, and once they heard the angry grunt of a bear, and the great brute regarded them with little fierce, piggy eyes from the tangled bushes.   The wild things of the country were bold, and a lone traveller would have found robbers even bolder, but Valens and his party were too strong and well armed to fear the savage brigands who watched all roads in the Britain of feeble kings whose rule put barbarian desolation in the place of strength and order. South, south, beyond Deva, with its river now empty of shipping, its towering brick fortress sparsely manned with ill-clad soldiers, and its city quarters deserted for the most part, streets of ruined shops clustering about a dilapidated forum.   The baths had done duty as a military storehouse for over a generation ; luxuries there were none, and beyond a Christian church and the beginnings of a monastery, growing by the inept hands of crude builders from miscellaneous materials, tiles, bricks, and marble, ravished from a score of ruined houses, no activities other than military stirred the life of the dead place.   Down at last to Viroconium (Wroxeter), where four big roads met, a white city touched by the long shadow of a towering hill, washed by a broad, silver-clear river, over which the road ran direct from the southward city gate on a three-arched bridge of red and yellow brick. It was the first live city Valens had ever seen, but he was compelled to skirt it, for guards placed far beyond the gates along the road told him that unless strangers

were covered by the local prince's protection they were
not allowed to enter Viroconium.   The city chiefs were
determined to keep the city safe : to that end all trade
was done beyond the walls.

Still south by a straight valley road he went to Glevum
(Gloucester), where he offered service to an officer, one
Artorius,[1] commanding a Legion under Ambrosius
Aurelianus, stationed for training at Glevum, which had
awakened from its long life as an easy-going city, and was
now a military centre.   Valens found in Artorius, whom
the local British soldiers and rustics called Urther, a
young man, old in wisdom, a wonderfully able soldier,
firm in the resolve to bring back the days his forefathers
had known when the golden eagles of Rome went back
and forth proudly along the roads of Britain.   His
soldiers were armed, exercised, and trained entirely in the
Roman tradition.   He wore the armour of a Roman
general, the helmet with its rasping plume of horsehair
dyed scarlet, the moulded breastplate, the short sword,
and a toga of white, edged with purple, gave his tall,
commanding figure a greater dignity.

"You know nothing of war," he said coldly to Valens
on his offer of service.   "You have fought in woods and
among trees and in the open in the army of some fool
against the army or mob of some other fool.   Brains win
battles, and we should have beaten the barbarian back
to the sea in my father's time if we had used this weapon
we have ; the weapon they have never had."

"I can learn," said Valens, "and I hate the barbarian
too deeply to be altogether useless as a fighter.   See, I
bring you six slaves, armed, and I give them to the
service of the *Dux Bellorum*.   As for myself, some small
command, when I have learned war your way, is all
I ask."

[1] The existence of Arthur, not as a king, but as a military chief, is now generally
admitted by historians.

Artorius gave him his chance, and in a year he was a centurion of the twelfth cohort of the legion Artorius commanded.[1] Followed five years of campaigning ; active, scientific fighting ; carefully-planned war, efficient, ruthless, and unceasing, until Ambrosius Aurelianus died, and there was a temporary check in the pushing back of the barbarian hordes. Came a great council, held at Aquæ Sulis (Bath), where Valens saw civilisation for the first time, saw a great city in the full flush of life, with its shops open, its baths intact, and crowded with slaves ministering to the needs of princes and wealthy gentlemen from the country round about Glevum and Corinium (Cirencester), saw a confusing crowd of people, merchants, doctors, lawyers, craftsmen, and magistrates, for the city still kept its Roman municipal system, although it owned allegiance to a Prince. The council was held in the forum, with its tall Corinthian columns and great mosaic-paved hall agleam with golds, greens, and reds, and amid that untouched splendour Artorius was proclaimed by the kings and chiefs and princes *Dux Bellorum* of *Britannia*, Leader of the Legions, General Supreme. Somebody with a sense of old-world fitness brought him a purple cloak, and as he strode forth to the broad paved space at the head of the forum steps and spoke to the vast crowd of soldiers and citizens waiting to hear the council's ruling, he seemed a very Cæsar. . . .

He was hailed as such, and the forest of right arms raised in salute possibly made some of the princelings who had elected this war chief doubt the wisdom of their faith in unity. But as the weary war continued intermittently, the quality of Artorius was too fine to bring doubts even to the meanest. Taking up the task of his great predecessor, Ambrosius Aurelianus, he proved the

---

[1] The retention of the title of *Dux Bellorum* suggests that the Roman military organisation and nomenclature were either maintained or restored in this corner of Britain where Roman civilisation yet lingered.

E

singleness and sincerity of his purpose, to drive the barbarian back and back and back, and win once more for a united Britain the peace of the old, lost province.

And in this giant task Valens helped, year after year, ever and again returning to that group of western cities where the arts of a happier time still flourished, Corinium, Calleva Atrebatum (Silchester), and Aquæ Sulis, living for a few weeks in surroundings that seemed always strange, although he became familiar enough with the streets and shops of those last refuges of civilisation. Manners had faded from their old standards, and military necessity, an ever-present influence for generations, had removed the last lingering traces of elegance. Conversation was concerned first with war and the possible movements of the barbarians, and then interest turned to the political intrigues of the various princes and all the petty scandal of a score of petty Courts. Even the great aim of Artorius could not dispel the menace of division ; it lurked in the background of men's thoughts. Of trade there was little talk. Cut off from Gaul, and with dwindling powers of production at home, the city states of Western Britain were now almost entirely agricultural, although the cities themselves contained rare things produced by a few craftsmen who spared time from the making of weapons and engines of war ; woodwork, pottery, and metalwork that a century before would have been condemned as incredibly inept gave a few traders the material for shopkeeping.

Valens never returned to his family, but in due time he sent for two of his sons ; the successful war-making of the *Dux Bellorum* having rendered communication safer throughout the west country. But ere they could reach him he was killed in a minor battle, little more than an affair of outposts, on the road that ran south from Calleva Atrebatum to the lost city of Venta Belgarum (Winchester). The young men both entered the service of Artorius, whose fame had now spread throughout all troubled Britain, and learned from his example to look for the final expulsion of the barbarian. But being British forest folk by upbringing, they thought of him, not as their father Valens had thought of him as Artorius, *Dux Bellorum* of *Britannia*, the leader of the legions, but simply as Urther, the Fighter.

CHAPTER V

Foundations of Saxon England

BY the time the great-grandchildren of Valens were men, Artorius was a legend. His deeds were magnified by the kings and warriors of the feeble patchwork of British states that endured as the monument of his life-work for unity, and to the barbarians he was a terrible memory. Nobody capable of organising the forces of civilised Britain and of bringing together in a common cause the dozen or more princelings of the western states succeeded the last of the Romans. Throughout the sixth century the gradual dissolution of that great dream of Britain united, the constant lowering of the old standards of civilisation, and the flourishing strength of the Saxon settlements, made life uncertain and uncomfortable

The seed of Valens was scattered. Of the two sons who came south to him, only one survived the military rule of Artorius, and having won honour in war, he ended his days as military governor of Corinium, where he married and his sons and daughters grew up in the comparative comfort and security of a city state. They knew nothing of the other branch of their family—the children of Valens's third son—that lived precariously and very hardly in the great forest of the kingdom of Elmet. So it came about that early in the seventh century two young men, directly descended from Valens, but differing in speech, manners, and training, lived through some interesting changes and saw those changes from very different points of view. Œwulf, one of these youths, was born in the south-west, in the lost city of

Corinium, and as a child of five he had escaped the massacre and sack of that city in 577, when the fierce soldiers of King Ceawlin made their great western march.[1] When the first eagerness of victory had been deadened by blood and slaughter, the Saxon conquerors bethought themselves of slaves, and Œwulf was captured with other children and a few wretched women who had fled the city, and renamed to suit the taste of his masters. He had grown up a theow in the service of Aulwyn, one of Ceawlin's most powerful leaders, a giant of a man who led his warriors to battle singing and shouting, great masses of yellow hair flying over his shoulders and shaming to a dull tone the golden torque that bound his brows and signified his rank of commander.[2] Aulwyn was a hard master, but he was able to appreciate and encourage the qualities that went to the making of a good soldier, as he understood that term, and he found as Œwulf grew to manhood that he possessed a rich endowment of those qualities. Œwulf became rather more than a slave, for by saving his master's life in a fierce battle during a war with a neighbouring kingdom, he won the rank of ceorl, or freeman. Aulwyn was an eorl, a noble by birth, standing high in the favour of his king, and under his protection Œwulf became a warrior of repute. In all things was he Saxon, and as he grew older he forgot utterly the early morning of his life in the fair white city of Corinium, with its gracious houses, its towers and sheltering walls, paved streets thronged with citizens, its well-being and comfort. Instead, he accepted the life of his adopted people. Physically he was not unlike them, for he was fair, blue-eyed, and tall. In time he was considered wise, for he inherited something of the power that had made his ancestors prominent men in their time.

As he gained fame as a warrior, so he acquired posses-

[1] *Anglo-Saxon Chronicle*, under date 577. [2] Cf. Anuerin, *Gododin*.

sions in reward. He served his king with a passionate loyalty, equalled only by his passion for advancement, though the latter emotion was restrained. He lived in a two-roomed house of wood,[1] one wall of which was of good brick, being the remaining wall of a Roman house, long since ruined.[2] It was a draughty, ill-built house, cold and uncomfortable in winter, for the fire occupied a central hearth and the smoke from it found its way eventually through a hole in the thatched roof. It consisted of one big room, a hall, where every one connected with the household lived. A smaller room gave to the master of the house a poor imitation of privacy. The windows were shuttered at night; the interior was black with the soot and grime of the fire and the hanging lamps which burned dim and odorously after sunset. The floor of stamped earth and irregular stone slabs, taken from Romano-British houses and roads, was filthy. Save for some roughly trimmed logs for seats and a crude trestle table, furniture was unknown to his household, and at meals the simple apparatus of eating consisted of a sharp hunting knife, and for drinking, a cow's horn. A nobleman might have these vessels mounted with silver or gold, but Œwulf was not a nobleman or rich, consequently he drank only mead and barley-beer, seldom tasting the poor wine of the country which a few wretched vineyards produced in the southland.[3] His food was chiefly pork, game, fish—especially eels—and barley-bread, with sometimes a few ill-cooked vegetables. Cooking had died as an art, and Saxon feasts

[1] The descriptions of Œwulf's house and the king's palace and their equipment are largely drawn from contemporary chronicles and from drawings in MSS. in the Cotton and Harleian collections.

[2] Tangible evidence of the practice of utilising ruined Roman buildings and building material has been laid bare in the course of excavations in several of the old Roman towns.

[3] Bede, *Hist. Ecclesia*, says: " England produces vines in some places." See also Oman, *opus cit*. Lambarde mentions vineyards at Haling, Battle, and Windsor, and speaks of the wine made there. There are also several references to vineyards in the *Saxon Chronicle* and in the *Chronicle of William of Malmesbury*.

were untouched by any subtlety of preparation, unsoft-
ened by the mellowing influence of planned flavours and
good wine. Gobble and gulp held the stage, and table
manners long awaited resurrection.

Conversation was dull and obvious, concerning itself
with hunting, war, falconry, and the doings of the Court
and the nobles. Jugglers sometimes visited a house and
entertained those who ate after sunset, and there were
bards, and musicians who played the harp, flute, horn,
tabor, panspipes, and a type of violin. But these entertainments seldom took place in houses other than those
of nobles, and it was at Court that Œwulf first heard music
played on stringed instruments. The king's great hall
was a little richer than the house of Aulwyn, which was
the richest and most luxurious place Œwulf had ever
known. At a great feast given by the king to his chief
warriors after a long war, Œwulf saw chairs—ugly,
angular, box-like chairs—for the first time, also stools,
and circular tables with legs crudely ornamented by
carving. The feasters were waited on by theows, who
carried cloths over their arms to wipe up the wine spilled
on the table. Toasts were drunk solemnly, and a tall,
thin man in a black robe, who sat on the right hand of the
king, was presently allowed to speak to the company.
He spoke haltingly, with many Latin words filling the
gaps in his broken Saxon, and he told them that he was
one of many soldiers of a new god, who apparently had
nothing to do with Thor or Woden. The king nodded
agreement, and the nobles and other guests were all
attention. It was after the stranger in black had made
an end of his speaking that Œwulf heard music ; then a
bearded bard, with a harp, entered the hall and sang a
saga in praise of a great chief who led the Saxons to the
British shores when the Roman ruled.

They were a strange company in that royal hall. Long-
haired, fierce-looking men, listening intently to the bell-

like voice of the singer, whose harp throbbed a trickle of sound, an undercurrent of melody, save in the pauses of his song, when it swelled with vibrant notes. In form their garments were identical, king, eorl, and thane wearing tunics of linen which reached to the knee, open at the neck, and having long sleeves set in rolls from wrist to elbow and kept back by heavy bracelets. Breek and hose they all wore, and over their stockings were bands of cloth, linen, or leather, wound from ankle to knee, crossed diagonally or wound spirally in close rolls. Laced-up shoes were on their feet, and a woollen or leather cap, a Phrygian cap in form, would be worn when they left the hall, and also they would don *mentils*, or short cloaks, fastened on the breast. Only by the richness of ornaments, belts, bracelets, buckles, brooches, chains, and rings, was rank indicated. The jewelled and enamelled work on such ornaments was brought out from the homeland of the Saxons; they had as yet no arts or crafts in their British settlements and kingdoms; war and agriculture were their only concerns.

The soldiers wore loricated armour, small plates sewn on to leather or coarse linen, iron rings sometimes taking the place of plates; helmets with four horns, or four-sided helmets with symmetrical serrations, four ridges that met in the centre; leaders like Œwulf would have shields of split wood with a metal boss, and would carry long spears. A long, straight and broad iron sword would always be carried, and a dagger called a seax. The axe, the double axe, the barbed spear and javelin were familiar to Œwulf, and he found himself wondering whether the black-clad stranger who had spoken of himself as a soldier of—who was it, Christus? Christ?—could handle any of the weapons he knew.

That stranger was to have a great influence in the southern kingdom of which Œwulf was a subject, and before a year was past, in 634, he had been baptised, together with many thousands of his countrymen ; but he did not know that it was his second baptism, and that in a Christian church in lost Corinium he had been blessed as a babe by a British bishop.

*   *   *   *   *

With his unknown relative in the north, in the kingdom of Elmet, the coming of Christian missionaries had an altogether different effect.   This descendant of Valens, by name Verthger, was British by upbringing and tradition.   There had been no violent uprooting of civilisation to disturb his early childhood, for in Elmet there was little enough civilisation to uproot.   There were Christian churches in the settlements in the vast forest where Verthger lived, and those churches kept alive the traditional abhorrence of the barbarian, who lay, settled and powerful, to the east.[1]   The father of Verthger had incurred many years of penance because he had the misfortune to be captured by a band of marauders from the neighbouring kingdom of Northumbria, and was compelled to guide them from the great forest to within sight of the ruins of Eoforwic (Eboracum).[2]   They had been raiding westwards and had got lost in the forest. Consequently, Verthger grew up with a dread and hatred of barbarians that made the suggestions of some of these strange foreign priests who came from the south seem wildly foolish.[3]

He knew nothing of the Saxon kingdoms or their ways. In Elmet their ways had been destructive and bloody ; and beyond the eastern borders of the kingdom these savages lurked, planning raids, stealing women and chil-

[1] For arguments in support of the continued independence of the British kingdom of Elmet at this time, cf. Oman, *opus cit.*
[2] By the Canons of the Synod of Lucus Victoriæ, A.D. 569, a thirteen years' penance was imposed on any Briton who acted as a guide to the barbarians.
[3] Oman, *opus cit.*, pp. 264 and 269, refers to the hatred of British Christians for Saxon Christians, with whom they refused to co-operate.

dren when they could. And now, it seemed, these
savages had been converted by Paulinus, a foreign priest,
who was actually building a church for them in Eoforwic.[1]
They were calling themselves Christians ; as if they could
ever be anything else but barbarians ; moreover, his own
priests in Elmet were being asked to help in Christianising
them. Altogether absurd in their demands were these
stranger priests who came armed with some vague
authority from a place called Rome. . . .[2]

Secure in the discomforts of his forest home, poor
enough in worldly goods, hemmed in by invincible ignorance but conscious of superiority to the barbarian, a
consciousness which was a last relic of the great civilisation
he had never known, the flame of which had died down
lower and lower until now it barely flickered north of
Deva, Verthger together with the other chief men of his
country opposed a step that might have linked the remaining British kingdoms in peace with the Saxon settlements.
He demanded that his religion should be exclusive, and
his priests were of the same mind, so that in Britain there
were two branches of Christianity : the older survival
from Romano-British times, a warped remnant of the
social life of those days, and the new and vigorous growth
planted by Augustine and extended by Bishop Paulinus
at York,[3] where three centuries before another Paulinus,
a Roman citizen of some distinction, had deplored the
growth of the " slave religion " that had provided him
with a distressing domestic problem.

Verthger was destined to repeat his father's experience
with barbarians, although he was to escape the penance
imposed by a nationalised Christianity. A Saxon attempt
to subdue Elmet brought war into his forest life, and

[1] In A.D. 627. Refer Bede, *Hist. Eccles.*, Book II., Chaps. XI., XII., XIII.,
and XIV.

[2] Cf. Bede, Book II., Chap. II.

[3] The Roman Eboracum, the Saxon Eoforwic, and the Norse Iorvic, mark
successive stages in the transition to the name York.

changed the whole course of it, for he was captured,
forced to act as a guide, and, being without hope of ever
regaining his home and property, and with the knowledge
that his family and nearly every one whom he knew had
been massacred, he resolved to make the best terms
possible with his captors and at least escape ultimate
slavery by proving his worth as a man of intelligence.
Within him lay the special quality and power of his race,
as yet unsunned by circumstance, but ready to develop.

The Saxons of Northumbria found Verthger extremely
useful.   His knowledge of the country helped their westward raids to a success of such magnitude that the king,
Edwin, desired to see the British prisoner.   Edwin and
his queen, Ethelburga, were both Christians, and Edwin
was in the first stages of zeal for the new religion,
having been converted only a few months before Verthger's appearance at his Court.   Ever since his baptism in
the timber-built church of St Peter in York [1] he had been
busy uprooting the heathen cults of his forefathers.
Coifi, his chief priest, forsaking his former faith, burned
the heathen temples with all the zeal of a proselyte.
Plans for the baptism of his loyal subjects were put into
operation.   It is possible, too, that certain Christian
principles of forbearance and charity survived the orgy
of ceremony accompanying wholesale conversions ; it
may have been Christian teaching that prompted Edwin
to reward a man whose race regarded the Saxons as
" barbarians," a term of hatred and bitter contempt, or it
may have been a purely mercenary purchase of allegiance.
However, Verthger was not concerned with the king's
motives when he found himself granted property in return
for his services.   His loyalty was easily bought with the

---

[1] This event took place on 12th April 627.   But Edwin and his queen had been
flirting with the idea of conversion for some time : Bede records correspondence
with Pope Boniface, in which the latter sends with a letter presents of a shirt, a
gold ornament and a garment of Ancyra for Edwin, and a silver mirror and
a gilt ivory comb for Ethelburga.

hope of future prosperity, and he settled down comfortably and earnestly to the building up of a fortune, modest but secure in the crude standards of those times, and found that Saxon ways were easily mastered.   Like his distant relative, Œwulf, he had something of the Saxon physical quality, and the child of his marriage with a high-born Saxon lady was altogether a man of the conquering race, albeit he inherited the gifts of his father's forbears—the adaptability, the keenness for a bargain, the vision that went a little further than other people ever imagined, and which was such a valuable military and trading asset.   Verthger's son, Urtfrid, prospered on a far more imposing scale than his father.   Entering the king's personal service he was finally created ealdorman (alderman), and his possessions and influence increased, so that his son, Bertfrid, by the beginning of the eighth century was a great landholder and a man of considerable influence.   Ealdorman Bertfrid of Neotheradæl,[1] thus was the grandson of Verthger known to his contemporaries.   He was the owner of all Nidderdale, in the kingdom of Northumbria, which at that time embraced Yorkshire, and his other lands included Craven, Wharfdale, Swaledale, and Wensleydale.   He had a hall in the heart of the Nidd valley, and houses in the capital city of York, Knaresborough, and in the royal city of Catterick, and among his possessions he counted many farms and mines and forests.   In the year 706 he was some thirty-eight years of age, an expert politician, playing a dominating part in the affairs of his country, affairs that were involved by one of those recurrent quarrels between Church and State.

The Golden Age of Anglo - Saxon England was flourishing in those opening years of the eighth century. Northumbria had been enriched by a scholarly king, Aldfrid, who had succeeded the ill-fated Ecgfrith, whose

[1] Neotheradæl = Modern Nidderdale.

disastrous war with Pictland had begun the decline of the Northumbrian kingdom.[1] But although the northern part of Northumbria had been lost after the Pictish war, the loss of strength and vitality was not yet apparent, and vigorous and ambitious men like Bertfrid would be unaware of it. The crudities of Verthger's day were passing, and learning was once more lighting the way of life,[2] although naturally its influence did not spread far beyond the Church. But Bertfrid would not be un-lettered, and as a nobleman would have enjoyed advan-tages of an exceptional kind under such a king as Aldfrid. He was in close touch with the Court, being a member of the Northumbrian Witanagemote ; his lands were in-creased, and he was created Governor of Elmet. Owning extensive property in the dales, he was the head of a hundred—that is, the chief of a hundred households—and his wealth was drawn from agriculture, timber, and minerals. It was the springtime of a new civilisation that was in some respects a parody of the old Romano-British days, like a rough wood imitation of some fine thing carved in stone. Customs were becoming laws,

[1] Ecgfrith was unfortunate in war. He was allied with Kent and Wessex, but was severely handled in a war with Mercia ; and although a peace was arranged by Archbishop Theodore in 679, Northumbria only enjoyed it until 684, when Ecgfrith sent a fleet to attack the Scots of Ireland, who had allied themselves with the Picts and had attacked the Strathclyde Britons who were vassals of Ecgfrith. The fact that he sent a fleet shows that the English had not forgotten the sea-manship of their pirate ancestors. In 685 Ecgfrith invaded Pictland and ravaged the country until he had passed the Tay ; but his army was annihilated by a local king, Bruide, near Forfar, and the Northumbrian king met his death in that battle of Nechtansmere.

[2] A school of Greek learning was started at Canterbury by Archbishop Theo-dore (668-690). Such men as Bishop Aldhelm (died 709) and Bede (died 734) were writing, also Cædmon, the poet, a herdsman and lay brother of Whitby Abbey, who wrote in English (died 680), and Abbot Ceolfrid, who was causing the *Codex Amiatinus* to be engrossed. The activities of these churchmen suggest that a high degree of culture, so far as literature was concerned, was by no means uncommon among the clergy. Nor were the crafts undeveloped. The conver-sion of the whole country to official Christianity during the seventh century implanted an enthusiasm for building and endowing monasteries, cathedrals, and churches ; and the gradual increase in the numbers of dioceses led to the beginning of a rudimentary diocesan organisation of the Church.

and with the development of a legal fabric the whole
social structure gained the stability that made the creation
of wealth possible.   But society did not yet think in
terms of money, for the holding of all land involved
service of some kind, whether personal service in the
army, or assistance in the building of defensive works
and the maintenance of roads and bridges, and actual
payments in money or kind were, for the most part,
brought about only by trade or by misconduct with fines
to follow.   In Verthger's view, his grandson would have
appeared to be living in a world of infinite comforts
and securities.   Verthger would have regarded the
innumerable churches as a satisfactory sign of a Chris-
tianised peacefulness ;   and those buildings that cari-
catured Roman basilicas in wood certainly indicated the
growing importance of the Church ; but the desire for
secular as well as spiritual power on the part of churchmen often involved them in undignified squabbles with
kings and nobles ; and even the cultured Aldfrid, who had
been trained for the Church originally before he succeeded
his half-brother Ecgfrith, did not escape a trying contro-
versy with Wilfred, the Bishop of York.   This early
English king quietly but firmly defied the Church's
ruling, even disregarding a Papal Bull, and later the
Archbishop of Canterbury, Bertwald, when the latter was
armed with instructions from the Pope.   The dispute
concerned the Abbey of Ripon, which King Aldfrid
wished to take from Bishop Wilfred, who held it
together with the See of York, in order to found a new
bishopric there.   There were resignations and protests
from Wilfred, expeditions to Rome, and exhibitions of
towering self-importance ; but Aldfrid died in 705 with
the dispute still unsettled ; a difficult legacy for those
who followed him in ruling Northumbria.

The ruling of that kingdom was not an easy task.
Aldfrid had kept a peace for twenty years, save for inter-

mittent warfare with the Picts,[1] but internal troubles
began immediately after his death, for his son Osred was
only eight years old, and the crown was seized by a pre-
tender, one Eardwulf, a distant relative of the royal
house; but he only held it for two months, for Ealdorman
Bertfrid, a dominating figure in the Witan, determined
to place the boy prince on the throne, and with the aid of
other noblemen this was accomplished, Eardwulf being
assassinated, and Bertfrid becoming regent of the kingdom.   Immediately after these events, in 706, Bertfrid
assembled a council on the river Nidd, which was attended
by the Archbishop Bertwald and all the bishops of the
north.[2]   The case of Bishop Wilfred was discussed, and
a compromise was effected whereby Wilfred regained his
Abbey of Ripon, but exchanged the See of York for the
much less important See of Hexham.

We may imagine that after the great Council of the
Nidd a feast would be held to celebrate a new era of
political alliances and the re-establishment of cordial
relations between Church and State.   This would
certainly be held in Bertfrid's hall, where priest and nobles
would be entertained with all the magnificence its owner
could muster.   There we may picture the great ealdorman at the head of the table, the Archbishop Bertwald as
the guest of honour, and the partially-mollified Bishop
Wilfred being assigned a seat of importance by way of
additional balm for his lifetime of ruffled dignity.   Bertfrid, ruler of Northumbria in all but name, presides
impressively, and his guests at the far end of the table
catch glimpses of him through the drifting smoke from

[1] Bede states that Aldfrid " nobly retrieved the state of a kingdom that had
been ruined, though it was now less extensive than of yore."
[2] Bertfrid, who has been associated with our hypothetical family because he
illustrates so vividly the political and administrative career of a nobleman of that
period, was an historical figure of considerable interest, being a diplomatist of
real ability.   His Council on the River Nidd was an event of some importance.
Possibly its memory is preserved by the village of Birstwith which may mark
the actual spot where it was held ; certainly the name is significant.

Bertfrid's feast after the Council of the Nidd.

80

the open fires of the hall.   To them he appears a commanding figure, his tunic of fine linen embellished by a brooch of coloured enamel (made by a skilful craftsman of York), and his golden hair carefully combed.   Yet he would have shocked his ancestor, Titus Paulinus, for the delights of the bath were almost unknown to him, and the very food he ate and the setting of the feast would have revolted that long-dead citizen of Eboracum.   And yet the meal was not without its order and ceremony. The dishes were of gold and silver, and servants offered meat on spits, bending on one knee while each guest cut slices for himself.   There were some traces of elegance, napery and tolerable service, but there was little restraint about eating and drinking.   Conversation would turn on politics, war, and agriculture, and there would be solemn condemnation from responsible men of the condition of convents.   The women would discuss such matters, too, and criticism would be expressed with a freedom that bordered on coarseness, until, as the feast advanced, the extreme fashions of the gay young nuns, their love of pet dogs and their addiction to cosmetics would cease to be the main subjects of scandalous gossip.[1]

The scene would change its character gradually, becoming instead of a sedate gathering of well-dressed people, a noisy and possibly disgusting orgy of drunkenness.   The priests and the more dignified nobles would withdraw.   We can picture Bertfrid leaving the scene when its riot and racket had passed the culminating point, and general stupor was supervening, donning his mantle and cap and strolling into the cool evening air.   He turns to look at the great wooden mass of his hall, with its lead-covered roof sparkling in the frosty moonlight. Within, the musicians are striving to drown with pipes and fiddle a drunken bard who twangs a harp discordantly,

---

[1] Many of the convents and monasteries were at this time, as later, ill-managed and the homes of all kinds of vice and excess.

F

but Bertfrid only smiles, for he knows that better bards
and music-makers will flock to Northumbria now that his
strong hand can guide the kingdom's peace, and make
the land secure for every trade and craft, and give the
farmer freedom from the constant call of war.

CHAPTER VI

CULTURE AND AGRICULTURE

HOME life in eighth century England acquired a definite routine, despite the intermittent alarms and disorders of war. The land imposed an unalterable calendar for the bulk of the population : January, ploughing ; February, pruning ; March, digging and sowing ; April, planting ; May, lambing ; June, haymaking ; July and August, harvest time ; with a break at September for hunting, although throughout the year wolves and wild boar claimed the attention of farmers and lords. Then in October there was sowing, and threshing in November.[1] As a system of life it was not very dissimilar from that prevailing in pre-Roman Britain. Agriculture was certainly more scientific, and farmers employed a greater variety of better implements for their work, including the wheeled plough with the metal ploughshare, and pitchforks, billhook scythes, spades, picks, flails, and sickles, and the adze and the harrow had come into use ;[2] moreover, existence was not weighed down by a dread of dark religious rites as a permanent and threatening background. Also there were important buildings and cities ; but the wattle and daub house of the common man, dark with the grime of an open fire, comfortless and insanitary, did not mark a great advance on the domed huts of the ancient Britons, and was probably inferior to any slave quarters attached to the great Romano-British estates of six centuries before.

But from the anarchy of the first Saxon settlements and

[1] Details taken from Saxon pictorial Calendar.
[2] All these implements are illustrated in illuminated MSS., of a later period.

the desperate and declining remnants of Romano-British life a comparatively ordered system had grown up, a social organisation with a king for its supreme head, and a carefully graded aristocracy of whom the eorls, the nobles, were either of the blood royal (athelings) or were created by the king, as Ealdorman Bertfrid was created. In the grade immediately below the nobles were the ceorls, freemen who owned enough land to support a household, and below them were læts, men with no proprietary rights, the cottagers and free labourers, many of them of the old British stock ; and at the bottom of the structure came the theows, or slaves.

The land would be worked, in the case of freemen, by a family group, or mægth. Such a settlement would consist of large arable fields, divided into narrow strips, each household of the group possessing several of these strips as well as a hedge-divided lot of meadow in the summer, though in the winter the meadow would become common land for the whole group.[1] Waste land would also be common, and the community would draw its wood supply therefrom, and pasture its swine on the coarse grass. The strip system of dividing fields doubtless gave an acrimonious turn to conversation on all occasions, and it is not difficult to visualise the constant bickering produced by this archaic individualism. We find that the chief offences against established law and order are brawling, homicide, and theft, particularly of live stock. Gang-robbery and rape are also popular among the criminal classes, which then represented a very large section of society. A Romano-British magistrate, accustomed to the peace and orderliness of the Roman Province, would have been distressed and seriously alarmed by a week's experience of most districts in the Saxon kingdoms of England. We can figure him writing a report to the Præfect, or to the Governor of Britain, asking for at least

[1] Crops cultivated would be chiefly wheat, barley, and oats, sown in rotation.

two cohorts of troops to quell the natives " who appear to be utterly out of hand. The civil power is constantly threatened."

Practically all offences were punishable by fines, but offences against the clergy or the Church were dealt with severely. Christianity had ample material safeguards. For example, a thief repaid a ceorl three times the value of what he had stolen, but to a priest nine times the value. Purely religious offences were met with great harshness, and the peasant was brutally restrained from such crimes as Sabbath-breaking, worshipping pagan gods, or failing to get a child baptised within thirty days of its birth.

The revival of the crafts, metalworking, and the production of enamel, the development of illuminating manuscripts, and the rise of literature and the encouragement of music and dancing may be attributed very largely to the strength and security of the Church, and to the comparative immunity of religious settlements, monasteries, and convents from the troubles trailed by war. It is true that many convents, monasteries, and abbeys were ill-managed, and sheltered people who occupied themselves with a variety of vices and excesses, but a very real intellectual life existed, although it hardly affected the ceorls, læts, and theows ; but the nobles saw something of it, and Ealdorman Bertfrid's descendants were not lacking in elementary education.[1] They could appreciate music and the sagas sung or declaimed by the bards who visited their great houses ; their taste in clothes and ornaments could not be identified with anything primitive and savage, and in their time decorative art advanced triumphantly.

But in Northumbria, where the family of Bertfrid lived

[1] In his work, *Anglo-Saxon Literature*, the Rev. J. Earle states that " There was in the Anglian region of Northumbria a development of religious and intellectual life which makes it natural to regard the whole brilliant period from the later seventh to the early ninth century as the Anglian period. Here we recognise the first great stage in the revival of learning and the first movement towards the establishment of public order in things temporal and spiritual."

and prospered generation by generation, brief reigns and almost constant civil war helped the decay that had really begun when the Picts had freed themselves from the overlordship of the English kingdom. War became the most important business of the nobles ; evading it probably became the most urgent task of the freemen farmers ; and even the prosperity of the Church was influenced, for we hear of Ripon Cathedral being allowed to fall into ruin. But even under such difficult conditions the common life of the land went on ; food was grown and families were reared, and in the intervals of warfare the nobles went about their hunting, arranged their feasts and entertainments, concerning themselves with the holding of their lands, intriguing to control the Witanagemote,[1] and thereby the whole kingdom, and administering the curious justice acclaimed by custom. But presently Northumbria, in common with other English kingdoms, was compelled to concern itself with an overseas menace, and before the close of the eighth century Viking raiders were repeating the tactics of the fourth and fifth century Saxon pirates, whose English descendants were as troubled and dismayed at the energy and ferocity of such foreign incursions as the Romano-Britons had been. England, dominated in the eighth century by the kingdom of Mercia and in the early ninth century by Wessex, was soon to experience the threat of Danish rule.

Despite the troubles and dangers that beset all England, Northumbrian kings and nobles kept internal squabbles vigorously alive, and when, in the third quarter of the ninth century, a Danish army entered the kingdom, a political crisis was in full swing, for the king, Osbert, had been temporarily ousted by a usurper, one Ælla. It was

[1] The Witanagemote, the legislative body of the kingdom, consisted of the king, the ealdormen who governed directly under the king various units of his domains, the bishops, and a few great thegns. English kings were generally dominated by their councils.

at this time that a great-great-great-great-grandchild of
Ealdorman Bertfrid was living at Beristæth [1] in Nidderdale, the Lady Ethelflæda, the last of the noble family that
had played a prominent part in the affairs of the kingdom,
ever since the days of its great founder. Her father,
Urtfrith, had been absent from his lands for some weeks,
for he was a gesith, a member of the king's war band, and
had followed Osbert into exile, leaving his daughter
securely guarded in a strongly fortified hall in the valley
of the Nidd, the most remote of his possessions and the
most difficult to approach, marking the spot where Bertfrid's Council had been held, and not far from a forgotten
Roman station where legionaries had once guarded the
road to the lead mines.

Ethelflæda found life at that hall a dull domestic round,
without feasts, music, or gossip. It was comfortable, as
she understood comfort. The great wooden structure
with the walls draped with hides and bearskins, and a
large woollen tapestry stretched across the master's end
of the hall, formed a setting that was richly though bar-
barically decorative and undeniably dirty from wood
smoke, the floor fouled, and the huge greasy surface of
the long table—a very crude piece of woodwork—dark
with ancient stains, crumb-littered, telling the history of a
hundred meals. In the more than usually disturbed state
of the country, rumours of raids and bloodshed, the burning of farms and the wholesale looting of live stock—
including theows—drifted in with every wayfarer, though
travellers to that remote settlement in a wood-begirt
valley were few ; but there were fugitives, and sometimes
a fragment of King Osbert's war band, a handful of
wounded and exhausted soldiers, would seek the shelter
of Urtfrith's strong retreat and claim the hospitality of his

---

[1] Modern Birstwith. This spelling, Beristæth, for which there is no docu-
mentary authority, is suggested by Professor Moorman in his work on the place-
names of the West Riding of Yorkshire (Thoresby Society).

daughter. Ethelflæda felt that it was all very remote, this warfare, something too distant and scattered to touch the securities of her home life, and fierce rumours left her unperturbed. She was a tall, blue-eyed, well-built girl, with long golden brown hair, which she wore in two plaits that came over her shoulders and hung down in front of her gown. But she was tempted by the desire to dress her hair in the more fashionable manner adopted by all the ladies she had met, curling it delicately with hot irons and sinking into the gathered and crowning tresses a semi-circular headband of engraved gold. She had often rehearsed this fashion in her father's absence, using a headband that her mother had worn, and had at last dropped into the habit of adopting it entirely, risking the rage of the peppery old nobleman, who hated her to make any changes, even when they were the accepted signals of maturity. Her father had been away many weeks, and having received no word from him, she was beginning to feel a double anxiety, first for his welfare, and secondly for his comments on her modish venturing when he should return. That return was unheralded and violent in its suddenness.

Supper in the hall was over, and it was a night of eddying moonlight, for rain clouds were laced over the sky, letting the beams through their gaps as they drifted slowly. The big room was full of smoke, and Ethelflæda sat in a clumsy chair sewing with a silver needle. In another chair was a fat monk mending the strings of a harp. A huddled old woman crouched on a bench by the great tapestry, Fritha, Ethelflæda's old nurse, who was now her duenna and personal attendant, a withered, wise old creature, of whom the monk, Adbert, disapproved, for it was rumoured that she still worshipped forbidden gods, laughing slyly at the Church. Only Urtfrith's protection had saved her from the correction of holy hands. A group of theows muttered among themselves as they lay on the rush-strewn floor at the far end of the hall, as near the fire as they dared to venture. The air was drowsy with the fumes of cooked food, and stale with other odours, for bathing was unknown to the noble lady in her gown of green silk with gold glinting above her brow and at her throat, or to the fleshy monk in his russet habit, the bundle of dingy red and blue cloth that was Fritha the ancient servant, and the dozen or so slaves of the soil who were gathered in the place ; all were unwashed, the theows a prey to parasites, nor was noble blood exempt from tribute to the nourishment of fleas. The monk, with a simple directness that did not embarrass his hostess in the least, would occasionally stay his task to imitate the manners of the monkey cage. And then this scene of natural ease after a full meal was interrupted. There were hails from the guard by the ford, and answering shouts from the men outside the hall ; a sound of horse's hoofs, and Urtfrith's voice raised in anger. Ethelflæda rose in absolute panic as her father strode into the hall. He reeled a little as he came towards her. She thought, of course, that he was drunk, but a second later she knew that was wrong, for he could never speak steadily when his draughts of mead had been too copious.

" The king marches to-night with Ælla," he said in the voice of a man unutterably weary.

" *With* him ? " said Ethelflæda curiously, wondering when the storm on the subject of hairdressing would begin.

" There is a truce," replied Urtfrith.

" But why ? "

" Ay, a truce—the Danes are here. The dark devils have taken York—they're on the march now, a thousand swords strong, each party, and mounted." [1]

---

[1] When in 867 the Danish army entered Northumbria in force and sacked York, Ælla and Osbert, too late, sank their differences and combined to face the common enemy.

" Where are they marching to ? "

" Everywhere—sacking what they can. Come, girl, no more questions, I must sleep ; I must march from here by dawn with every man who can stand."

He stumbled towards the big curtain of tapestry and collided with the monk who was standing meekly obsequious, waiting for his lord to greet him. He was not disappointed.

" Out of the path, nithing ! " shouted Urtfrith in a sudden spasm of fury, grasping the corpulent creature by the scruff of the neck and slamming him across the hall. " Fat priests have brought all trouble to Northumbria," he said, the jealousy of a threatened politician surging within him as he thought of the power the Church enjoyed with a calm serenity that war left undisturbed ; never mind, though—these Danish raiders would respect the Church and its property as they respected a woman and her chastity. He staggered to his rough plank bed behind the curtain and dropped off to sleep, awaking instantly, so it seemed to him, to a world of violent uproar. Shouts and screams were tearing the night air. He heard Ethelflæda's voice calling him, and leaping up, still drowsy, he lugged his sword from its wooden, leather-bound sheath, and burst through the curtain.

The hall was full of black-clad armed men led by a roaring blond giant, manifestly drunk, who was waving a blood-bathed double-bladed axe in sweeping circles above his steel-clasped leather helmet. Iron rings on leather streaked with scarlet glittered on his broad chest. On the floor lay Adbert, the monk, his head smashed to pulp, while Ethelflæda cowered screaming in a corner. Fritha, the old nurse, was yelling strange words to the mob :

" Sons of Odin ! Sons of Odin ! Welcome to your heritage ! " she screamed. Urtfrith had a momentary pang of regret that he had ever protected the hag ; but at least the woman was wise, and she might serve

The hall was full of black-clad armed men led by a roaring blond giant.

his daughter yet, despite a change of masters, so he cried :

" Look well to your mistress, woman."

But she only answered : " Your word is naught ; your god is dead ! " And as he hurled himself at the gigantic Viking he felt that she spoke truth. He was beaten down by that great axe, his head broken and split by the whirling strokes. The conqueror kicked aside the corpse and bawling with drunken joy advanced on Ethelflæda.

*　　　*　　　*　　　*　　　*

Ethelflæda's captor was a hersir, or clan chief, named Ulf-Ketil, a follower of Ivar the Boneless, the great Danish general who with Halfdan had captured York, and who had tricked so many English forces. Ulf-Ketil was in command of a raiding party some three hundred strong, and they were sweeping up Nidderdale, burning farms, wasting lands, and massacring and ravaging from York to the slopes of Whernside. They had taken Beristæth in a well-timed rush, after an hour of crafty, silent killing of sentries and guards. Mead by the gallon they had drunk that afternoon in the taking of an outlying farm on Urtfrith's estate, some miles from the hall ; but no carousing could make their cunning sleep, and they saw to it that no warning of their approach went through the forest.

They did not burn the hall, but after setting guards and searching for survivors they rested. The terrified theows prepared a tremendous meal in the dawn, and after spoiling the place of everything that could be moved and carried, they rode back towards York, Ulf-Ketil bearing Ethelflæda on his saddle, his sturdy little pony carrying their joint weight easily. Ulf-Ketil had been compelled to kill two of his followers in order to give point to his explanation that Ethelflæda was his own exclusive share of the Beristæth loot. Discipline having been restored and property rights firmly established, they drove all the live stock before them, together with a score of theows who had failed to escape to the forest; and old Fritha, who had welcomed them and praised their gods so readily, was given a seat on a pack-horse.

York, as Ethelflæda saw it at the close of the next day, was partially ruined. No house had a door, and many were charred remnants only, walls and roof having sunk in flames to a black heap. And everywhere the Danes were encamped, lording it over the cowed inhabitants of the ancient city, driving them in gangs to work at the repairing of the great walls, designed by some forgotten Roman engineer centuries before, and pulled down and rebuilt, breached and patched as wars and raids touched the city, but following the old lines imperial military science had laid down. In the great house of an English nobleman, who had given up the tenancy and his life somewhat painfully when the city was taken, the Danish chief, Ivar the Boneless, had made his headquarters, and it was there that Ulf-Ketil reported the return of his raiding party.[1]

Ethelflæda could only understand a little of the talk that went on in this improvised Court. Ivar sat in a box-like chair that had been crudely carved with the Danish raven emblem on the back and sides, a couple of raven's heads also rising as clumsy finials at the back, so that he looked as though misshapen birds were trying to perch on his shoulders. He was dressed in black, his sombre, silken tunic being edged with scarlet, while his arms shone dully yellow with bracelets of massive gold, half a dozen to each muscle-bulged arm. Trousers of black cloth with ornamented borders at the ankle covered his legs, and leather sandals with straps and buttons were on his feet. He was a well-kept man, with carefully combed hair, bearded, majestic. Ulf-Ketil showed him great reverence. The raw grief at her father's death, the

[1] See Appendix II., Note 1.

confusion, horror, and bewildering succession of sensa-
tions that had been crammed into the last twenty-four
hours could not dull Ethelflæda's curiosity. She was
apprehensive, naturally, but she was under the protection
of this great chief, Ulf-Ketil, and conceivably she might
be more to him than a slave concubine. Her captor's
interview with Ivar was very important to her ; she
listened eagerly ; and piecing together the scraps of talk
she comprehended, she gathered that the lands and hall
at Beristæth were passing into Ulf-Ketil's possession.
Her name was mentioned. She found the cold eyes of
Ivar upon her. Ulf-Ketil was looking anxious ; but
Ivar's gaze lacked interest ; he nodded assent to his
gigantic follower ; and then there was more talk, and
presently a huge interminable meal ; the second and final
meal of the Danish day, supper.

These two vast meals were exactly alike. Early morning and early evening saw the consumption of colossal
quantities of meat, not unappetisingly prepared, and mead
and beer would flow in gallons into the drinking horns
of the monstrous men whose physical endurance and
build made them such superb sailors, warriors, and
horsemen.

The next day there was a marriage ; and old Fritha
prepared Ethelflæda for the course of heathen rites that
accompanied the social proclamation of Ulf-Ketil's proprietary interest. The prospect of being wedded to her
father's murderer was not so utterly revolting to one who
had heard of war and death, and had seen the gaps in
family life created by intermittent fighting, from her
cradle. She placidly abandoned Christianity, and changed
her life to suit its new conditions with the ease she had
inherited from a long line of ancestors, all able and
adaptable folk, changing their ways to conquer newer
and often better modes of living.

Ethelflæda stayed in York for a few years after her

marriage, and there her son, Thor-Ketil, was born. The war passed on, the warriors of the raven striding from triumph to triumph. Now they would ride north and set up a puppet king of their own choosing beyond the Tyne;[1] and presently Mercia would submit to their commands. Edmund, king of East Anglia, was granted the immortal privilege of martyrdom by Hingwar and Hubba; and the Danes raged this way and that across all England, from Mercia to Wessex and back again, with their headquarters now in Reading then in London. Ulf-Ketil became a very famous warrior indeed, but when he was seriously wounded, in 876, nine years after his marriage to Ethelflæda, retirement to his great estates in Nidderdale became imperative. Here he re-built the hall at Beristæth. In the same year Halfdan was dividing up Northumbria, and encouraging his followers to cultivate the war-torn countryside. The Danish social order was imposed upon the country, and with the jarl (earl) at the head, society was graded with the same rigidity it had known in Saxon days. The chiefs of clans, the hersirs, came immediately below the jarls, and then were hölds, yeomen, bóndi as they were called, the freedman or leysingi being the lowest rank above the thrælls, who were slaves, the equivalent of the Saxon theows.[2]

Ulf-Ketil had been made a jarl before he retired to his Beristæth home. That home he enriched as befitted a great warrior and a nobleman; and his son, Thor-Ketil, grew up amid surroundings that boasted all the luxuries offered by that rough age. The boy was brought up as a worshipper of those Northern, war-like gods of Scandinavia, learning from a renegade Christian monk the tenets of his father's faith. He was taught to ride very

[1] Ecgberht.
[2] For the Saxon social ranks and the services due from each, see Appendix II., Note 2.

soon after he could walk, and he was also taught to handle weapons, and was taken to York periodically and accustomed to ships and shipping, learning the ways of a seaman before he was twelve years old, sailing from the city quays down the Humber to the tumbled grey sea. His education was a very practical affair. Reading and writing had no place in it ; but he learned about the organisation and management of a farm, and physically he was trained to far pleasanter habits than his grandfather, Urtfrith, would have tolerated. A weekly bath was included in the scheme of things, for example, and a certain fastidiousness in the matter of personal cleanliness, the combing and careful dressing of the hair, and attention lavished on small details of dress all combined to render Thor-Ketil, and his father, Ulf-Ketil, more agreeable people to look at and live with than any inhabitants Britain had possessed since the final disappearance of Romano-British towns.[1]

When his father came to live permanently at Beristæth, Thor-Ketil's recreations were extended. He accompanied Ulf-Ketil on hunting expeditions, and in the winter evenings he would play chess with him.[2] Life was packed with interesting things to do for a hardy, energetic youth of the ruling caste. Before he was twenty he was a soldier, taking part in the great wars against the English king, Alfred, who was determined to break Danish power ; but although his arm was long it did not reach Northumbria. And so war flowed over the land, and, a veteran warrior at twenty-five, Thor-Ketil married a Christian girl from East Anglia, the daughter of a jarl who had been a counsellor of the Christian Danish king,

[1] John of Wallingford says that the Danes were hated by the English because "they were wont, after the fashion of their country, to comb their hair every day, to bathe every Saturday [Laugardarg, ' bath day '], to change their garments often, and set off their persons by many such frivolous devices. In this manner they laid siege to the virtue of the women."

[2] Cf. *Scandinavian Britain*, by W. G. Collingwood, F.S.A.

Guthrum.[1]   The Danes let in once more the faith they had driven out.   Although Thor-Ketil would not leave his gods, he let his son, Sweyn, be baptised and taught later on to read and write by a Christian priest.   Culture was slowly climbing back to power, despite the wars and massacres and raids.

[1] King Guthrum died in 890 in East Anglia, where he had settled.

G

CHAPTER VII

AFTER THE DANE

ARKELL "SCRUFA" (the curly-headed) was the great-great-great-great-grandson of Ethelflæda and Ulf-Ketil, and, like his fathers before him, he was a hersir, the head of the Wapontake of Claro, which included all Nidderdale. His hall at Beristæth stood in a great field named after his Danish ancestor, Ketilsing (Ketil's Ing), and there he lived a life of ease and enjoyment, as ease and enjoyment were understood in his day. All England was ruled by Edward the Confessor, a pious weakling addicted to Courts and culture, but representative of supreme governing authority, with sufficient backing to make civilisation united from the savage Scottish border to the south coast, while in Wales petty princelings still played with faint memories of Romano-British times and posed imperially in their mountains. Northumbria, under Earl Siward, still included Yorkshire, and the Danes in settling the country had divided that county-to-be into ridings, and the ridings into wapontakes, which were the equivalent of the hundreds of Saxon England.

Four scenes from the life of Arkell Scrufa during a week in the spring of the year A.D. 1046, when he was a man of forty, married, prosperous, and the absolute ruler of a large tract of country, will throw some light upon the customs, powers, and conditions of his time.

The four scenes are set in the hall at Ketilsing.[1] It is a long, high room with blackened oak beams bearing the

---

[1] The hamlet of Kettlesing exists in fact in Nidderdale, some five miles from Harrogate. Though it is the scene of most of the events in the ensuing chapters, considerable liberties have been taken with the local history and topography.

weight of the lead-covered roof; the walls being hung with skins, fabrics, and crude tapestries now mellow in tone for their original bright colours have been dimmed by smoke from the open hearth, which whirls and drifts about the great barn-like space before it trickles through the pinnacled cowls that are perched on the roof ridge; day and night, summer and winter, it stings the nostrils and eyes of those who use the hall. There is a rough trestle table occupying about half the length of the place, the top composed of ill-trimmed boards—a heavy, crude piece of furniture, stained and dirty. There are box-like chairs at the head of the table for the hersir and his lady and for two chosen guests; but the only other seats are benches formed of rough boards supported by thick upright logs.

SCENE I.

The first scene opens when Arkell is about to begin the second meal of the day, supper. He is a tall man with a mass of copper-coloured hair, carefully combed and washed, and his beard is trimmed to a point. His clothes are simple in form, but rich in their quality. He wears a tunic of dark red cloth that reaches to his knees and is girdled at the waist with a belt of leather and gold. The sleeves of this garment are clipped to his forearm with gold bracelets; at his throat is a jewelled brooch. Stockings with embroidered tops cover his legs below the knee, and he wears shoes of soft leather. His wife, Inglefred, has a long tunic or gown of green with gold embroidery of a flower design at the neck. She wears black shoes which peep out from under the long skirt of her gown. The sleeves of this gown are wide below the elbow, allowing a glimpse of the gold rings on her arms.

The hall is filled with the harsh voice of Anlaf, an unwashed, raucous anchorite who has left his hermitage, a cave in the bank of the river Nidd, to accuse Dage, one of Arkell's thrælls, of theft; and theft, moreover, of the blackest kind, no less than a lamb taken from the lands of Aldeburgh (Aldborough) Church

*at Hompthveit (Hampsthwaite).   Church property is especially
sacred.   Arkell, who has no love for Anlaf, is inclined to impatience.   The anchorite has never lost an opportunity for outspoken disapproval of the riotous, pleasure-loving ways of the
lord of Ketilsing.   The curtain rises as Anlaf concludes his
accusation, one skinny, grime-grey finger pointing at the big,
wooden-looking thræll Dage, who seems absolutely unmoved by
the saintly eloquence.*

ANLAF.   A lamb, Lord Arkell, a lamb, thieved from
    our church.   With these eyes have I seen him—
    thief, cursed one, Dage—one of thy flock, Lord
    Arkell.

ARKELL.   So you said before, holy one.

ANLAF.   Ay, and I repeat the charge—judgment, judg-
    ment ; pronounce it, oh lord.

ARKELL.   By God's eyes, holy one, are you lord here
    or am I ?   There must be trial with proper form.

ANLAF.   Dage must be brought before a higher court
    than thine, Lord Arkell.   He has thieved from
    the Church ; from Church lands hath he ravished
    a lamb ; and there he stands—his belly crammed
    with meat that should have fed more sacred bodies.
    His life is forfeit.

ARKELL.   After trial—perhaps.   (*To Dage*) : Speak,
    thræll—shall justice be done on you for this ?
    You've heard this holy witness of your guilt—
    if guilt there is.   A matter that I doubt.

ANLAF (*enraged at the insult but turning its meaning from
    himself adroitly*).   You hold unguilty those who
    steal, Lord Arkell ?   Yet do I recall three bodies
    lacking heads not many moons since, slain by
    your orders, lord, for ravishing your flock ; and
    yet how small their sin compared with this dark
    crime, this thieving of a lamb owned by the Holy
    Church.

ARKELL. I have not yet heard Dage reply; your voice is somewhat loud, holy one, and I must repeat my question to my thræll about your lamb.

DAGE. Lord, I have taken no lamb. I have seen no lamb. I have eaten no stolen meat. I am your thræll, and my meat is not lacking.

ARKELL. The man is innocent. You may go—holy one. (*To his steward*): Thort, bring mead—and my supper. (*The steward, who has been holding a silver-mounted drinking horn, kneels and offers it to his lord.*)

ANLAF. I demand trial!

ARKELL (*with feigned surprise*). Still here, holy one— I thought I had released you from my presence. My voice, perhaps, is too quiet for your ears. (*He leaps to his feet and roars*): Get to your unclean cave, holy wolf, and howl there with your blood brothers, the wolves!

ANLAF. I demand trial of a thief!

ARKELL (*grasping the drinking horn with both hands so fiercely that he spills the mead*). I will baptise you afresh, holy one! (*Bellowing with laughter he shoots the contents of the horn across the table, drenching the rigid figure of Anlaf.*) There, holy one, take cheer from this unholy rain!

ANLAF (*unmoved*). I demand trial of a thief!

ARKELL (*to a group of armed men crouching by the fire*). Thrælls! Fling this filth from my hall!

ANLAF. I demand——

(*He gets no further, for the guards drag him roughly from the hall, one of them clapping a hand over his mouth. The scuffling dies away outside, although a faint cry of Trial, Trial! comes echoing back to the hall. Arkell nods to Dage who kneels to him for a moment and then creeps quietly to his place at the far end of the hall just within the circle of firelight.*)

ARKELL (*to his wife*).   I've drowned his holy mouth !

INGLEFRED.   I fear there will be trouble, my dear lord.

ARKELL.   Agreed, wife ; there will be trouble if I lose
Dage.   (*He sinks his rumbling voice to a whisper*) :
The thrӕll knows the pasturages like the lines on
his hand ; and am I to part with my best huntsman
and tracker ?   Besides, he will father more brats
unless he kills that wench of his with blows when
he is in mead.   (*He raises his voice*) : Anlaf can
squall till the blood washes his dirty neck—lamb
or no lamb, Dage is my thrӕll.

INGLEFRED.   But, husband, what if he is guilty ?

ARKELL.   Of course, he's guilty.   Do you suppose I
don't know that ?   I saw him toasting slices of
the meat on a spear head in the fire outside his hut
down by the marsh. .   (*He empties the horn which
the steward has refilled, and passes it over his shoulder
to be filled again, but Thort is not there, and his absence
draws a bellow of fury from the lord*) : Thort ! Thort !
Blood drench you, stinking rush rat !   My cup
lacks mead ;   fill, fool, fill !   (*Thort tremblingly
refills the drinking horn and Arkell drinks in eager gulps.*)

INGLEFRED.   Dear lord, the Church will try Dage and
the ordeal will prove his guilt.

ARKELL.   If there is a trial—if there is a trial, the ordeal
will prove what I wish, or else—(*To the steward*) :
Have you no eyes for an empty cup, fool ?

   (*Once more his horn is filled, and then supper is served.
It is a gigantic meal.   Meat seethed and roast is carried
round the table, every one dipping coarse baked cakes into
the gravy and cutting off slices of meat with their knives.
There is silence so far as spoken words are concerned,
every one eating with earnest vigour.   Arkell keeps his
great curly beard clean by wiping it every few minutes with a
square piece of linen.   The meal has passed its more solid
stage when Cedric, priest of Hompthveit, enters the hall.*

He is a man of courage and culture, and is respected by Arkell, who has found him useful. His church at Hompthveit has been burned down a few days before, fires that destroy individual buildings and whole villages being common and absolutely unpreventable owing to the universal use of timber and the equally ubiquitous open fire.) [1]

CEDRIC. Pax vobiscum. Lord Arkell, greeting. Lady Inglefred, greeting also.

ARKELL (*thickly to the steward*). Bring back that meat. Father Cedric, you will meat with us ?

CEDRIC. My thanks, lord.

ARKELL. Sit, Father. (*He indicates one of the guest chairs.*)

CEDRIC (*sitting*). Lord Arkell, I have a small matter on which to crave your hospitality.

ARKELL. Given as it is claimed, Father. Is the hospitality for yourself ?

CEDRIC. Nay, lord, for another.

ARKELL. Your friend will be welcome.

CEDRIC. My friend is—Justice. Let me explain. You know my holy house at Hompthveit died in flames more than a week ago ; therefore I am without a place wherein to hold a trial, and wish to consecrate your hall for trying by ordeal a man accused of grievous sin against the Holy Church.

ARKELL (*who has been drinking steadily and has now reached the maudlin stage*).[2]   How well you put your wishes, Father. Who could refuse you anything ? Not I ! No, no, not I ! Take my—take my (hic) hall and all therein for your trial when you will.

CEDRIC. That wide permission saves me much, Lord Arkell. Your word is better than a chain of iron. One thing from your hall must I claim now : the

---

[1] Cf. Collingwood, *opus cit.*, p. 143.

[2] That gluttony and drunkenness were the besetting vices of the Danes the sagas abundantly prove.   For example, when Edred held his Court at Abingdon, the Northumbrian visitors became so drunk by nightfall that they had to be removed.

man accused, who must meet justice at the trial—the
thræll, Dage !

ARKELL (*slowly clenching his huge freckled fists*). Are you
but Anlaf's thræll in this thing ? By God's eyes !
I will not be driven in my own hall—a pig that stinks
in a river cave orders this and that for me, Hersir
of Claro, to perform ! The river will be in his cave
ere long if his pride be not bitted ! No and no and
no !

(*He beats his fists on the table until the sturdy wood
quivers beneath the rain of blows, glaring at the priest
meanwhile. Cedric returns his savage gaze quite coolly.*)

CEDRIC. Anlaf, Lord Arkell, is but a witness. The
Holy Church gives orders to all men alike.

ARKELL (*gulping down mead*). The Earl Siward and the
king alone give orders to Arkell, Hersir of Claro !
I lend you my hall and give you charge of this
unguilty thræll because, in friendship—in friendship,
I say—and regard for you, I promised. But remember well, Father Cedric, that the man is innocent,
and remember also (hic), remember also, I say, that
I can ill afford to lose thrælls to suit the whim of a
(hic) wolf like Anlaf.

(*He staggers to his feet, but he has drunk far too much
mead to make standing possible. He falls across the
priest's knees and is violently sick. Cedric rolls him off
on to the floor, drawing his robe aside to prevent it from
being soiled. The steward and two thrælls drag Arkell
through the gap in the tapestry at the end of the hall.
Inglefred glances nervously at the priest : her husband's
spirited behaviour to the Church always worries her.*)

INGLEFRED. Dage will be delivered to your keeping,
Father.

CEDRIC. He is safe in yours. Lord Arkell's word will
be his jail and fetter.

(*Curtain.*)

SCENE II.

The hall at Ketilsing, prepared for the ordeal.   The table has been moved to one side, leaving the stamped earth floor free.   The stone slabs of the square, open hearth are hidden by a crackling wood fire, in the centre of which a round, rough bar of iron has been heated until it glows dull red.   Near the fire is the " stapela," the pile of wood on which the iron will be laid when it is judged to be hot enough for the trial.   The hall has been consecrated by Cedric, and the priest and Dage are its only occupants as the curtain rises.   Cedric, a crucifix in his right hand and a heavy, hide-bound book in his left hand, stands looking into the fire.   Dage, stolid and silent, stands beside him.[1]

CEDRIC.   Pace the mark, Dage.   Good steps, such as you always take.   (*Dage paces slowly from the stapela across the hall while Cedric counts*) :   One, two, three, four, five, six, seven, eight, nine.   Enough !   Stay while I mark the spot.   (*The priest places two pieces of wood one over the other in the form of a rough cross.   Then he returns to the fire while Dage walks back to the stapela. The iron bar is now almost white hot, and Cedric cries out*) :   Four may enter.

(*Four men come in, two representatives of the accused, of whom one is a soldier unarmed but wearing his thick leather tunic sewn with iron rings and holding in both hands his iron-clasped, leather helmet ; the other is a thræll, a farm hand with tousled, dirty hair, his bare legs and feet disclosed by his torn and filthy garment, a long tunic of dingy green.   The two representatives of the prosecutor are thrælls from Church lands, both clad in dirty rags of cloth.*)

CEDRIC (*addressing the four men*).   Judge ye if the iron of the trial be hot.

(*The men look apprehensively at the furnace of wood with*

---

[1] Trial by Ordeal for serious offences was the general rule.   See Appendix II., Note 3, where the procedure is described,

its white-hot iron heart, and carefully avoiding the eye of Dage, they mumble a low, nervous affirmative.)

CEDRIC (*calling*). Enter those who have fasted in preparation.

(*Twelve men enter, including Arkell's steward, Thort, and stand six on each side of the path Dage has paced out from the stapela to the mark. The priest first sprinkles them with holy water, letting each man drink from the ewer ; then taking up his book and crucifix he passes again from man to man, letting each kiss the rood. The fire is now falling lower, powdering the floor about the hearth with white ash, and when the hallowing is over, the priest addresses himself to the soldier and the thrælls who judged the heat of the iron.*)

CEDRIC. Let the iron be laid for God's judgment.

(*Two of the men addressed, one of whom is the village smith, move the iron gingerly with a pair of iron pincers, placing it on the stapela, where it sizzles on the dry wood and sends up a mist of smoke.*)

CEDRIC. Let no word be said, but pray ye all in your hearts to Almighty God to set the seal of His Holy Justice on this trial. (*He walks slowly to the mark, speaking as he goes*) : May Almighty God reveal to us the innocence or guilt of this thræll of our Lord Arkell, after the passing of the time appointed. (*He reaches the mark, and turning about looks down the path with the eight silent men each side of it to where Dage waits by the stapela, unmoved and apparently quite unafraid. There is a moment of tense silence, and then the priest addresses Dage*) : With thy right hand, take up the iron and bear it to this mark.

(*Dage stretches out his hand and grasps the glowing bar, which hisses and steams as it burns into the skin of his palm. He walks quickly to the mark and lays the bar at the priest's feet. He makes no sign of pain, and holds his blistered hand out to Cedric who binds it, saying*) :

Thus shall your hand remain until after the third day. If it be unbound (*he seals the linen strips with lead*) before that time and by any other than I, then is the trial void, and will the king need six score shillings as fine.

(*Curtain.*)

SCENE III.

The same as Scene 1, two days after the Ordeal. The curtain rises upon the Lady Inglefred, who is sewing iron rings on to a leather jerkin, her chair pushed back against the big tapestry that screens the lord's end of the hall. Three hounds lie in the flickering light of the low fire, replete with the leavings of the last meal eaten in the hall, leavings upon which they had first call, before the thrælls could venture on the scraps. Lord Arkell values his hunting friends, but it is not apparent as he strides in at this moment, his neat, curly hair disordered, his eyes red with rage, muttering in his beard; he kicks the hounds away from the fire, and crashes into a chair near his wife with a metallic rattle, for over his breast and back is leather armour faced with overlapping iron plates. Inglefred glances at him anxiously, but is too wise to speak. Arkell draws his sword and looks at it for a space, then hurls the naked blade to the ground and roars out : Ahoy!

(*Thort, the steward, runs into the hall. Arkell rises deliberately, picks up his sword and strikes the shrinking servant with the flat of it. Thort falls on his knees.*)

ARKELL.   Find your feet, fool—and let me always find mead for my cup when I come here ! (*He kicks the man savagely as he staggers to his feet and reels in terror from his lord's presence. There is silence for a moment, and then Arkell explodes to his wife*): That cave wolf is watching Dage ! I've tried to be alone with him since noon.   May Anlaf's bones stink naked in their rottenness before——

INGLEFRED (*interrupting with horror*). Oh, dear lord, do not curse the Church's holy ones. Spare me the fear of some ill fate for you, husband.

ARKELL (*picking up his sword*). I am my own Fate's master, wife.

INGLEFRED. Such boasting is but blasphemy, dear lord.

ARKELL. What ! Blasphemy to plan the things I wish —think you that some thing dear to my desire must not be worked for lest I anger Heaven ? I buy with blood or gifts the things I want ; and as I cannot use my sword in this, blood will not buy security for Dage.

INGLEFRED. No price paid makes the guilty innocent.

ARKELL. The wood and labour needed for rebuilding a church may at least influence those who proclaim guilt—or innocence.

INGLEFRED. You mean a bribe for Father Cedric ?

ARKELL. No, a gift to the Holy Church. It will sound well, too, and draw the teeth of that mangy cave-dweller, Anlaf.

INGLEFRED. Father Cedric will see what you want.

ARKELL. I hope he will, and lest he should miss my meaning, I'll explain his obligation in the matter. (*The steward limps in bearing Arkell's drinking horn, brimming with mead.*) Ah, this will lay the dust within my throat. (*He takes the horn, drinks a huge draught, and motions to the steward to leave him. The man goes.*)

INGLEFRED. When will you tell Cedric ?

ARKELL. At meat, within an hour.

INGLEFRED. Dear lord, cannot you tell him first ? Wait not until mead overtakes your wits.

ARKELL. Good sense, wife. Fetch him here.

(*Inglefred puts down her sewing and leaves the hall, and after finishing his mead, Arkell slips through an opening in the curtain, returning almost immediately with a leather-*

bound book. He turns the thick parchment leaves and looks at the pages sparkling with decorative drawings in vivid colours. He can read a little, but his reading is confined to legal documents ; it would never occur to him that it could be a recreation, and the book that represents his library also represents the forerunner of that form of ostentation that impels an illiterate captain of commerce in the twentieth century to install a few hundred yards of bookshelves, the freight of which he disregards entirely. Arkell's book is an earnest of culture, and he has fetched it into the hall because he wants to impress Cedric. Presently Inglefred returns with the priest.)

ARKELL. Good Father, welcome.

CEDRIC. Greeting, Lord Arkell.

ARKELL. Leave us, wife. (*Inglefred goes through the gap in the tapestry, and Arkell regards the priest for a moment before speaking. When he speaks he sinks his voice to a confidential, ingratiating level, vastly different from the bull-throated tones in which his views and orders are usually delivered*) : Since you sprinkled the holy water over my hall the place ill-fits me, Father. I cannot drink with my usual pleasure ; the place is still half church.

CEDRIC (*smiling*). A strange fancy for you to possess, Lord Arkell.

ARKELL (*missing the irony of the remark*). Isn't it ? If I may say so, Father, I should have thought mead would have washed away the memory of water, even if it has been priest-blessed. But then I have been disturbed. (*He snorts with rage at the thought of Anlaf.*) Disturbed by a mangy wolf ! (*He swallows his rage and smooths his voice again.*) And disturbed also by knowing that your holy house is ruined. Now if you want to raise a roof once more to praise Almighty God under it, well, Father Cedric, I am not ungenerous.

CEDRIC (*mechanically*).   Lord Arkell has always been the friend and helper of the Church.

ARKELL.   Just so.   As you know, Father, I am not without wealth and the fine things of living.   (*He permits himself a gesture which includes the book and his silver-bound drinking horn.*)   And for a new church at Hompthveit, I can order trees to be felled and sweat to run from a score of thrælls.   No doubt you have saved the lead from the ruins ?

CEDRIC.   Much of it, Lord Arkell.

ARKELL (*grandly*).   I will supplement it, if needs be, from the mines.   Am I not Hersir of all Nidderdale ?

CEDRIC.   Almighty God will bless your generosity, Lord Arkell, and I, his poor servant, will thank you gratefully.

ARKELL.   Enough of thanks, Father Cedric.   Now let me think—I must get the trees marked for felling. Dage must do it—but, what am I thinking of ? Dage is under ordeal, and we shall not know until after to-morrow whether we shall be able to put him in charge of this work.   That makes it difficult, Father.

CEDRIC.   It is in the hands of Almighty God.

ARKELL (*very softly*).   And yours, good Father.   (*There is a long pause, during which Arkell watches Cedric, smiling in his beard and waiting patiently.*)

CEDRIC (*half to himself*).   A house for my flock to weigh against the life of one wolf, if God prove him to be a wolf.   (*He rises to his feet.*)   Lord Arkell, do I understand your gift is but a price ?

ARKELL.   Something of that, Father, and yet something also of goodwill towards you.

CEDRIC.   Yes, Lord Arkell, I believe that too.

ARKELL.   It is a good price, Father.

CEDRIC (*repeating the words slowly as he walks out of the hall*). It is a good price, Lord Arkell.

ARKELL. Ah, and now for ease after all that bargaining.
(*He calls*) : Ahoy !

(*Inglefred appears through the gap in the tapestry.*)

INGLEFRED. And what said the good Father, husband ?

ARKELL (*irritably*). Didn't you listen ?

INGLEFRED. My dear lord, you sent me from you, and
I went.

(*The steward brings in an earthen vessel from which he
fills Arkell's horn ; Arkell drains the horn ; it is refilled
and the steward leaves.*)

ARKELL (*with a roar of laughter*). Bought—bought—
bought ! But (*he wags his finger at his wife*) not paid
for !

(*Curtain.*)

SCENE IV.

*The same as Scene 2, only there is no " stapela," and the
fire glows small like a red eye on the blackened stone hearth.
Cedric is standing near the fire, staring at it, lost in meditation.
Outside the hall the high, unmusical voice of Anlaf is heard
crying :*

God's judgment will reveal ! God's judgment
will reveal ! Repent all ye sinners, for you are to
witness God's will revealed in holy justice.

(*Cedric, roused by the voice, looks towards the door
irritably ; and the spasm of irritation is followed by a
gesture of apprehension. In a few minutes he will have to
break the seals on Dage's bandages and pronounce his
verdict. He kisses the rood he holds in his white fingers.
The voice of Anlaf continues its monotonous chant*) :

God's judgment will reveal ! God's judgment will
reveal ! God's judgment will reveal !

(*Then comes an interruption, and Arkell's great voice
roaring*) :

Whine in your own lair—wolf! Get you to your cave, holy one.

(*Arkell enters the hall, followed by Anlaf.*)

ANLAF.   I come to witness God's justice.

ARKELL.   And you may yet taste man's wrath.

CEDRIC.   My Lord Arkell, the time appointed is nigh. I ask for Dage to be given up from your safe-keeping so that I may read the signs of God's judgment upon him.

ARKELL (*shouting to three soldiers who have slipped into the hall*).   Fetch in Dage.   (*To Anlaf*): You took good care to watch that Dage was kept a prisoner.

ANLAF.   Three days and nights, sleepless and fasting, have I watched this guilty sinner.

ARKELL.   Guilty! Do you presume to speak before God's judgment has been given?

ANLAF.   I was the witness of his guilt.

ARKELL.   And now you will be the witness of his innocence.

(*Cedric starts nervously at this remark. Dage is marched in, his right hand enveloped in the sealed and soiled bandage. He is brought to where Cedric is standing, and the priest examines the seals carefully. Then one by one he breaks them, and as he unwraps the linen he prays.*)

CEDRIC.   All powerful God, whose wisdom is as a mighty river to the little pool that we, Thy servants, know, grant justice to this trial. Let the marks of the iron speak Thy wisdom, and if the flesh of this sinner's hand be healing, then shall we see Thy proclamation of his innocence.

(*He has now finished unwrapping the linen. Arkell fidgets impatiently, anxious for the formalities to be finished, for he wants to make plans for hunting with Dage the next day. There have been rumours of a boar in the thick woods near Hompthveit. Cedric is examining*

Dage's hand. The palm is scarred by two blisters, one broken and angry-looking, and they are stamped across the palm in the form of a cross. The priest is intensely moved. He tries to speak ; his tongue falters ; presently he mutters) :

The Cross !   The Holy Cross !

ARKELL.   What's that—guilty or innocent, Father ? (*He glares at Cedric, almost threateningly.*)

CEDRIC (*making his choice and letting his courage flame high*). Almighty God proclaims him—guilty !

ARKELL (*roaring*).   What ?

ANLAF (*with tactless vehemence*).   Praised be Almighty God !

ARKELL (*with cold ferocity in his voice*).   I think you are mistaken, Father Cedric.

CEDRIC (*giving Dage the rood to kiss*).   God's justice must be done ; God's judgment followed ; and may the healing of Almighty God's forgiveness come to the soul of this sinner whose body must be slain for his dark sin against the Holy Church.

ANLAF (*raising his hands and looking upwards*).   Oh, God, may I pray to Thee to save the soul of this poor sinful one whose body is now forfeit to Thy Holy Church.

CEDRIC.   Let him be taken from this place.

ARKELL (*snarling*).   Orders, orders, orders, in here—and not my orders.

CEDRIC.   The Church's orders.

ARKELL.   The Church—(*He swallows an oath. Suddenly the utter hopelessness of the situation crushes his truculence. He draws his sword, and then flings it on the ground*) : Your church at Hompthveit will rot in ruins.

CEDRIC (*quietly*).   It is the will of God, Lord Arkell.
       (*At a sign from the priest the soldiers take Dage from the hall. Anlaf follows them.*)

ARKELL.   And my sword is beaten by the rood !
               (*Curtain.*)

H

A Norman castle.

CHAPTER VIII

ENTER THE NORMAN

SIGFERTH, the grandson of Arkell Scrufa, was sixteen years old when the country was again conquered, fresh influences released, and the social life of the land furrowed and turned over like ploughed earth. And the plough was the Norman, who beat down opposition, and occupied place after place with a military wisdom almost Roman in its efficiency. The men in the iron-scaled hauberks and acorn-shaped helmets with the long nose-guards went everywhere, penetrating, like the pioneer legions of Julius Cæsar's first expeditions, into the hidden dangers of a country more hostile than an angry sea. Sigferth's father, Eric, fought at Senlac, where he was wounded, flying north to the fastness of Nidderdale with a handful of weary Anglo-Danish troops. His arrival at Ketilsing after that flight gave Sigferth the first glimpse of the vast change that was coming to England. Eric, fierce soldier and lord of the wapontake of Claro, chief of a line that had ruled in Nidderdale for centuries, a name respected and feared throughout Evorwicshire,[1] this powerful nobleman came to his home as a refugee.

The values, ideas, and ambitions of young Sigferth were overset in a single night. He learned that he must fight not for glory or personal advancement, but for the very roof over his head and the soil that provided his food.

Life and manners had not changed much at Ketilsing since his grandfather's day. Farming, the cares of an estate, hunting, feasting : such matters were to command the time of Sigferth when the future promised the careless luxury of wealth and rank to be inherited. He had been well educated at the College of Secular Canons at Ripon,[2] and could read and write Latin and speak it with a fluency and sympathy that would have enabled him to talk with ease to his Romano-British ancestors of some twenty-five generations back. Had he been guided to accept Norman overlordship, he might conceivably have helped to bring nearer by a generation the ultimate welding of the two peoples ; but his hand was set against these brigand adventurers who had scored a serious success in the south, and as he regarded the Duke William and his followers much in the same way that the Romano-Britons regarded the Saxons, and later on as the ostensibly civilised Saxons regarded the Danes, the vision that might have been possessed by a man of his culture was dimmed by his outraged and extremely localised patriotism. The home had already become very sacred in England ; and Ketilsing was historic in the intimate family sense.

In a few years life at Ketilsing changed beyond all

[1] The Saxon rendering of Yorkshire, the stretch of country between the Humber and the Tees. Cf. Thierry's *Norman Conquest*, p. 77.

[2] The former Abbey had, *circa* 995, been converted into a College of Secular Canons.

knowing, and even the face of the country altered.   Once
more armies marched and counter-marched over the land,
spreading destruction.   Nineteen-year-old Sigferth took an
active part in the attack on the forces of one of Duke
William's great military lords, Robert de Comines, who
was killed with all his men at Durham, and in the early
autumn of the same year, 1069, both he and his father
were prominent in the siege of York, which was sacked
with the aid of ten thousand Danish soldiers.   The city
and its Minster were burnt, and the Norman garrison
fled.   So far, the peace of Nidderdale and the hall at
Ketilsing had been untouched, but now came the Norman
leader's war of revenge, a war designed to smash down
opposition so that Saxon England could contemplate the
conqueror's power amid the ashes of a lost prosperity.
York was retaken, and Sigferth and Eric were outlawed,
flying to the depths of Knaresborough forest for refuge,
but in touch with their home and property, to which they
returned when the ravaging army had swept away to the
north.   The main Nidderdale valley suffered in that
punitive war.   Farms were burnt, male thrælls flayed
and hanged, the women attached to the train of the
military machine, live stock that could not be driven
away for the use of the commissariat department was
killed, property looted, buildings left mere empty shells ;
it was a planned and deliberate breaking up of a social
system ; a largely successful attempt to render organised
opposition impossible by wiping out civilisation.[1]

[1] Thierry, *opus cit.*, says : " They precipitated themselves on the land of
Northumbria in a very frenzy of vengeance ; they burned the fields under culti-
vation as well as the hamlets and towns, and massacred the flocks with the men.
. . . William planned to make Northumbria absolutely uninhabitable."   And
again on p. 294 : " Another rising at Durham in 1080 was repressed by the forces
of Bishop Odo of Bayeux, who pillaged the church of Durham and renewed
throughout Northumberland the ravages made there by William in 1070.   This
second devastation, added to the first, impressed upon the northern counties of
England that aspect of desolation and gloom which they presented for more than
a century afterwards.   In this county, ruined as it was, the population, half
Danish, half Saxon, long preserved its ancient spirit of independence and of

Without modern weapons, high explosives, bombing aeroplanes, and poison gases, destruction was a prolonged process, fatiguing to the destroyers, and although forests blazed and blackened all over Yorkshire and away up to the Scottish borderland, there were some patches that escaped, and the lateral valley of the Tang Beck, in which the hall of Ketilsing stood, missed the devastation and depopulation of the main Nidderdale valley.

So presently Sigferth returned to his hall, bringing with him that shadow of a powerful lord, his father Eric, who was broken in health and weakened in mind by his hardships and misfortunes, so that Sigferth was virtually the lord of Ketilsing. There he lived on the edge of starvation,[1] mocked by the memory of plenty, his meagre mode of living in violent contrast with the suggestion of wealth conveyed by the tapestries and furniture of the great hall, for no Norman had spoiled Ketilsing. With a few retainers, Sigferth ruled this little community, their lives being dependent on the wretched crops that could be raised and what little game an arrow could bring down. And in the winter, month by month, wolves grew bolder, threatening live stock and even the lives of those who ventured into the woods alone : hunger shadowed all the land.

In 1071 the Norman power settled at Knaresborough, where Serlo de Burg, a favourite baron of William the Conqueror, took the very necessary precaution of building a castle. The Norman lord farmed the manor of Knaresborough from William, who held it in demesne, and brought something like order to the surrounding district. His castle was built on a cliff on the bank of the

somewhat savage pride. The forests sheltered countless bands of outlaws. Norman ordinances required all inhabitants of the cities and boroughs to hunt the outlaw as a wolf, to pursue him from hundred to hundred with hue and cry. But the English sang ballads in honour of these outlaws."

[1] Thierry states that following the Norman campaign of destruction there was a famine in which 100,000 persons perished.

river Nidd, and was immensely strong, an impregnable shelter for the baron and his little body of retainers. He never suspected the existence of the hall at Ketilsing and its brooding, impoverished owner. He had heard of Sigferth, naturally, and knew that there was a price on his head ; but he imagined that the grim forests that had escaped burning, sheltered most of the refugees from Norman power. He seldom ventured more than a few miles from his castle, nor did any Norman attempt to penetrate the Yorkshire wastes, for the natives were playing that same deadly game the old, forgotten British tribe of Brigantes played so many centuries before upon the Roman legions, so that all roads and tracks were hedged by hidden dangers for the Norman, and the ways of the country were dark with silent butchery.

Life at Knaresborough Castle would have interested Sigferth, the scholar and man of taste, turned by circumstances into an embittered organiser of an unending guerilla war. The Norman day was well planned :

Lever à cinq,	(To rise at five,
Diner à neuf,	To dine at nine,
Souper à cinq,	To sup at five,
Dormer à neuf.	To bed at nine.)

There was a richness and finish about the home life of the wealthy Norman, which had not been known in Britain since the Saxon barbarians undermined a rich and finished civilisation in the fifth and sixth centuries. Serlo de Burg enjoyed his comforts at Knaresborough. The great hall, or salle, of his castle was the scene of well-appointed meals, abundant in their variety, and planned with a conscious artistry that English lords did not command, although they had the same materials available.

A few years of settlement at Knaresborough enabled the Norman lord to entertain his occasional visitors with

agreeable luxury, wringing excellent service from the
cowed inhabitants who had gradually drifted back to the
district, for the Normans tamed even that hardy mixture
of old British blood of the Brigantian strain crossed with
Saxon and Danish characteristics.[1]   So when the Domesday commissioners visited Knaresborough in the year
1086, the lord of the manor, who held the property
from Serlo de Burg, helped them to forget a weary and
dangerous journey by reproducing the comforts of the
settled southland, and giving to their difficult and prolonged investigations a background of ease and good
living, embellished with the courtesy and conversational
ability of which he, a cultured Norman gentleman, was
master.

The state of the country, the obstacles in the way of
the commissioners' researches, and methods of extracting
information regarding the names of places and estates,
the ownership of lands, the numbers of villeins and serfs,
the acreage of arable, waste, and wood, and other details
required in the compilation of the great inventory, would
be discussed, and the lord would be a very helpful and
accommodating host to these important representatives
of the powers of law and property.   There would be
anecdotes concerning English perversity, the mulish
stubbornness of the peasants ; some speculation, too,
concerning the activities of the many outlawed English
nobles who lived—or at least were supposed to be alive
—isolated and in hiding.

The commissioners learn that their host is quite
ignorant of the surrounding country apart from a few
well-used tracks.   He is of little assistance to them in

---

[1] " The foreign lord was a master ; the inhabitants of the domain trembled in
his presence, and approached with terror his manor, or hall, as the Saxons called it ;
an abode once hospitable, whose door was ever open, whose fire ever lit ;
but now fortified, walled, embattled, garrisoned with men-at-arms and soldiers,
at once a citadel for the master and a prison for the neighbourhood." Thierry's
Norman Conquest, p. 261,

their endeavours to assess the taxable value of the lands in the wapontake of Claro. What answers would they be likely to get to their long list of questions regarding the lost lands of Nidderdale, and whom should they question?[1] The lord of the manor cannot tell. He understands that the hersir, Sigferth, was lord of all Nidderdale, unless his father, Eric, son of Arkell Scrufa, be still alive. How can the commissioners question this outlawed Sigferth? The problem is examined during supper at Knaresborough Castle. The meal has been long and appetising, beginning with boar's head, this preliminary dish being carried in to the accompaniment of a flourish of trumpets, a musical and also a decorative opening to the meal, for the head is garnished with flowers. Then come venison and wild geese, flesh and fowl being spiced and seasoned and washed down with wine, white and red, imported from France, for wine-making in England has been forbidden by King William, and mead is a little heavy for the palates of the Norman gentlemen who eat so daintily, and are so skilfully graceful in the management of the daggers or knives with which they slice their meat, taking care to wash their fingers and their blades after each course. Large sweetmeats conclude supper, and by the firelight the commissioners' plans are shaped and finished. The lord of the manor will send out a strong body of men-at-arms to proclaim that at least six men who have served the outlawed Eric or his son, Sigferth, must attend forthwith at

[1] A list of some of the questions asked by the Domesday commissioners has been preserved, and is given in *England under the Normans and Angevins*, by H. W. C. Davis, C.B.E. (Vol. II. of *A History of England*, edited by Sir Charles Oman), p. 45. The list reads as follows : " What is the name of your manor ? Who held it under King Edward ? Who holds it now ? How many hides does it contain ? How many ploughs are there on the demesne, and how many belong to the tenants ? How many villeins, cotters, slaves, freemen, socmen are there ? How much woodland ? How much meadow ? How many pastures ? How many mills ? How many fish-ponds ? How much land has been added or taken away ? What used to be the value of the whole ? What is the value now ? How much did each freeman and socman hold ? How much does he hold now ? "

Knaresborough to answer certain questions asked in the king's name. Failure to attend will mean the burning of every farm and hut in Nidderdale, the confiscation of all live stock, the burning of all crops and woods, the death of all males, slaves or freemen, and the slavery of all women.

"Even with that threat, I doubt whether the sturdy, stubborn pigs will budge from their wallows," said the Norman lord sadly.

"But with the king's name to back it, my lord— surely that will impose immediate obedience?" The eldest commissioner was obviously incredulous.

"Sirs, I respect your belief in law and order," replied the lord of the manor; "but you are fresh from the south, where the king's arm is strong and long; here, I am the king's arm, or rather the feeble hand and weak fingers at the end of it; and I know how far I can reach, and how little I can grasp when I do reach forth with all the strength I command."

"But surely you make good every threat?" said the commissioner.

"As a soldier I never threaten that which I cannot execute," the lord returned; "but although I can kill them, and flay them first, or put out their eyes, cut off their hands, or give them a dark life for ever in some dungeon, I cannot make these English obey or even promise obedience, and even now, twenty years after Senlac, there is no place in these parts save this castle where a Norman could in safety lay his head at night, or be alone by day."

"This is a very strong position for a castle, is it not?" asked one of the commissioners nervously.

The lord smiled with grim contempt. "The walls and the cliff enable me to have the pleasure of offering you hospitality," he said; "it is poor, judged by your southern standards, for I cannot show you good hunting and only a little hawking. (He nodded towards the perch for falcons at one side of the hall.) Nor can I give you music, now that Brother Lessip has parted with his tongue."

In reply to the questioning looks of his guests, he said : " It is a sad tale, and I blame myself for trying to think that the English can ever behave. Brother Lessip was my wife's chaplain ; a worthy fellow, with a voice like a romance and a knowledge of all the songs in Christendom, I fancy. But one night, when I was entertaining some of the king's friends, this cursed land, with its chills and ice, had so thickened the good brother's voice that he could only wheeze and wipe his nose on his gown and croak like a raven. So I was without music, and my seneschal persuaded me to invite one of these English bards who lived nearby to supply the want. The fellow was to be well rewarded ; gold pieces and a full meal—more than the English gain in their dreams these times. He came, sirs, and brought his harp. And do you know what the wretch had the audacity to sing ? By the splendour of God ! [1] I would never have believed such madness possible ! He sang a ballad in praise of the deeds of Eric and Sigferth, those two outlaws we have talked of to-night ; praised them for their valour when they helped to butcher poor Lord de Comines at Durham fifteen years ago ! He sang in his own tongue, of course. I had him flayed at once and flung from the battlements, quietly and without informing my guests, who had not seen anything amiss because they had no Saxon or Danish, fortunately, for the insult was deadly."

The commissioners shook their heads, and then one asked : " But how did this affect Brother Lessip ? "

" Oh, half a dozen English decoyed him to one of their villages two months later, and cut his tongue out and took his fingers off so he cannot sing or harp, and

---

[1] According to Thierry (p. 282) this was William's favourite oath, and consequently, no doubt, the popular oath of the Court.

returned him to me. Naturally, I burnt the village and killed those belonging to it on whom I could lay hands, but, sirs, the laugh is with them—I lack a musician."

The commissioners did not enjoy much sleep that night. This Domesday circuit was a much more perilous enterprise than they had imagined. Their beds were comfortable enough, consisting of feather-stuffed quilts on which they lay, for there were no mattresses, linen sheets and cloth coverlets faced with cat's hair, badger, or marten. They slept in the hall, the lord and his lady alone having the privilege of a separate bedroom.

Early next morning the proclamation party set forth, two of the commissioners reluctantly accompanying the lord and twenty-five mounted men-at-arms, all clad in glittering hauberks, their pointed helmets gleaming, and their shields slung ready to ward off English arrows. They were armed with sword, mace, axe, or bow, and they looked extremely business-like and grim. A herald who could speak Saxon rode with them up the valley by the boiling, rushing river Nidd.

They did not come within a mile of Ketilsing, but Sigferth heard of their approach, and watched them from safe cover in company with a score of his thrælls, all armed with bows. He longed to shoot them down, but he knew that it would mean the ultimate destruction of every living thing in the valley, so he cursed them softly under his breath and ordered his men to let them pass in peace.

At every hut and every village the party halted, and the herald, blowing blasts upon his trumpet, proclaimed the king's will for the Domesday assessment.

That night Sigferth took counsel in his hall with his men. His father, Eric, sat limp and withered and dumb at the head of the table, and Sigferth, blond, fierce, and savage, sat and planned difficulties for the Domesday commissioners. Dage, his most trusted servant, and a descendant of that thræll whom Arkell Scrufa had tried to preserve from justice forty years ago, volunteered to attend the inquisition, and to confuse the king's servants.

"Nay, Dage," Sigferth forbade him; "I would go myself, but that would leave you all without a leader, for is there not a price upon my head, and no immunity is promised to outlaws in this thief's proclamation? But I cannot sacrifice your wits."

Father Cedric, an old priest nearing eighty years, who had served the church at Hompthveit and the family at Ketilsing for three generations, urged that he should go.

"Nay, Father," Sigferth objected, "you are full of useful knowledge of the lands and people therein, but you are also too full of truth to be of use in this matter of deceit. This is a task for thick heads and brave hearts."

"Of which there are plenty, Lord Sigferth," smiled the old priest. And the proclamation was answered from Ketilsing promptly and in accordance with the plan of confusing the Norman. Six stubborn English thrælls, one from each township within the manor, presented themselves at Knaresborough Castle, and with the aid of an interpreter were questioned by the king's representatives.

After an hour of examination, the commissioners began to realise what a hopeless task was before them in this bleak and wretched countryside. The English thrælls were incredibly stupid, hardly able to comprehend the simplest of queries; slow and gruff, lacking respect for the authority from which the questions proceeded.

"Come, come, now," snapped the eldest commissioner, whose temper was going fast, "remember we are speaking in the king's name."

His remark was translated, and it brought a smile and a muttered comment from the dirty, wild-haired man to whom he had spoken.

"What was that?" asked the commissioner sharply.

The interpreter stammered, and said :
" Insolence, my lord."
" Then translate it ! " was the order.
" He said : ' Lord de Comines also spoke in the king's
name ! ' " answered the interpreter.

The threat was obvious, and this man had probably
taken part in that very attack on Durham, years ago,
when Robert de Comines had perished with all his men.

" Take that man away," ordered the commissioner ;
" the lord of Knaresborough will deal with him."

There was another growl from the Englishman, who
understood what the commissioner had said, which
on translation proved to be : " Take heed that Knaresborough is not dealt with as we once dealt with York ! "

When the lord of the manor learned the result of their
questioning he shrugged his shoulders.

" There is nothing to be done," he told them. " You
will never learn the size of one field or pasturage, or know
the place of a single fish-pond or mill in all this waste.
Why not write it down as waste, and let our children's
children assess it when it has grown rich and the memory
of these feuds has grown old ? "

" But we must try again," insisted the commissioners,
" we cannot give such an account to the king."

" Try then, and with all the aid I can lend you,"
answered the lord of Knaresborough. " Meanwhile, I
must do justice on these insolent pigs who have insulted
the king and the law."

Justice consisted in removing the noses and hands of
the six thrælls, who returned thus to the hall at Ketilsing.
Sigferth was finishing his meagre supper—porridge and a
scraggy hen—when he was informed of the treatment his
men had suffered. Rushing from the hall in blind rage
he confronted the six hideously mutilated thrælls.

" Listen," he cried, " for the good of your ears and
the healing of your wounds : from now on I spare no

"Take that man away," ordered the Commissioner.

126

Norman; would that I had shot down with my arrows every one of the party we saw and spared three days ago. While I live all Nidderdale shall be a death-trap to these armoured wolves."

And that promise was kept, and civilisation was at low ebb in and about Ketilsing until Sigferth's son, Edmund, the year after his father's death, made his peace with the ruling powers, and later married a Norman lady. Edmund's son had lost every hint of that rugged blend of Saxon and Dane that formed pre-Norman England, and even his name marked the firm establishment of new ideas, for to the name of Robert was added a surname linked with the locality this family had known for so many centuries, and the grandson of Sigferth was called Robert de la Nidde.[1]

[1] For the character of the Normans, see Appendix II., Note 4.

CHAPTER IX

FEUDAL ENGLAND

LIFE changed but little in its essentials during the hundred and fifty-eight years that elapsed between the death of that implacable conservative, Sigferth, in 1100, and the sunny August morning in 1258, when his great-great-great-great-grandson, Brian de la Nidde, set out on a tour of inspection round the home manor of Ketilsing, accompanied by his bailiff, Edward Rathebayne. Although the life of the countryside flowed on, controlled by the needs of agriculture, bound to its course by the necessity of growing food, imposing on the peasant the same tasks and the same time-table generation by generation, the character of that life altered, even if its quality remained unchanged.

Opposition to Norman rule died down ; and following its final acceptance came intermarriage between Normans and Saxon-English and the ultimate fusion of the two peoples. Norman-French was the language of the king's Court ; it became the language of the Law, and the English vocabulary was enriched by many hundreds of Norman words and phrases and the English ruggedness smoothed by the adoption, in a modified form, of Norman manners, customs, and costume. A period of unparalleled religious fervour helped to turn men's minds from hereditary feuds and hates, diverting the energy of English craftsmen and their masters to the building of churches and religious houses, thereby helping the rapid growth of monasticism, and setting the eyes of English chivalry towards the Holy Land, inspiring the Crusades. But even more far-reaching in its effects was the gradual consolidation of the countless and varying customs and services associated with feudal tenure, welding them into something approaching a uniform system—so far as anything may be termed a " system " that is subject to endless local modifications. This consolidating process actually touched the daily lives of the people, adjusting or rearranging their obligations, without altering their work.

Sigferth's descendants responded to the influences and the wonderful and vital religious inspiration of the period, and in common with other substantial land-owners two of them risked life, health, and fortune in the shining adventure of the Crusades, and one of those lords of Ketilsing was wounded at the siege of Acre. At home those lords were generous in their gifts to the Church, helping with lavish contributions of labour and money the building of local churches in stone ; and Roger de la Nidde, the father of Brian, had surrendered several hundred acres of moorland at the head of the Dale to the recently founded Abbey of Fountains, as well as giving large sums towards the cost of certain new build-ings there. Both Roger and his son had, on reaching manhood, made the pilgrimage to Canterbury, an act of piety that was particularly popular in Nidderdale, for Knaresborough Castle had sheltered Becket's murderers, and the Dalesmen were anxious to display their dissocia-tion from the crime, which for centuries was held in abhorrence as a vile and atrocious deed. For the same reason, Hampsthwaite Church was dedicated to the martyred and canonised Archbishop.

In 1258 the descendants of Sigferth still owned seven or eight sub-manors, amounting to a knight's fee, within the superior manor or lordship of Knaresborough, for which they rendered knight service. Although the family had been deprived of much of their original estate by William the Conqueror and his sons, they were still comfortable and secure, so long as due service was given

I

to uphold their title. " Knight service " meant that the
head of the family had to follow his lord (in the case of
Brian de la Nidde it was Richard, Earl of Cornwall) in
the field for forty days in the year at his own expense ;
and it had also become customary to pay a small annual
rent as well as the traditional dues.   The Niddes had not
yet taken up the knighthood to which their property
entitled them, because they felt that their income, derived
from the poor grazing ground they held, was insufficient
to maintain the standard of living required of a knight.
So each successive head of the family had paid a small
fine for not " taking up knighthood " when he came into
his inheritance.

Since the days of Sigferth's grandson, Robert, the
family had borne the surname of de la Nidde, the outcome
of their long association with the valley of that river.

On the morning of the particular August day which is
to show us something of the life and surroundings of a
home in Feudal England, Brian de la Nidde was aroused
from a heavy sleep in his comfortable though none too
clean bed in the solar of Ketilsing by a man-servant soon
after half-past five, before the sun had caught up the thin
sheet of low dew-mist that shrouded field and moor.
After the warmth of the deep feather bed and equally
voluminous feather-stuffed quilts upon which and under
which he had slept, with Alicia his wife by his side, the
morning air chilled his body and made him gasp, for in
the manner of the times he slept stark naked.   He is not
concerned with washing, and dresses with his skin unre-
freshed and scarred with flea bites.   He shaves his cheeks
and chin every two days.   First he slips on a linen
undershirt, over which comes a well-cut under-tunic
of thin green woollen material, falling to the knee and
having long, tight, buttoned sleeves.   Over this he draws
a short upper tunic or cyclas of a darker green cloth
spangled with stars of silver thread, and girt round the

waist with a silver and leather girdle. He also dons knee drawers of the same material, which can be seen through the open front of the under-tunic, which is divided from the waist to the hem for freer movement. He covers his legs with green woollen stockings, and on his feet he puts a pair of stout leather shoes with long pointed toes, to the heels of which are attached prick spurs. After combing his fair hair, which falls in ringlets on his shoulders, he crowns it with a fur-trimmed green velvet bonnet. Had the day been wet, he would have added a voluminous cloak or super-totus (overall). The final touches to his costume are a pair of strong leather riding gloves and the inevitable sword and knife.

His wife, on ordinary occasions, wears a close linen gown, a super-tunic of brightly coloured silk, fitting her figure closely, a vivid sheath for her body above the waist and falling freely to her feet, and over all she favours a gaily-patterned, voluminous, fur-trimmed mantle of some rich material. Like most married gentlewomen of her time, she wears the stiff linen wimple, her elaborately plaited hair being confined in a caul of gold thread and covered with a veil.

As Brian de la Nidde sits on the bedside drinking from an earthenware cup of thin, home-brewed beer which a servant has brought him, he looks about the solar with the warm satisfaction of agreeable possession. To him the place seems wonderfully comfortable, though actually it is not a great advance on the bedroom of his ancestor Sigferth. The solar is about 25 feet long and 20 feet wide, with a lofty timber roof, the beams of which are clouded with cobwebs and black with the smoke of the occasional open fires that had burned there on the few occasions when Brian or his wife were sick. The uneven board floor is strewn with rushes and rosemary. The roughly-plastered walls are enriched by painted decoration, a small and simple geometrical design in two or three vigorous hues, repeated in diaper fashion. The August sun shoots golden shafts through a couple of narrow windows, deeply splayed on the inside and barred by an iron grille. The shutters that protect the room from the bitter winds and driving rain and snow of winter nights are now folded back. The room is sparsely furnished. Three massive chests of oak,[1] simple in form, innocent of ornament, and crude in construction, provide accommodation for an assortment of clothes, armour, weapons, jewellery, and prized possessions such as plate, bedding, and napery. These chests stand against the wall and serve as seats, together with a long cushioned bench. The only other pieces of furniture are two low trestle beds, one for Brian and his wife, and one for any honoured guest, who would not feel the slightest embarrassment at sharing a room during the night with his host and hostess.

In one of the outer walls of the solar is a garde-robe or urinal, from which a pipe leads through the thickness of the wall and drains into the moat.

A stout oaken door, with massive ornamental hinges of wrought iron, leads from the solar—the one private room of the manor house—to an exterior stone staircase by which the courtyard is reached. This stair is the only means of entrance to the solar, which is on the first floor, the ground floor room below serving as a storehouse. The hall, which shared the same roof as the solar,

[1] *The Encyclopædia of Furniture*, edited by Dr Hermann Schmitz (Schloss Museum, Berlin). English edition, London, 1926, Chap. IV. In Chap. I. of Vol. II. of *Early English Furniture and Woodwork*, by Herbert Cescinsky and Ernest R. Gribble, a thirteenth century chest from Great Bedwyn Church, Wiltshire, is described thus : " It is roughly constructed, yet in a characteristically thirteenth century manner. The front is a solid board of oak of great width, roughly finished with the saw marks left in its surface, tenoned into heavy uprights. These project over the ends, and are united from front to back by two heavy cross pieces, the tenons of which are carried through to the front. The lower one supports the bottom of the chest, which is made from stout wood to carry heavy weights. The ends are housed into the heavy styles, and are fixed to the cross pieces. There is no attempt at ornamentation, although, originally, the bottom of the upright styles may have been carved with simple cusping."

was the common room wherein the family and their guests spent their day, ate their meals, conversed, and listened to music. It was 60 feet long by 20 feet wide, paved with stone flags quarried from the head of the Dale. In the middle of this floor was a large flat stone slab on which a big fire of peat and wood burned in winter, filling the hall with smoke before the chimney, a hole in the roof protected by a louvre, did its work. Although this wood smoke irritated eyes and throat, it was bearable and even welcome, for its pleasant smell fought with and vanquished other smells, inevitable in a room crowded with unwashed and unsavoury humanity and numerous dogs.

Several single light, square-headed windows were set high in each wall ; but it was only a pale ghost of daylight they supplied. The hall was always sombre with twilight by day and was plunged into darkness at the first touch of twilight outside.

At the end nearest to the solar was a dais, raised about 9 inches from the floor and occupying nearly the full width of the hall. Here stood a long trestle table at which the family and principal guests dined, sitting on a long bench placed against the wall, which was here hung with a gaily-hued tapestry. Under their smoke grime the remaining walls were enriched here and there with very primitive paintings, depicting hunting scenes or incidents from sacred history : additional decoration was provided by a few tapestries and trophies of the chase. Near the table a simple cup-board accommodated the earthenware and pewter cups, plates, and dishes, and, on important occasions, the few pieces of silver plate. A number of chests stood against the walls, those with flat tops serving as seats, the larger chests having lids that sloped like a roof, rising to a central ridge ; [1] storage

[1] ". . . the most distinguished form of receptacle is the chest raised on high legs with a sloping lid like a gable roof, and which is doubtless a descendant of the wooden sarcophagi, mediæval roofed coffers and chests."—*The Encyclopædia of Furniture*, Chap. IV.

places for armour and weapons, hunting gear, and miscellaneous household equipment. In one corner there was a perch to which a couple of falcons were secured by slender chains.

At the farther end of the hall a carved oak screen, a strong but not very skilful piece of woodwork, occupied almost the whole width, and was surmounted by a gallery for the minstrels. The narrow space between the screens and the end wall of the hall formed a passage, at one end of which was the main entrance to the manor house, a massive door of oak studded with iron nails, reinforced with bands of the same metal and equipped with elaborate iron hinges and bolts ; at the other end of this passage was a door that led through the hall wall into the kitchen, a room as large as the solar. The walls of the kitchen were hung with pots and pans, knives and spoons, and a miscellany of utensils, for the art of cooking had, under Norman influence, passed beyond the stage of primitive apparatus. At one end of the room stood an immense and sturdy trestle table, and on the floor, near the walls, were ranged basins and jugs, cauldrons and baskets by the dozen. There was an open fire over which was suspended a reckan to hang pots and cauldrons on, and in front of the fire, which occupied the centre of the room, was a huge revolving spit. The ceiling beams were hung with hams, sides of salted beef, dried fish, and bunches of herbs. A ladder led through a hole in the ceiling to a small, dark upper chamber, which served as a larder and a bedroom for the kitchen staff.

Outside, the manor house of Ketilsing appeared as an unsymmetrical group of buildings. At the north-eastern corner of the solar a three-storeyed stone-built tower rose, a bulky hint of military necessity. This tower was about 15 feet square, and the only entrance to it was through an iron-banded door in the solar ; its immensely thick walls were pierced only by long, narrow slits through which arrows might be shot and spears hurled by defenders. The battlemented coping rose breast high above the flat lead-covered roof, affording a protective screen from which missiles of all kinds could be cast upon the heads of any attacking force. This pele tower was a purely defensive structure, built primarily as a refuge against possible Scottish raids, for the northern raiders were bolder and more powerful and successful in the England the Normans remoulded than they had ever been in the orderly days of the Roman province ten centuries before, the golden days of the *Pax Romana*, now utterly forgotten and unknown, save for the antiquarian gleanings of some erudite monk. Scottish raids were a permanent threat in the northern counties, and one that was to be fully realised little more than half a century after this year, 1258. The tower also afforded a safe retreat against the bands of robbers that infested the forest, and in times of civil commotion or rebellion. During such troubles—as, for example, the Revolt of the Barons—a lookout would be stationed on the roof of the tower, where he could command a vast view over the surrounding country. But in more peaceful days the three superimposed, dark chambers of the tower—the upper ones being reached by ladders from the lower ones—were used as storerooms and granaries. The main walls of the manor house were built of local gritstone, which was as plentiful in the vicinity as timber, though more expensive to prepare and more difficult to use : the Niddes were proud of this relatively uncommon feature of a small manor house. The whole hall was built over a range of cavernous, rat-haunted cellars, which had tiny windows just above ground level, so that the main floor of the building was some four feet above that level, the entrance door being reached by a short flight of broad stone steps. These cellars were used as tool sheds, barns, cowsheds, and stables. The waters of the adjoining

Tang Beck had been led into a channel above the hall, forming a wide and deep moat around three sides of the building, the Beck itself guarding the fourth side. A rude drawbridge raised by beams and counter-weights gave access to the bridle path that led to Hampsthwaite.

Over this drawbridge, falcon on gloved wrist, accompanied by his verderer, Henry Hunter, rides Brian de la Nidde a few minutes after he has finished dressing and has drunk his rising cup of home-brew. He is off to the nearby moor for a little early hawking; nor is he unsuccessful, for he returns to the Hall about eight o'clock, leaving his bag—a heron and two grouse— to be cooked, while he rides down to Hampsthwaite to hear morning mass at the parish church.

Dinner, the first of the two daily meals, is served at nine o'clock. The trestle table in the hall has a linen cloth spread over its rough boards, and is set with trenchers and drinking cups, dishes, and bowls. Each member of the family brings to the table his or her own spoon and knife; forks were as yet unknown. The meal begins with porridge followed by trout, fresh from the Nidd, the heron and grouse, and a great joint of boiled salted beef. Large quantities of coarse wheaten bread and thin oat cake are eaten with the fish, fowl, and beef; and the men drink huge draughts of beer, the women drinking the sweeter metheglin.[1]

At the end of the meal Brian sends for Rathebayne, a man who combined the offices of steward and bailiff, and together they set out on a tour of inspection round the manor, mounted on the small but sturdy moorland ponies. Rathebayne carries with him bread, cheese, and a large leathern bottle of beer for midday refreshment.

Passing over the drawbridge they skirted the edge of one of the three immense common fields of the manor. The arable land within the manor was cultivated on the

[1] For description of thirteenth century table manners, see Appendix II., Note 5.

three-field system, one field lying fallow while the other two were under crops of barley and oats. These great fields were divided into strips of an acre, each strip being separated from those on either side of it by a narrow piece of unploughed land called a " baulk." The holdings of the villeins were scattered through these fields. A man might own five or six strips in a single field, and yet none of them might adjoin ; his entire holding of both arable and meadow land was scattered about over the whole of the cultivated land within the manor. The villeins held this land from the lord of the manor by service. In return for the land and permanent loan of implements and their initial stock both of animals and seeds, they worked three days a week on the lord's own demesne land which, like their own, was scattered through the three fields. In addition to this regular work they were required to put in extra work, or " boon " work, at haymaking, harvest time, and other occasions. The three-field system led to the communal conduct of all agricultural operations. Each villein, for example, contributed his share to the oxen team when the whole of the fields that were not lying fallow were ploughed. Similarly, every one reaped his crops at the same time, all helping to reap the crops on the lord's demesne lands. With difficulty and extreme industry some of the more thrifty tenants had, in some districts, commuted this service for a money payment ; but they were still bound to observe the customs of the manor ; and in earlier times such com- mutation of service would have been impossible. The customs of the manor and the rights of its lord con- stituted a heavy tax on the property and liberty of tenants and a detestable invasion of their privacy. Each " customary " tenant was bound when he died to leave his best beast to the lord as a " heriot." His son, upon entering into his father's land, paid what was termed a " relief " either in money or kind. No tenant could allow his daughter to marry without the lord's sanction, which was only given subject to the payment of a small fine known as *merchet*. Although there has doubtless been much exaggeration concerning one particular privilege enjoyed by the lord of the manor, the *droit du seigneur*, its existence cannot be denied, although its practice may conceivably have been restricted.[1] Tenants were also bound to perform the office of reeve, constable, wood-ward, hay-ward, corn-ward, and so forth when called upon. In return for these services, and by way of compensation for the humiliating conditions accompanying them, they received the protection of the lord and the permanent loan of a small acreage of land. It may be asked whether the lives of Brian de la Nidde's serfs were as worth living as those of slaves in Romano-British times, when, thirty-five generations earlier, that cultured ancestor of the lord of Ketilsing, Titus Paulinus, had owned a vast estate in Nidderdale and had supervised the administration of the lead mines on Greenhow Hill.

The dawn to sunset working-day of the thirteenth century peasant demanded intense labour if sufficient produce was to be wrung from the land to maintain himself and his family and the lord's requirements fulfilled also ; and there was no possibility of shirking the latter. When Brian de la Nidde and his stern bailiff ride through one of the great fields of the manor, they pass men hard at work reaping the golden grain with sharp sickles, men dressed in ragged tunics that come to their knees, with their legs bare, or else with garters of plaited straw criss-crossed over coarse breeks, with shoes of the roughest make upon their feet. These men redouble their efforts as they catch sight of their lord and his

[1] We would refer readers to Mr G. G. Coulton's remarks in Appendix XIV., p. 465, of *The Mediæval Village*.

bailiff, their taskmaster. Rathebayne was an ill man to cross, and was capable of making a serf's life even more insupportable than it was already. Passing through the big oat field and skirting the fallow, the two horsemen came to the village green, around which clustered the timber and wattle hovels of the tenant-farmers and labourers. Each hut consisted of a single room where the whole family ate, slept, and lived in the greatest squalor, without any suggestion of sanitation. Each hut was surrounded by a toft, and each had its croft or patch of meadow. By the side of the river Nidd stood the lord's water mill, at which every tenant was compelled to grind his corn, the miller taking a small proportion of the grain in payment for his work. Behind the village the slopes of Swincliffe were dark with dense and silent woods that stretched, with an occasional clearing to east and west, as far as the eye could see. In these woods, and on the moors to which they gave place on the heights, the tenants had common rights of pasture for their swine, sheep, and cattle, and here they were allowed to cut such timber as they needed for fencing, building, and firewood, and to dig their turfs of peat. Although the houses of the villeins, who in the manor each held thirty acres of arable land and their share of meadow, were abominably squalid, the hovels of the cottars were the vilest and most miserable of places. Home life for the cottar class might indeed be compared very unfavourably with the home life of the Britons before the Romans came. The cottars held no property, but worked as general labourers either for the lord or his villeins, and usually filled the manorial offices of shepherd, swineherd, bee-keeper, and so forth in exchange for just enough coarse food to keep them alive and profitably active for the benefit of their masters. Their miserable timber and wattle huts were ill lighted, ill ventilated, insufferably hot in summer, dark, damp, and draughty in winter, and altogether more like fœtid pig-stys than human habitations ; and a marshy patch of ground near the Nidd had been selected as a site for a cluster of these dwellings.

Brian and Rathebayne rode through this rural slum, entirely oblivious to its condition, and naturally untroubled by any stirrings of conscience regarding the human life condemned to rot in such surroundings. The women folk at the doors of the huts curtseyed as their lord rode by, and glanced apprehensively at the bailiff.

Brian's tour of the estate occupied four hours, and they were nervous hours for Rathebayne. The lord asked innumerable questions on agricultural matters, approving here, complaining there, suggesting improvements, and giving orders. At two o'clock they arrived at the courthouse for the monthly court baron.

The great barn-like hall of the court-house was packed to overflowing with hot and dirty people. So mephitic was the atmosphere that even Brian, who was hardened to most odours, and whose daily life was encompassed by the stench of the moat at Ketilsing, had recourse to a small silver box of dried herbs, which he sniffed from time to time. At one end of the hall was a bench and trestle table at which Brian, as president of the court, Rathebayne, as chief steward, and John Flower, a friar of St Robert's-juxta-Knaresborough and vicar of Hampsthwaite, as clerk, took their seats. Nearby was a massive oak chest, iron banded and locked, wherein were kept the sheepskin rolls upon which the proceedings of the court were recorded. Standing behind the table were the constables of the various townships within the manor, also the jury of sixteen villeins or tenants-at-will. The remaining tenants stood in the body of the hall, leaned against the walls, or squatted on the stamped earth floor.

The proceedings opened with the constable of each township making his " presentments," that is, presenting various men for such minor offences as could be tried in this court. There were many cases of assault with violence, house-breaking, theft of stock, selling of ale or bread below the quality required by the assize, and not a few cases of slacking while working on the lord's demesne. In most cases evidence of guilt was forthcoming and fines were duly inflicted ; some of them being very heavy. Such fines were payable in money or kind. The verderer next presented charges against several offenders for poaching, for wounding animals of the chase that had ruined their crops (for villeins were only allowed to drive these animals off their fields, but were not permitted to wound or even seriously harry them), and for taking wood, bracken, and peat beyond the amount officially sanctioned. Two of the defendants were ordered to be branded on the hand as well as being fined. The miller "presented" no less than twenty tenants for refusing to repair the mill dam, which was an obligation they incurred by the terms of their tenancy. An all-round fine of sixpence met this case.

The final business of the court concerned the transfer of property. The outgoing tenant, if he were alive, paid a fixed fine on transferring his land, and the incoming tenant paid another fine, called a " relief," on taking over the land. If the tenant bequeathed the land on his death, a " heriot," generally his best beast, or if there was no live stock, the best piece of furniture, was paid out of his estate in lieu of a fine. Where the dead man's successor was a minor, the lord assumed the wardship of the property until the successor should come of age. All the transactions regarding transfer were laboriously recorded by the clerk. Not until the vesper bell sounded from the church did the proceedings end, enabling Brian to mount his horse and ride back to Ketilsing Hall, accompanied by agreeable thoughts regarding the revenue the court had brought in.

After washing his hands and feet and thighs in a bowl

of cold water, brought to him by his groom when he reached the Hall, he went into the solar, where he found his wife embroidering a brightly coloured tunic for his small son. Presently they sat down to supper in the great hall, together with a knight and his squire, who were passing through the village on their way to Lancaster, and who claimed the hospitality which was always readily accorded. Supper was the principal meal of the day and took place round about six o'clock.

Men-servants bore in an impressive succession of dishes, beginning with a kind of pot-au-feu of mutton and vegetables. This was followed by grilled trout and crayfish, roast rabbits and hares, a roast sucking pig stuffed with plums, a boiled shoulder of mutton, venison in pastry, and finally buns and biscuits from the manor bakehouse, and a form of soufflé of eggs, saffron, and cream. The squire himself waited upon his master, the knight, before sitting down to eat. In honour of the guests a great leathern bottle of French wine was added to the usual liberal cups of beer and metheglin. Alicia contented herself with sheep's milk. At the far end of the hall sat the servants of the manor who were not engaged in cooking or serving, and they took a tribute from the substantial remains of each successive dish as it was removed from the head table. What little food remained was then distributed to the handful of poverty-stricken wretches who gathered outside the Hall every evening to receive this kindly mark of their lord's regard for the welfare of his tenants.

During the meal Brian's own minstrel, in company with others from the village, occupied the gallery above the screens, and discoursed music—of a sort. At least their efforts made up in vigour and volume what they lacked in melody. The minstrel sang a passionate French chanson ; then all the musicians played the popular songs of the day, simple songs of hunting and war, love and drinking, with now and then a reference to the farmer's round of work, and the whole hall, lord, guests, and serfs, bellowed the choruses. In between songs the place echoed with loud voiced conversation, and the barking of the many dogs who awaited scraps and bones, which the diners flung to them from time to time. As tongues loosened and passions rose, and the thin veil of restraint

A late thirteenth century hall.

present at the opening of the meal was withdrawn, the lady Alicia retired to the solar. Torches were brought and stuck in iron sconces on the walls, and their flames and those of the central fire flickered in a blue haze of resinous smoke. The hall was lit by a few patches of light, and the flickering illumination here and there revealed the coarse and inflamed features of the men. Simple and crude jests went the rounds at one end of the hall together with tales of violence ; at the other end the host and his knightly guest discussed the chase, the tournament, church matters, such as tithes and building, the growing independence of the villein class, and their own personal adventures in love and war. Every one drank steadily until Brian, now truculent under the influence of beer and wine, had the hall cleared of his men ; the incapably drunk being flung out. A mattress and bedding were brought into the hall for the squire, and Brian and his guest staggered unsteadily into the solar, where the lady Alicia had already been asleep for nearly two hours despite the noise in the hall. The two men had just enough steadiness to strip off their clothes and get into the right beds.

CHAPTER X

Fourteenth Century England

WHEN the battle of Bannockburn had decided the fate of the great idea of one government for the whole island, that was as tempting to English kings as it had been in the remote past to Roman governors of Britain, Northern England suffered terribly from the effects of this military disaster. Hard times came to Nidderdale and the Nidde family during the three years following Bannockburn, for the victorious Scots, meeting with no organised opposition, overran the northern counties, burning, slaughtering, and pillaging like the savages they were, for Scotland only enjoyed a rudimentary civilisation, and North Britain was as wild and threatening as it had been when the Picts troubled the minds of Roman officials and Saxon monarchs. Such raids had occurred for centuries ; and they were to occur again.

In 1317 the Scots ravaged Nidderdale, putting to the sword all who ventured to resist their sweeping southward advance. They burnt every house and hut, killed or drove away the live stock, and fired the crops.[1] When he was warned of the approach of the raiders, Henry de la Nidde, then a man of thirty-five, had gathered his family, his servants, and retainers in the pele tower adjoining the great hall at Ketilsing ; and before long this little defending force beat off with well directed arrows a straggling

---

[1] A Royal Commission appointed to investigate the damage done within the Honour of Knaresborough, reports that the Scots had burned in the town of Knaresborough 140 dwelling-houses, leaving only 60 ; crops and timber had been destroyed by fire and cattle driven away. Similar damage had been done in all the townships within the Honour. *Close Rolls,* 12th, Edward II.

band of some twenty or thirty Scots. The raiders, leaving behind them a dozen corpses bristling with feathered shafts, passed on to Hampsthwaite, where prey was easier and resistance feeble. It was the first phase of the raid ; but when a wounded and exhausted swineherd crawled into Ketilsing with the news that a body of Scots, at least five hundred strong, had crossed the Monk Wall, six miles distant, the lord of the manor knew that his home and lands must be abandoned immediately. An attempt to stay such a force would be madness : the tower would be rushed and scaled by sheer weight of numbers, and there was no help to be looked for from Knaresborough, for the castle and its garrison would be closely invested. Time was short, and with a few clothes and valuables carried on a pack-horse, the whole party left Ketilsing and sought shelter in the forest. Henry, clad in light armour, mounted on his war horse, his wife Eleanor on her ambling pony, the two children, ten-year-old Stephen and eight-year-old Matilda, and four armed men-servants, all on sturdy little moorland ponies, made their way by a circuitous route to York, where they stayed with friends until the Scots, having stripped Nidderdale, turned their attention to fresh and more fruitful territory. They returned to find a village of charred ruins, the church a blackened shell of four bare, burnt stone walls, and their old home gutted. . . .

The next few years were tinged with want and poverty for the Nidde family—years when the lord of Ketilsing endured the discomfort and indignity of eating and dressing like one of his own villeins. Henry died in 1333 at the age of fifty-one, which was a good old age for his day, when disease and violence followed lord and serf alike in close attendance from the cradle to the grave. His body was found in the forest after he had been out hawking ; violence had claimed him before disease could strike, for there was an arrow in his head. His belt,

knife and sword, and furred cap and doublet had disappeared with the assassin. His son, Stephen, who
succeeded him, was twenty-three, very much a man of
the world, polished as a result of his apprenticeship, first
as a page and then as a squire to a neighbouring lord,[1]
trained in the arts of war, the usages of chivalry, and the
etiquette of hall and table, courageous, blandly insensitive
to the sufferings of others, a capable farmer and admin-
istrator. When he was seventeen he had been married,
much against his will, to Catherine de Burun, a child
of fifteen. The marriage was a convenient commercial
arrangement between the parents of the parties concerned,
uncomplicated by any consideration for the tastes of the
young people involved, and simplified by an entire disregard for such matters as mutual affection or sympathetic
temperament.[2]   Henry de la Nidde was in need of money,
and Catherine brought with her a substantial dowry :
Edward de Burun desired freedom from the expense of
his daughter's maintenance : a marriage between their
children solved both problems ; and it was, fortunately,
an age of docile and disciplined children.

When Catherine was seventeen she bore her husband
a daughter—stillborn. A second daughter and a son

[1] It was the general practice for men of rank and position to apprentice their
sons in this way.

[2] G. G. Coulton in that remarkable book, *Chaucer and his England*, p. 204,
writes : " Child marriages were the real curse of mediæval home life in high
society. The immaturity of the parents could not fail to tell often upon the
children." And on p. 207 he refers to " the scandalous frequency of formal
child marriages." Many examples are quoted in the same chapter. The commercial aspect of these marriages is bluntly described in *Piers Plowman*, Chap. XI.,
p. 256, in these terms :—

" . . . they give their children
For covetise of chattels and cunning chapmen ;
Let her be unlovely, unlovesome abed,
A bastard, a bondmaid, a beggar's daughter,
That no courtesy can ; but let her be known
For rich or well-rented, though she be wrinkled for elde,
There is no squire nor knight in country about,
But will bow to that bondmaid, to bid her an husband
And wedden her for her wealth ; and wish on the morrow
That his wife were wax, or a wallet full of nobles."

both died in infancy. A third daughter, born in 1338, managed to survive the dark perils of disease and ignorance that assailed childhood, as did a second son, Nicholas, who was born three years later.

By the year 1346, in which our first scene is laid, all signs of the Scottish ravages of 1317 have vanished from Nidderdale. Ketilsing Hall has been rebuilt with but little variation of its original plan—it now includes a great hall, parlour, solar, kitchen, and cellars ; and clustering at one end are penthouses that serve as dairy, bakehouse, and store chambers. The pele tower still raises its three storeys at one end of the building, but its walls are stouter than before. All the walls, except the party walls, are now of dressed local stone, and the thatched roof of earlier days has given place to a low-pitched roof of stone tiles borne by strong oaken trusses. Although the new Hall differs little in plan and construction from the old, it can boast many new comforts and conveniences, and its mass of dressed stone is far more pleasing to the eye ; it is less of a rugged military refuge and more of a home ; a stronghold still, but also a centre of civilised life, the pivot of a community.

Inside, a little more privacy has been secured for the lord and his lady by the addition of another room at the dais end of the hall. This room is, in effect, the forerunner of the " parlour," where the family may retire when they wish to escape from the unavoidable publicity of the hall. During the winter months this room would be far more comfortable than the great hall, that damp, chilled setting of the general life of the place, where icy draughts sent the wood-fire smoke swirling about on dirt-distributing errands, until rafters and walls were darkened by soot. The central fireplace in the new building was provided with a rough conical chimney, suspended above the flames like a giant candle extinguisher, which led much of the smoke straight to the roof unless the draughts were especially vigorous, which was the case whenever strong winds were blowing.[1] Any one sitting near the fire was nearly roasted on one side and half frozen on the other, despite the protection afforded by high-backed settles.[2] Both the parlour and the solar had fireplaces now ; gaping, fuel-devouring gashes in the side of the room they were ; but they marked an immense advance in the achievement of comfort.

The gloom of the old hall has been largely dispelled by an increase in the size and number of windows. When Hampsthwaite Church had been rebuilt after the great Scottish raid of 1317, Henry de la Nidde engaged the skilled masons who had been responsible for that work to supervise the rebuilding of Ketilsing Hall ; and it was on their advice that the great hall was brightened by four square-headed windows, two on each of the long sides of the hall. Two of these windows were divided by a single stone mullion ; the others were larger, having two stone mullions ; all of them were headed with simple geometrical stone tracery.

Bright decoration did much to counteract the dinginess that comes from a sooty atmosphere. The walls, where they were not hung with arras or enriched with crudely-executed pictures, were painted pale blue and spangled with white stars and golden crescent moons. The oak trusses of the open timber roof were carved and painted.

Furnishing was still crude, but showed a greater though an ineptly expressed regard for comfort. The same clumsy trestle tables were set firmly and solidly above the rush-strewn floors ; but bare forms were occasionally replaced by the cushioned settles with high backs already mentioned, and restful, draught-screening pieces

[1] Cf. Coulton, *opus cit.*, p. 86.
[2] *Ibid.*, p. 87. " It is not generally realised what draughts our ancestors were obliged to accept as unavoidable, even when they sat partially screened by their high-backed seats. A man needed his warmest furs more for sitting indoors than for walking abroad."

of furniture they were.   One or two chairs of very simple
form and rough finish might even be found, although
chairs, except in palaces, were extremely rare.

The sanitary arrangements remained primitive : the
garde-robes still drained into the moat, but the latter had
been reconstructed so that the water ran fairly swiftly
over a pebbly bed around the hall and into Tang Beck,
and although it was still both cesspool and dust-bin, it
was much less foul than before.   Still it was undoubtedly
the cause of the frequent fevers that attacked the inhabitants of Ketilsing, ills that were invariably regarded as
evidences of Divine wrath, rather than of human ignorance.   Kipling has condensed the situation into four
lines in his *Natural Theology (Mediæval)* :

> My privy and well drain into each other
> After the custom of Christendie. . . .
> Fevers and fluxes are wasting my mother,
> Why has the Lord afflicted me ?

However, Stephen de la Nidde is comfortable enough,
and although the stench of the moat occasionally pene-
trates even to that inner retreat, the parlour, he is not
unduly critical.   And on a particularly sunny day towards
the end of September 1346, he is quite prepared to regard
his home as an earthly paradise of comforts, for he has
been back barely a week from the French wars, disabled
for further service by the loss of two fingers of his right
hand and a troublesome wound in his right thigh—
painful souvenirs of the victory of Crecy.   Upon this
day when the English climate is in genial mood and all
Nidderdale is serenely luminous with the sunshine of
early autumn, the Nidde family is preparing to attend the
three-day Michaelmas fair at Hampsthwaite, which had
opened that same morning.   To celebrate the holiday
and to keep her lord in agreeable humour, Catherine de la
Nidde had seen to it that an unusually elaborate dinner was
served.   She had planned it with care, and its scale and

A game of loggats in the solar.

quality were such that the kitchen staff had been tremendously busy all the previous day in preparations.

The meal began with eel pasty, served with hard boiled eggs, cloves, saffron, and rissoles of marrow. Hippocras, or spiced wine, washed down this opening course. Next came minced fowl, highly spiced and served with boiled thistle roots, followed by stuffed hare and a salad. Red wine from Auxerre accompanied these two dishes—a greatly treasured drink of which Stephen had managed to secure a small cask some years before. Various kinds of roots and also leeks served with spiced sauce and herbs formed a vegetable course, which was followed by light pastries, pear pie, and cream cakes, and finally by fruit and further draughts of Hippocras.[1] The villeins and peasant farmers had to be content with very different fare ; no subtleties of flavour, no art in preparation or grace in serving touched their meals ; and the strong contrast between their food and that enjoyed by their lords and rulers may be seen from the following words that William Langland puts into the mouth of Piers Plowman :

Says Piers : " I have no penny pullets for to buy,
No, neither goose nor pig but only two green cheeses,
A few curds, a little cream, and a haver-cake,[2]
And two loaves of beans and bran baked for my little ones ;
And, by my soul, I say I have no salt bacon,
No, nor a cook boy collops [3] to make.
But I have parsley, cabbage, leeks, and a cow and a calf,
And a mare to draw the dung afield while the drought lasteth ;
And on this living we must live till Lammas [4] time,
By then I hope to have harvest in my croft,
Then may I do thee thy dinner as I fain would do."
But all the poor people fetched their peascods,[5]
Their beans and baken apples they brought them in their laps,
Onions and salads, and many ripe cherries,
And prepared Piers this present to please Hunger withal.

---

[1] From the recipe book of Taillevant, chief cook of the Kings of France in the fourteenth century.

[2] Oatcake.   [3] Bacon and eggs.   [4] 1st August.   [5] Pea-pods.

Vast was the difference between lord and serf; between noble blood and the common life that clung to the land and laboured on it and wrung food from it.   Small wonder that Stephen de la Nidde should regard with disfavour the prospect of mingling with his own villeins, even on an annual occasion of such local importance as the Hampsthwaite Michaelmas fair; but Catherine had coaxed him into taking her, and had been careful to keep him from brooding irritably on his grudging promise when once he had given it.   That elaborate dinner on the first day of the fair was only part of her plan for keeping his mood pleasant, for she wished to enjoy the fair without the company of a glum face and a harsh voice; and the weather was her friend, for the lord of Ketilsing loved sunshine.

Like most women of her class, Catherine led a hard and monotonous life, and the annual fair promised as dazzling a prospect of enjoyment to her as it did to any villein's wife.   Mewed up in that cold stone hall, her days were passed in supervising the work of the house and the dairy, in sewing and embroidering, and her short evenings in conversation with her husband.   On rare occasions she rode with Stephen through the muddy, winding lanes and forest tracks to visit the few people of her own class within half a day's journey of Ketilsing; and such visits would occasionally be returned.   But still more rare was the arrival of unexpected and unknown guests at the hall, travellers delayed by weather or some accident on their way through the forest.   Such visits were really thrilling events, for they meant new faces and news from the outside world, a world of which Catherine knew practically nothing, for beyond two journeys to London—an incredibly marvellous city she found it— a few brief stays in York and four yearly expeditions to Knaresborough, she had no knowledge of or contact with places other than Ketilsing, her home which she sometimes thought of as her prison. Strange visitors brought more than news ; they brought exciting possibilities of romance, and that brave, misleading word romance stood nearly always for illicit love in the days of Catherine de la Nidde.[1] Twice already she had been unfaithful to Stephen ; but her own infidelity became utterly insignificant when compared with her husband's open disregard of his marriage vows and his ready satisfaction of the desires roused by any woman who came within his power.

However, Stephen was not unwilling to please his wife, and he overcame his distaste for attending the fair, for he was anxious to have first-hand knowledge of the prices farm produce and live stock would fetch there ; moreover, there were one or two purchases he wished to make himself. In any case his presence was advisable at the "Court of Pie Powder."[2] So we find the lord and lady of Ketilsing dressing in their finest clothes for the occasion. As their wardrobes had been enriched by the loot brought back from France by Stephen, they were able to wear clothes that would have been deemed the last word in fashion even by London town.[3]

Stephen's personal servant, who combined the duties of groom of the chamber and groom of the hall, helped him to don his long trunk hose of which one leg was yellow and the other blue. Over an under-tunic of silk he then buttoned his close-fitting cote-hardie, also of silk, which had a well marked waist and which came down nearly to his knees, having slits about twelve

[1] Coulton, *opus cit.*, p. 227, writes : "Seldom indeed could the course of true love run smoothly in an age of business marriages. . . . The large majority of mediæval romances celebrate illicit love." This indeed is the whole tenor of Chap. XVII. of the book quoted, which should be read by those who desire evidence in proof of this statement.

[2] Pie Powder, from *pieds poudre* (=dusty feet), was an emergency court held in the fair ground to deal summarily with offences committed during the period of the fair.

[3] It was through the booty secured by the English forces in France that the extreme French fashions were first introduced and popularised in England.

inches long in the back and front to allow freer movement. This gay garment was parti-coloured, one half being a rich red and the other a vivid grass green; it was fastened down the front by a number of large, brightly-hued enamel buttons, and the tight, full-length sleeves were secured by a row of small silver buttons from elbow to wrist. The skirt of the cote-hardie was scalloped, each scallop having a flower worked on it in gold and silver thread. My lord now puts on a cape and hood of grass green. The cape just covers his shoulders and has a scalloped edge embroidered in the same manner as the cote-hardie. The hood itself is thrown back from his head, its long liripipe being brought over one shoulder and passed over the other to be out of the way. Around his hips he fastens a silver and enamel belt or baldric, from one side of which depends a scarlet leather gypciere or purse and a short dagger or anelace. Blue leather shoes with long, pointed toes, open at the instep and strapped round the ankle, and a pair of brightly embroidered leather gloves complete his costume. He selects a fur cap with a rolled-up brim, which gives a somewhat sinister touch to his pale, clean-shaven face. At all times he is a stern-looking man, and wounds and war have brought physical distress to mark his features harshly.

Catherine makes a brilliant figure in a bright green close-fitting upper tunic with a gaily embroidered narrow panel of white silk inserted in the front from throat to hem; her sleeves are tight to the wrist, and the skirt falls in ample folds about her feet. A long scarlet cloak worked with silver thread and lined with green is fastened in front with an enamelled clasp and is thrown back from her shoulders, hanging behind her in graceful folds. A white silk coverchief hides her hair, which is confined in a golden caul, and the hard beauty of her face is framed by a white linen wimple. Over the coverchief she wears a flat, broad-brimmed hat of scarlet cloth. When she lifts her skirt, scarlet cloth stockings are disclosed, also pointed-toed shoes of supple green leather. She refrains from wearing her two massive rings with their clumsily cut rubies and emeralds—it would be unwise to put temptation before a drunken and disorderly crowd, and as she wears gloves, such parading of jewellery becomes pointless. Some time is occupied after her dressing is done while she adds colour with more earnestness than skill to her pale face.[1]

Just before midday, Stephen and Catherine ride down to Hampsthwaite, accompanied by a groom and the lord's reeve, a clean-shaven, severe-looking man who wears a red hood with its long liripipe wound round the neck for convenience, a russet surcoat reaching to his ankles, and a leather belt round his waist from which hangs a leather purse on one side and a long sword on the other.[2]

The whole village of Hampsthwaite is in an uproar, for during the fair it holds at least four or five times its usual population and everybody is out in the single village street. Rough booths made from boughs lopped in the neighbouring woods form a continuous line around the village green and down each side of the street, and several have even been erected on sacred ground in the churchyard. The lord of Ketilsing's first duty is to

[1] Geffroi de la Tour Landry, writing a little later than this period, refers with horror both to the extensive use of cosmetics and to the practice of plucking eyebrows.

[2] " The Englishman haunted so much unto the folly of strangers " [foreigners] says Dowglas, the monk of Glastonbury, " that every year they changed them in divers shapes and disguisings and clothings, now long, now large, now wide, now strait, and every day clothingges new and destitute and devest from all honesty of old arraye or good usage ; and another time to short clothes and so straight waisted with full sleeves and tapetes [tippets] of surcoats and hodes [hoods] over long and large, all so nagged [jagged] and knib [nibbled ?] on every side, all so shattered, and also buttoned that I with truth shall say, they seem more like to tormentors or devils in their clothing and also in their shoying [shoeing] and other array, than they seemed to be like men." *MS. Harleian Coll.*

proclaim the fair open, and there is some little ceremony attached to this, for he includes in his proclamation orders various injunctions for keeping the peace—for instance, there is a warning that football will not be allowed [1]—maintaining honest dealing, and restricting the malign activities of vagabonds.   There are a few local shopkeepers looking on sourly at the opening scenes, for in the villages within the manor all shops and markets are closed for business to enable the fair while it lasts to enjoy the complete monoply of trade.[2]

As Stephen de la Nidde rides slowly down the village street after the opening ceremony, his eyes reveal to him a changing sea of colour in the flow of gaily-dressed people of all degrees and classes coming from York, Knaresborough, Skipton, Ripon, and many other towns, cities, and villages round about.   Pedlars and traders are there by the score, bringing their pack-horses and loads of merchandise: homespun and imported fabrics, fripperies, crocks and earthenware, kitchen utensils, trinkets, charms and relics, horse furniture and saddlery, spices and condiments, dried fish, boots, shoes, and clogs, weapons, and small agricultural implements.   Villeins have come in from many outlying districts bringing in on sledges such goods and provisions as skins, homespun fabrics, cheese, honey, horse furniture, and spurs. The lord of Ketilsing does not disdain to be a trader, and his representatives sell such of his live stock and farm produce as are surplus to the needs of his household and staff.   The noise of a multitude of verbal trading transactions effected almost entirely by barter is deafening.   Money was by no means plentiful, and the haggling and arguments created by diffi-

[1] As early as 1314 the Laws of London forbade the playing of football, and the game was again forbidden in 1363.   It generally resulted in fatal accidents, brawls, and faction fights.
[2] Cf. *Mediæval England*, ed. H. W. C. Davis, p. 316.

cult problems of exchange did not make for peaceful business.[1]

There is also a spiritual side to the fair, and pardoners and sompneurs attend for the selling of relics, of which the supply is plentiful enough to suggest that these holy traders anticipated the practices of the less creditable sections of the twentieth century antique furniture and curio trade, and faked the relics a gullible public found so acceptable. The official licensing of peccadilloes and the consolation of the holy minded are also good reasons for the presence of these curious by-products of mediæval Christianity.

For the more wordly visitors there are acrobats and jugglers, tale tellers, and performing bears ; in fact, the fair is a pleasant though somewhat boisterous union of business and recreation. To the peasants it comes as a rare relief from endless toil, and they take full advantage of it, and not unnaturally their extremely high spirits are productive of a good deal of licence and excess. The hostelries and taverns of the villages around the neighbourhood are crowded. The lord of the manor provides at supper time—five o'clock—a feast for his dependants and serfs, and all who care to come are bidden to partake of the ox that is roasted whole nearby the kitchen of Ketilsing Hall under the strict supervision of the master cook. There is dancing and also cock fighting, wrestling for the prize of a ram, sword and buckler combats and displays of archery which, backed by royal and official encouragement, is becoming increasingly popular. The emphatic disapproval of the Church had little effect in checking these sports and games, many of which certainly led to trouble, broken heads, and bloodshed. There is much drunkenness, and brawls are frequent ; and to counteract the flow of simple sin, relays of friars preach continuously at the

[1] See Appendix II., Note 6.

market cross, and their exhortations are echoed in
graver key and with greater ceremony in the church.
Cut-purses and such predatory visitors are singularly
active, and the " Pie-Powder " court is kept busy.

Presently, in spite of the definite orders in the opening
proclamation, a game of football is started on the village
green.   Hundreds of men go surging down the village
street, kicking, pushing, fighting, trampling on the
fallen and even overturning the booths.   The lord of
Ketilsing decides that an attempt to stop it will mean
more bloodshed than the game itself will produce ; and
as matters are reaching the stage when even the lord
and the lady of the manor are not altogether safe from
insult or even assault, he retires with his wife and servants
to the Hall.   The groom bears their purchases : dolls
and " loggats," or nine-pins, for the children, a pair of
spurs, a silk gypciere, and a hunting knife for Stephen,
and an enamelled fillet, several yards of purple velvet,
and some scarlet bone buttons which he had bought for
Catherine as a " fairing."

To judge from the obvious prosperity of the country
people, the number of traders, and the considerable
wealth that has been brought to the making of this fair,
it might be said that the French war had not yet seriously
affected the life of the land.

As Stephen returns to the Hall, ready and eager for the
second meal of his day, supper, he cannot refrain from
making a wry face at the stench from the moat.   Had
he but known it, his nose was receiving the gravest
of all messages : warning of death and disaster and of
happenings that were to fill his middle years with anxious
sorrow and perplex his old age with a host of problems
beyond his solving. . . .

Fevers and diseases were too common to cause much
comment in mediæval England.   The blind and the
lame were found upon the highways, and ever and again

travellers through England would hear the sound of a leper's bell as, hooded and hideously bandaged, some poor wretch would plod from place to place, tolling the warning of his uncleanness and crying for Christian charity.

The Black Death came to England in 1348.[1] The pestilence was worse than any war or Scottish raid. Its terrors were unknown; it struck at lord and serf, churchman and layman, without discrimination, without mercy. It imposed a helpless terror on the people, for even prayer failed to stem its grim march through the country. The very thieves of the highway were cowed and killed; homes both great and small suffered dire losses, and famine followed the plague, threatening whole communities. Agriculture was paralysed, the harvest rotted in unattended fields. Terror begat hopelessness, and presently grave difficulties of administration began to crowd on one another, and perplexed landlords were at their wits' end to work their estates. Prices rose, the cost of living soared to unheard of altitudes, and Stephen de la Nidde was by no means the only landlord who turned his thoughts to pasturage owing to the shortage of labour and the growing expense of meeting high wages.

We may take one glance at life in Ketilsing Hall some years after the Black Death has gone by, although the troubles it brought have by no means abated. Quite half the population of Hampsthwaite and the surrounding district has perished, and the lord of the manor sits down to far poorer fare than in pre-plague days. Mutton, a few beggarly rabbits and fish, followed by blancmange and some fruit, and his supper, ill cooked and ill served, is completed. Conversation at the Hall turns on the troubles of the times. Stephen is emphatic upon the importance of landlords paying only the legal rate of

[1] See Appendix II., Note 7.

wages and not tempting serfs to mutiny by offering higher rates.   He is urgent, too, for the enforcement of all the penalties for keeping men at work upon the land,[1] although the vicar of Hampsthwaite, who is a guest at supper, reminds him that a man in prison does not help the harvest.   Stephen is particularly bitter because his last few remaining labourers have run away in the hope of finding some lord who offers higher wages, and although he has hunted three days with hounds and mounted men-at-arms, he cannot trace the deserters, and he is compelled to turn the last of his rich fields into grazing grounds and to see sheep in place of men.

To this end Stephen de la Nidde followed the practice of other lords and began the enclosing of common lands for the pasturing of his own sheep, enclosing, too, the demesne lands which had hitherto been intermixed with the holdings of the villeins.   Sheep and fencing were becoming the most important things in England, which alike for lord and serf was to be a lean land for many years, wherein innumerable homes were impoverished or deserted and allowed to fall into ruin.

[1] See Appendix II., Notes 8 and 9.

L

CHAPTER XI

The End of the Middle Ages

GENERAL prosperity in England did not materially suffer during the Wars of the Roses, for " the wars concerned the nobility and gentry far more than the great mass of the people; as a foreign observer (Comines) put it, in England, the troubles and misfortunes of war fell on those who waged it." [1] The struggle " was a baron's war and did not concern the commonalty. It was regarded by participators as a somewhat serious sport for kings and noblemen—a sort of glorified tournament." [2] Despite the distractions of intermittent warfare and the consequent collapse of law and order, the prosperity of the masses who worked instead of fighting steadily increased, so that even when the struggle ended, "the splendour of the households of the magnates, with their elaborate regulations, and the hosts of servants exceeded anything hitherto known, and sumptuary laws show that the dress of labourers also was rising in quality. Citizens were able to pay higher rents for their houses than heretofore." [3]

The del Niddes, with the business acumen that had always distinguished their family, contrived for the greater part of their lives to avoid taking any active part in the war, though the position of Nidderdale was a particularly difficult one. As part of the Duchy of Lancaster it was Crown property, and strongly Lancastrian in its sympathy, whilst the territory to east and south was

---

[1] *England in the Later Middle Ages*, by Kenneth E. Vickers. (Vol. III. of *A History of England* in seven volumes. Edited by Sir Charles Oman), p. 495.
[2] *Ibid.*, p. 439.   [3] *Ibid.*, p. 501.

as strongly Yorkist. There had, of course, been a few faction fights at Knaresborough, but no serious encounter had taken place in the district. A few of the Dalesmen had left their homes to join the Lancastrian forces, but there was no general exodus until the battle of Wakefield and the battle of Towton in 1461, when Hugo del Nidde had raised a local company to serve with the Earl of Northumberland's forces. He had no personal feeling in the matter—his action was inspired purely by motives of self-interest; with the war brought within easy distance of his manor, it would have been thoroughly bad policy to have showed no anxiety to serve King Henry VI., from whom he held his land, and in whose good graces it behoved him to remain—whilst the king was still in theory king

The family fortunes had steadily grown, thanks to a series of cleverly-planned marriages which had brought with them further estates, and also to the flourishing woollen industry. By 1484, when old Hugo del Nidde died at the advanced age of sixty-three, his son, Hubert, entered into an inheritance that included, not only the original Nidderdale property, but great estates in other parts of the Riding. Hubert found himself sufficiently affluent to support a knighthood had he thought it politic to take up that honour. But he did not take this step because, as a knight, he would have found it more difficult to keep out of the wars than if he had remained a plain esquire, and he was not the man to let war interfere with business.

Kettlesing Hall had been reconstructed some few years before Hubert became its master. Of the fourteenth century building only the great hall remained, and that had been much improved. At either end of the dais, the side walls were carried outwards into two bay windows, divided equally by a transom and into many vertical lights by a series of mullions. Both bays were fitted with stone window-seats spread with comfortable velvet-covered cushions. The remaining windows in the old hall had been replaced by long, low, mullioned windows of many lights. The roof of the old hall had also been taken down and replaced by a panelled ceiling, and another floor had been built to accommodate three new rooms, a long gallery, and two bedchambers. At each end of the hall were two gabled wings, both of two storeys, one accommodating the parlour, the great chamber or living room, the private chapel, and several bedrooms, and the other the kitchens, buttery, brewhouse, scullery, larder, and other domestic offices, and the servants' quarters. The buildings formed a sombre but impressive group. Inside, the various rooms had every comfort afforded by the age. Furnishing was beginning to receive serious attention. Beds with panelled heads and four posts supporting testers were emphasising the growing importance attached to comfort. There were feather mattresses and quilts, fine linen sheets, coverlets of silk and fur, and Chalons blankets, and from the tester hung curtains of elaborately embroidered fustian. Occasionally a big tub, with a tent-like covering, was used as a bath. In the hall and great chamber fireplaces were built in the walls, smoke, soot, and a good proportion of the heat being drawn up chimneys built in the thickness of those walls. Chests and benches are still used almost exclusively for seats, but there are one or two chairs, sacred to the use of the lord and lady of the manor. The hall still has a large trestle table, and there are one or two other smaller tables to be found in the house. There are cupboards also; very simple receptacles they are, solidly made of oak, and there is a buffet on which plate is displayed. The buffet is slightly more elegant in form, being a consciously decorative piece of furniture with carved panels whereon a local craftsman has expressed himself with more vigour than grace. Fabrics and tapestries

adorn the walls. The hall has been paved with
tiles.

Behind the dais in the hall is a withdrawing-room.
The parlour is used almost as a boudoir, and the chief
living room of the house is the great chamber or
chamber of parements.[1] The chapel is divided into
two storeys by a floor, the upper storey being open at
the east end to a chancel which was the entire height of
the building ; the two rooms forming the nave could be
cut off from the chancel by curtains and used as ordinary
living rooms. The upper room was called the oriel.

Our introduction to Hubert del Nidde and his wife
Margaret takes place when they are discussing in company
with their chaplain, Sir Laurence Thackewray,[2] plans for
the entertainment of a number of their friends and (more
important from the del Nidde point of view) several
influential men and officials. New appointments have
been made at Knaresborough, and Hubert is anxious to
stand in the good graces of officialdom. Priest and lady
sit on cushioned benches in the small parlour, which is
by far the most comfortable room in the house, and the
lord of Kettlesing is enthroned on one of the chairs the
house boasts. It is a throne-like box of a chair, squat
and sturdy, and without its cushion it would be extremely
uncomfortable, for its lines take no account of human
contours. A blazing log-fire gives a cheerful importance
to the fireplace and lights the room far more effectively
than the latten candelabra which holds its trio of reeking
tallow candles. The walls are warmed by textiles, which
make a dark setting in the firelight for the three richly
clad figures. The lord of Kettlesing wears a tight
murrey[3] doublet, padded at the shoulders to increase
their width, and in length barely reaching to the thigh.

[1] Parements = ornamental furniture.
[2] The courtesy title of " Sir " was commonly given to priests.
[3] Murrey was a dark wine red, a mulberry hue.

It has a high collar, and is pleated down the back. The collar and hem are embroidered with deep bands of pattern in which leaves and flowers in bright colours are entwined; and the doublet is edged with marten. A narrow leather belt fastened by a jewelled clasp is worn round the waist, and through it is thrust a dagger with an ornamental silver hilt. The wide sleeves of the doublet are slit from shoulder to wrist, the scalloped sides of the slit being loosely laced together with a cord of gold thread; and through the slit the close-fitting sleeves of a shirt of Rennes linen are seen. His tight hose are of a tawny orange hue, and his green leather shoes have toes of extravagant length. Wooden pattens are strapped to these shoes for use out of doors. He is clean-shaven and his curly hair falls about his shoulders, a shining bronze cloud. When he goes out he will wear on his head a hat of murrey cloth, rather like a flower-pot in shape, and with a closely turned-up brim; a feather will curl over the crown of this hat, being secured at the back with a button of gold and enamel. On his fingers he wears several large rings.

Margaret del Nidde wears a gown of blue fustian which fits tightly to a high waist, and falls about her feet in such voluminous folds that when she walks she must gather them up and carry them over her arm. The gown is V-shaped in front, cut very low, the bottom part of the opening being laced rather loosely with a cord of gold thread. The turn-over collar and edge of this V-shaped opening is of a deeper blue shade, trimmed with fur. The sleeves are tight with turned-down cuffs of white linen. A broad belt, brightly embroidered, accentuates the waistline. Around her neck is a loose collar of beads and gold filigree medallions. Her hair is taken straight back from her forehead and crammed into a gold net or caul trimmed with semi-precious stones, and attached to it is a butterfly head-dress of white gauze stretched on wires.

Her shoes are the same as her husband's, and heavy rings adorn her fingers.

The chaplain, save when he is performing his religious duties, wears clothes that are not unlike those of his lord, but his costume is invariably free from the extravagances imposed by fashion and from any kind of ornament.

The scale of the entertainment has been discussed, and it is decided to include a tournament, Hubert del Nidde looking very sour as the extent of the cost is brought home to him. A tournament will make pleasure not only for their guests, but for all the war-weary countryside, for folks will come from afar to see jousting ; and pedlars and puppet shows will gravitate to the neighbourhood, and an impromptu fair will take place.

The menu of the feast is settled. The next day preparations begin. Beyond the moat to the north is a herb garden, the sweet scents from which do something to mitigate the stench from the insanitary moat, and beyond this garden is a great level field that is to serve as the tilt yard. Here carpenters are at work, erecting the sheltered stand for the privileged guests and spectators, and building up the barrier that divides the lists, a stout low wall of oak boards topped by a smooth and partially rounded plank. Tents for the knights and esquires who will take part in the tournament will be pitched at each end of the lists. The rest of the field will be thrown open to the people : peasants, pedlars, and the servants of the gentry who are being entertained at Kettlesing will all have their share of the excitement of the tournament and its accompanying pleasures.

When the guests arrive, the lord of Kettlesing shows the gentlemen some very pretty sport hawking across the spongy turf and heather of the moor uplands, where the air is like wine and the sun pours over the green shoulders of the hills, making the winding Nidd valley look cold and dank by comparison, with its dark woods shrouded

A fifteenth century tournament.

in deep blue mist. They hunt, by the courtesy of the lord of Knaresborough, in the Forest, and follow a red deer for two-thirds of a long day, the hunt ending when they are a good fifteen miles from Kettlesing, having wound in and around many miles of the forest tracks with their hounds. Returning to the Hall, the hunting party wash and change their clothes,[1] and sup in a manner worthy of their estate. They are dainty eaters, although they still use their fingers, only employing silver spoons for some courses.

Silver and pewter shine on the table, dishes and cups glittering in the candlelight. The guests are squires and big neighbouring landowners—Stephen Scrope, Christopher Stead, Robert Atkinson, Sir Leonard Hardcastle, and Nicholas Metcalfe, all with their wives ; and the Seneschal and Constable of the Honour of Knaresborough ; all dressed with the richness that formed in nearly every great house of that period so striking a contrast with the comparatively poor furnishing and equipment of halls and rooms. Two meals a day still satisfied lord and peasant. Dinner was the great meal ; breakfast, merely a necessary preparation for the toil or pleasure of the day, a fairly brief attack upon meat and ale ; but for dinner the lady of Kettlesing has given her visitors day by day a huge variety of dishes, drawing her materials from farms near and far, buying spices and other embellishments for flavouring from Knaresborough, and even sending as far as York to give special point to some dish.

And as for the service, it was most punctilious, the

[1] In the Prologue to *The Master of Game*, by Edward, Second Duke of York, written between 1406 and 1413, being the oldest English book on Hunting, the cleanliness of the hunter is described : " . . . when he cometh home he cometh joyfully, for his lord hath given him to drink of his good wine at the curee, and when he has come home he shall doff his clothes and his shoes and his hose, and he shall wash his thighs and his legs, and peradventure all his body." From the edition edited by Wm. A. and F. Baillie-Grohman, published by Chatto & Windus, London, 1906.

servants being trained and drilled in the art and ceremony associated with feasts. The character of this service is best indicated by the following notes from " A Generall Rule to teche every man to serve a lorde or mayster." [1]

" The marshall in the morning ought to come into the hall and see that it be clean of all manner thing that may be found unhonest therein : the stools, trestles, or else forms if any be, that they be set in their owne places at meals at the boards, and before and after meals in corners farthest from encumbrance ; and all the hallings and costers dressed in their kind places and shaken or beaten with rods if need be : and that no hounds be abiding in the hall from morn to even.

" Also in winter time the groom of the hall shall bring into the hall as much wood and coals as shall be spent daily in the hall. . . . The groom shall also be continually in the hall at the first meat (dinner) or supper to bear away the dishes and keep out hounds, and fetch sauces. . . . And the yeomen, grooms or groom, or usher shall set up boards and make ready the stools before meat and bear them away afterwards : and when the lord is set the marshall and server shall fetch in his courses and make an obeisance to the lord. When the lord is served then shall another esquire serve the other messes at the borde. And forthewith the almoner shall bring in the alms dish with a loaf therein and set it beneath the lord's salt or else upon the cupboard, and a little before the second course the almoner shall take of every ' great meat ' in the first course a serving and put it in the alms dish."

(Same procedure with second course.)

[1] British Museum MS., Addl. 37969. The fifteenth century spelling has been modernised by the authors.

" Three-quarters of an hour after the last course, all broken meat and bread is to be cast into the alms dish. Esquires and wayters to take ewers of water and towels to those who would wash."

All bits are put in the alms dish, which the almoner then takes to the lord's table where he orders certain additions to be made from the various dishes. Then fruit is served and cheese by itself. The marshall assigns rooms to guests.

The contents of the alms dish were afterwards distributed among the poor. Explicit directions are also laid down regarding the service an esquire is to render to his lord. For example, an esquire is to say :

" ' God-speed,' on entering his lord's room, and after saluting all present to kneel to his lord. He is to stand until told to sit. At noon, which was dinner time, he is to fetch clean water for his lord to wash his hands with, and to give him a towel. He is to cut his bread on a trencher and not to break it ; by no means to dip his meat into the salt cellar, nor put his knife into his mouth. He is to taste every dish brought to him and to have a clean knife and trencher for his cheese. When the meat is finished he is to clean his knife and put it away." [1]

By the close of the century, food had become specially important, and cookery enjoyed such elaboration that " a carver had a different term for dismembering any joint." [2]

Those who dined at Kettlesing Hall at this time of lavish hospitality can have such gentle nourishment as almond milk, rice, gruel, fish broth, or soup ; and they can sample *jussell*, which is compounded of eggs and grated

[1] Harl. MS., 5086 (1475).
[2] *Social England*, edited by A. D. Traill, Vol. II., p. 435.

bread, seasoned with sage and saffron,[1] or perhaps *tansy,* which is an omelette made chiefly with eggs and chopped herbs, in all probability rather like a modern omelette, *fines herbs.* *Moile,* too, can be tasted ; it is made with marrow, grated bread, and haggis. In addition to fish soup there is wine soup, also ale soup. Meat fried, roast, or boiled is served ; and there are among other good things a sort of fricassee of fowl, collops, minced pork, sausages (which had just been introduced to English tables), and a *froise,* corresponding to the modern French *omelette au lard,* having strips of bacon in it ; there are also venison, a boar's head, geese, and duck. There are pies, shaped like castles with battlements modelled in browned pastry, containing meat or fruit ; there are tarts, too, and the bakers of Hampsthwaite and Kettlesing have supplied simnels, buns, cakes, biscuits, comfits, and cracknels, as well as the finest pain bread and manchet, which is white bread.[2] Figs, almonds, dates, prunes, and nutmegs provide an assembly of flavourings ; and some of the meat dishes are stuffed with raisins, almonds, or prunes. The spice box is generously filled, and salt, pepper, and sugar —the latter a very great luxury indeed, imported chiefly from Cyprus and extremely costly—are available, as well as other agreeable assistants to appetite. Beer brewed from hops accompanies each meal, and there are several wines, which are often drunk spiced : Rumney from Hungaria, Malmsey, and Hippocras.

[1] An extensive description of such dishes together with ample notes on the food of this period will be found in *Old Cookery Books and Ancient Cuisine,* by W. Carew Hazlitt. Another indication of the attention that was given to the preparation of food, even for hounds, is given in *The Master of Game,* when the "Sicknesses of Hounds" are considered. For a complaint "which cometh to them in their throats and sometime cometh so to men in such wise that they may not keep down their meat . . ." the following advice is given : ". . . give them to eat flesh right small cut, and put in broth or in goat's milk a little, and a little because they may swallow it down without labour, and give him not too much at once, that they may digest better. And also buttered eggs doeth them much good."

[2] Wheat bread, barley bread, bran bread, bean bread, and oat bread are among the varieties baked.

It was an age in which magnificence became allied with quantity at meals.   A special dinner in a wealthy fifteenth century home was a well staged entertainment, and such decorative wooing of appetite sometimes became impressively ornate, as witnessed by the following menu :—

DINNER : *First Course.*

Brawne with mustard.

Furmenty (wheat husked and boiled in milk) with Venison.

Mawmeny (an extremely highly seasoned dish of minced meat cooked in wine with cinnamon, pine-nuts or cones, sugar, cloves, almonds, ginger, salt, and saffron).

Pheasant.

Swan.

Capon.

Carpeis of Venison.

Young Heron.

Bream.

Royal Custard (marrow and marrow broth, pounded almonds, cinnamon, ginger, and sugar, baked in pastry cases at the bottom of which are raisins and dates).

A subtlety : St Andrew sitting on a high altar with a bishop in full canonicals kneeling before him.   (Of sugar, paste, and jelly.)

Second Course.

Crane roasted.

Venison roasted.

Conyng (rabbit).

Betore.

Partridge.

Curlewe.

Carp.

Tart Royal.

Third Course.

Cremes.
Jelly.
Brows.
Chickens boiled.
Melons.
Plover roasted.
Rabbits.
Quails.
Blancmange.
Queens bakyn.[1]

The company at Kettlesing address themselves to their varied and well-cooked dinner with relish. There is far less drunkenness in this period, but over-eating is quite common. Table manners have been shaped to a certain gentleness, although what crudities are curbed may best be judged from contemporary books on etiquette wherein injunctions such as, " Do not spit upon the table " are frequent, and those who dine are urged " not to return back to your plate the food you have just put into your mouth. . . ."[2] Conversation turns on hunting, crops, and the shopping to be had at York. The sporadic warfare of the troubled reign of that troubled king, Richard III., is tactfully avoided. Presently minstrels will bring the feasting to its close, and heads made a little heavy by spiced wine will be comfortably lulled by flutes and fiddles, guitars, and singing voices. The ballads of the time tell tales of love and war, and the bell-clear lines of the verses in " The Nut Brown Maid "[3] delight the lord of Kettlesing and his guests. The ballad relates the story of

[1] Notes from " Two Fifteenth Century Cookery Books," E.E.T.S., Vol. XCI., Book II. (*circa* 1450).
[2] Quoted in *A Short History of Social Life in England,* by M. B. Synge, F.R. Hist.S.
[3] This ballad, " the masterpiece of English Poetry in the fifteenth century," was first printed in Arnold's *Chronicle* about 1521, but is undoubtedly of earlier date. The ballad is given in *Readings in English Social History,* Book II., by R. B. Morgan, M.A., M.Litt.

a proscribed squire who, on the point of being captured, has to make his choice between a shameful death or exile in the depths of the forest. The lady of noble birth, to whom he is betrothed, desires to share his dangers. Here are two of the verses sung by the minstrels ; describing the conversation of the squire and his lover :—

> *He.* It standeth so : a deed is do !
>   Wherefore much harm shall grow,
>   My destiny is for to die
>   A shameful death I trow ;
>   Or else to flee : the one must be,
>   None other way I know,
>   But to withdraw as an outlaw,
>   And take me to my bow.
>   Wherefore adieu, my own heart true !
>   None other rede [1] I can
>   For I must to the green wood go
>   Alone, a banished man.
>
> *She.* O Lord, what is this world's bliss
>   That changeth as the moon,
>   My Summer's day, in lusty May
>   Is darked before the noon.
>   I hear you say Farewell : Nay, nay,
>   We depart not so soon.
>   Why say ye so ? whither will ye go ?
>   Alas ! what have ye done ?
>   All my welfare to sorrow and care
>   Should change if ye were gone,
>   For in my mind, of all mankind,
>   I love but you alone.

Other ballads follow, and presently a drinking song rouses the company, and many at table join the jovial chorus in praise of good ale : [2]

> Bring us in no brown bread, for that is made of bran,
> Nor bring us in no white bread, for therein is no game,

---

[1] Plan.

[2] A fifteenth century song in praise of good ale, reprinted in T. Wright's *Songs and Carols* (Percy Society).

But bring us in good ale, and bring us in good ale ;
For our blessed Lady's sake, bring us in good ale.

Bring us in no beef, for there is many bones,
But bring us in good ale, for that goeth down at once ;
        And bring us in good ale, etc.

Bring us in no bacon, for that is passing fat,
But bring us in good ale, and give us enough of that ;
        And bring us in good ale, etc.

Bring us in no mutton, for that is often lean,
Nor bring us in no tripes, for they be seldom clean ;
        And bring us in good ale, etc.

Bring us in no egges, for there are many shells,
But bring us in good ale, and give us nothing else ;
        And bring us in good ale, etc.

Bring us in no butter, for therein are many hairs ;
Nor bring us in no pigges flesh, for that will make us boars ;
        But bring us in good ale, etc.

Bring us in no puddings, for therein is all God's good,
Nor bring us in no venison, for that is not for our blood ;
        But bring us in good ale, etc.

Bring us in no capon's flesh, for that is often dear ;
Nor bring us in no duck's flesh, for they slobber in the mere ;
        But bring us in good ale, etc.

Presently the entertainment concludes ; an end is made
to drinking.   The ladies betake themselves to such gentle
recreations as spinning and weaving and embroidering.
Margaret del Nidde sees to it that her handmaidens are
fully and worthily employed, for she has three young
ladies of good family who have been sent to her by their
parents for training in the very serious business of house-
keeping.   Games are played too, including draughts and
chess, and the lady of Kettlesing sometimes relaxes her
close attention to the affairs of her establishment, and
permits herself and her handmaidens the indulgence of a
little music and dancing.   Also there are romances to
be read.

Altogether, home life has become more comfortable and gracious for the wealthy. Wealth is being created and distributed to better purpose than hitherto, and apart from flourishing traders, a prosperous tenant-farmer class becomes sufficiently prominent and imitative for laws to be directed against it for curbing extravagance in dress.[1] Well-born, wealthy, and educated people are becoming more polished and accomplished. New ideas are stirring in the European world, and a hint of change touches

The beginning of fireside comfort.

many things in England—clothes, architecture, and presently the comfort of many homes. Soon are the foul moats of halls and manors to be drained, filled in, and replaced by flower-beds, so that the English house may become an altogether sweeter place, free from tainted air and the grim limits of fortification, while gardens grow up around these transformed dwellings, and flowers and groups of trees replace dirt, refuse, and disorder with trim beauty.

With enlarged windows and the fuller development of

[1] The Statutes of Apparel of 1463 and 1482 are aimed at the farmer and the labourer because of their elaboration in dress.

M

furnishing, home life gains vastly in cleanliness and comfort. The del Niddes see such changes gradually taking place in their own home and the houses they visit ; but it is left to the next generation to reap full benefit from the general rise in civilised standards that marks the end of the Middle Ages and the beginning of the " Scientific Commercial Age."

CHAPTER XII

REFORMATION AND WRECKAGE

DURING the childhood and youth of Robert de Nidde, the owners of Kettlesing Hall possessed vast estates. Robert was a man great in his generation, fired with real power and fine courage; in appearance a reincarnation of a very remote ancestor indeed, for seventeen generations spanned the gap between his day and that of Arkell Scrufa, the curly-headed red giant in whose likeness he was formed. Applying himself very closely to the matter of personal advancement, Robert spent much of his time at Court, where he gained the friendship of many powerful people likely to be of use to him, and also found favour with the king himself, for Henry was ever a judge of men, and saw in this able, intelligent Yorkshireman an excellent servant; and after the Scottish war of 1513 Robert de Nidde was to be known to the king as an excellent soldier also. The distinguished conduct of the young captain at Flodden Field came to the notice of that great English soldier, Thomas Howard, Earl of Surrey.

Robert prospered and married in accordance with one of King Henry's simple but unmistakable hints in these matters, for royal suggestions concerning matrimonial alliances for his gentlemen were frequent and were invariably followed. But Robert was too wise to remain at Court all his life, and by too constant a devotion to the source of all material blessings, to outwear the welcome accorded by the king to wit and intelligence. So he begged the royal permission to retire to his great estates in Yorkshire, pleading a failure of health. Permission was given, Henry graciously hoping that a yearly visit to the Court would be possible for his devoted courtier, and even sending Robert to his own medical adviser to discuss the possibilities of such an annual pilgrimage. This was exactly what Robert wanted ; a key to the palace, but the security of a home, and the chance to develop his estates still further with the aid of the fortune he had acquired, modest enough by Court standards, but very satisfying to a country squire. He had never made the mistake of being too ambitious, and there was something about this personal reticence which attracted that temperamental robber, Henry VIII., for Robert de Nidde left London a knight in the year 1521.

Sir Robert's first act of homecoming to Kettlesing is to modernise much of the Hall, using the old stone house as the core of a new, T-shaped building of stone and oak. The moat is filled in and its place is taken by gardens encircling the Hall, a flower garden, a herb garden, a formal garden, and an orchard. In the new building the walls of some of the smaller rooms are warmed by oak panelling, and in the winter parlour the mullioned windows have small lead-framed panes of glass, a comparative rarity except in churches and palaces. A final touch of modern luxury is given to the furnishing by chairs, not only in the winter parlour, but in the bedchamber, great chamber, and hall. Chests of oak still serve as seats and store places in every room ; and Sir Robert adds to the two cupboards he has inherited a standing cupboard, carved and made by a Flemish craftsman whom he has tempted into the Yorkshire wilds for a time from a prosperous London business. The big table in the great hall remains, a long oak board on trestles; and there is a smaller oak table in the winter parlour.

It is in the winter parlour that the first of four scenes, illustrating certain aspects of the home life and political influences of the time, is staged.

Inside the Tudor bedroom.

... of this room is of the linenfold pattern, ... by a coloured plaster frieze, the arms of ... amily being emblazoned in a big plaster panel ... he stone fireplace. The room has a door, also ... linenfold panels, and the glazed windows overlook ... drained moat of the old hall, now partly filled up and on the south side forming a long sunk garden, bright with flowers. Sir Robert has retired to the parlour after a comfortable six o'clock supper in the great chamber, for the hall is now seldom used for meals : supper included venison pasty, beans served with butter, coarse but well baked bread, oatcake, and spiced trout, finishing with a variety of sweetmeats, cheese, and fruit, and accompanied by satisfying draughts of double ale, and followed by Malmsey wine, drunk from a silver cup. Silver spoons help to keep his hands clean during the different courses, and he uses a special knife for cutting his meat. He sits in the parlour with his wife, his big limbs relaxed and his body fitting tightly into an X-shaped chair that has an embroidered velvet seat and back. He is dressed in a short doublet of deep red velvet with enormous puffed sleeves " slashed " or cut to show the silk of his shirt beneath ; at the shoulders it is preposterously broad ; at the waist it fits tightly. The doublet is open from throat to waist disclosing a high collared shirt of fine silk embroidered in black. His long curly hair falling to his shoulders is carefully trimmed and delicately scented, but he has neither beard nor moustache. His shirt sleeves have lace ruffles, also embroidered in black silk at the wrist ; on his legs are scarlet stockings and puffed and slashed trunk hose, and square-toed shoes of black leather give his feet a very sturdy look.

His wife, the Lady Anne de Nidde, who brought more gold than beauty to the marriage, is dressed very plainly in a vivid green gown, which has a long train, edged with white. Her sleeves are slashed and puffed, and caught in at the wrist with a ruffle.   The throat of her gown is open, showing a deep necklace or collar of gold, enamel, and pearls.   A white linen kerchief covers her mouse-coloured hair.[1]

SCENE I.

As the curtain rises there is a knock at the parlour door and a servant enters.   Sir Robert looks up from the parchment roll he is studying and growls :

SIR ROBERT.   Well ?

SERVANT.   The Worshipful Master of the Priory of St Robert desires speech with you, Sir.

SIR ROBERT.   Conduct him hither.

LADY ANNE.   As the Prior does not follow game, it must be some special purpose that has brought him.
   (*As she speaks she moves from her chair, gathering up her needlework, and takes her seat upon an oak chest beneath the window.*)

SIR ROBERT (*with a touch of impatience*).   Without doubt.

SERVANT (*entering and announcing*).   The Reverend Prior of St Robert's.[2]
   (*A tall, soft-footed man enters.   He has the face of an ascetic and the quietly persuasive voice of a man who rules other men with courteous dignity.*)

THE PRIOR.   My greetings to you, good Sir Robert, and to you also, Lady Anne.   Nay, Lady, pray do not leave us.   (*Anne has risen as if to go.*)   I have that to tell you which concerns your peace as parents.   (*He pauses, and Lady Anne glances at him apprehensively, but Sir Robert smiles slightly.*)

SIR ROBERT.   Pray do not hesitate to bring your charge, whatever it may be, against my children.

[1] For the cost of clothing at this period, see Appendix II., Note 10.
[2] The House of St Robert's-juxta-Knaresborough was a priory of the Order of Trinitarian Friars.

THE PRIOR. Sir Robert, your son Henry has robbed our Church.

SIR ROBERT. " Robbed " is a word that should be carefully used.

THE PRIOR. But used it should be, when it stands for truth.

SIR ROBERT. Without a doubt ; but still—a greater delicacy in allowing it to fall upon the hearing of a tender mother should, methinks, have had some thought from the Reverend Prior of St Robert's.

THE PRIOR. Sir Robert, I am not here to play with words.

SIR ROBERT (*sternly*). Or facts, I hope, sir. Come—tell this story straightly about Henry.

THE PRIOR. A lad out hunting ; an arrow in the throat of a deer ; the feet of that deer upon Church lands, our lands at Hampsthwaite that lie within your own, and my tale is told, save for a mention of the insolence with which the lad accompanied his deed, preventing those with orders from the Church from doing that for which they had been sent. The deer he caused his servants to remove, beating two friars and Brother Laurence Beckwith, who has ward of this land, and is, moreover, thy chaplain, Lady Anne —these holy men he beat unmercifully because they begged him to desist and save his soul from sin against the Church.

LADY ANNE (*wailing*). Oh, what a son is this ! No son of mine, Reverend Father, no son of mine ! To beat my chaplain upon his own land. (*She collapses sobbing. Sir Robert raises his eyebrows expressively.*)

SIR ROBERT. My wife is ever apt, Sir Prior, to cry the verdict ere the evidence is weighed.

THE PRIOR. The Lady Anne is guided right in this, and reads the tale I tell in its true light.

SIR ROBERT (*dryly*). While I, for my part, prefer to sift the evidence, sorting true statements from those made in passion.

THE PRIOR. Your son is but a boy, Sir Robert. I bring no case in courts to hurt his name; yet there is punishment due unto him, moreover compensation must be paid for theft and for the beatings he hath given to the servants of the Holy Church.

SIR ROBERT. Sir, we will not barter over the price of a slain deer like Jews in a market——

THE PRIOR (*interrupting coldly*). Jews, Sir Robert! Is it seemly for a gentle knight thus to insult himself and the Prior of St Robert's by comparison to that foul race which crucified Our Lord?

SIR ROBERT. At least I was giving credit for the wit possessed by Jews, and I would remind you, Sir Prior, that Our Lord was of the same race as those who crucified Him.

THE PRIOR (*rising abruptly from the chair on which he had enthroned himself*). Sir Robert de Nidde, have ward of your tongue.

SIR ROBERT (*calmly*). Nay, Sir Prior, you mistake my intent. I do but give back some of that knowledge which you religious so generously dispense. You do not dispute the statement, but because it is inopportune when Jews are being cursed you find yourself disturbed; and it is as foolish to kindle anger over such a matter as it is to make a mighty crime of a boyish prank.

THE PRIOR. Then theft of Church property is no crime in your good eyes, Sir Robert, and the beating of your own chaplain is to be called the pastime of a playful child? And yet I have seen your justice executed for thefts from your lands and for assault upon your servants.

SIR ROBERT. Play not with words, sir, else I be tempted to deal in parables concerning the strength of swords compared with words.

THE PRIOR. You threaten the Holy Church?

SIR ROBERT. Nay, I end a matter in which the Church is mistaken, even as I ended the matter for my son Henry an hour or more ago, and he is still bewailing the beating he received.

LADY ANNE. Then you knew about it all, and told me nothing?

SIR ROBERT. What need? (*To the Prior*): Come, Reverend Prior, your price? That is all that now concerns the Church.

THE PRIOR. Are you so sure, Sir Robert? What if I ask for further punishment?

SIR ROBERT. The price will be withheld—and also other things within my gift. Sir Prior, this bargaining ill befits your dignity or mine. Speak plainly with plain words, and speak your meaning.

THE PRIOR (*after a pause in which he gazes earnestly at Sir Robert, the faintest shadow of craftiness marring for an instant the fineness of his features*). My chancellor will put a price in gold : justice alone is my concern, Sir Robert. (*He bows to Sir Robert and Lady Anne and leaves the room silently and swiftly.*)

SIR ROBERT (*after a pause*). Justice or gold : now which would a fat friar choose?

LADY ANNE (*primly, as she resumes her chair by the fire*). The Reverend Prior is not at all fat. Much fasting and prayer have thinned his holy body.

(*There is a knock on the door, and before Sir Robert can speak, a fat and fussy little man, greatly dishevelled, comes tumbling in : a man who is familiar enough with the de Nidde family to enter the parlour unannounced, and flurried enough on this occasion to speak before he is addressed by either lord or lady, for he is Laurence Beckwith, the chantry priest of St Anne, Hampsthwaite, and private chaplain to Kettlesing Hall, greatly disturbed in mind and somewhat bruised in body.*)

BECKWITH.   Oh Sir, oh Lady Anne—I hear the Worshipful Master of St Robert's has been with you—my bruises have forbidden me to hasten hither earlier to bear witness.

SIR ROBERT (*grimly*).   You find Henry has a strong arm, Sir Laurence—well, he hath found my arm is strong too, when I belassch [1] him.

LADY ANNE.   He must be punished by Sir Laurence, too.

SIR ROBERT (*curtly*).   My punishment suffices, Lady Anne. Tell me, Sir Laurence, did you bear tales of Henry's prank to the Reverend Prior ?

BECKWITH.   I—I came upon his reverence on my way from—your son.

SIR ROBERT.   When you were running, eh ?

BECKWITH.   Yes, Sir Robert, when I was running from the devil that possessed your son.

LADY ANNE.   Possessed—my son possessed ! Help thou a wretched woman, Mother of Heaven——

SIR ROBERT.   Peace, woman, peace—'tis but part of a good tale.

BECKWITH.   A good tale !

LADY ANNE.   Unworthy charge—the good Prior——

SIR ROBERT (*abruptly*).   The good Prior likes a good tale well told.   Church lands must be guarded, even from the lord-to-be of Kettlesing.   Look well to your lands, Sir Laurence, look well.   Learn wisdom, too, in small matters.

(*The priest opens his mouth to speak, thinks better of it and, after a glance at Lady Anne which tells him that she neither understands nor has a shred of power over her suave husband, he bustles his way out of the room, limping and groaning with an eye to effect.*)

LADY ANNE.   More reverence for the Holy Church would not become you ill, Sir Robert.

[1] Thrash.

SIR ROBERT. More reverence for holy silence would become you well, Lady Anne. Patter your prayers, woman, patter your prayers, but keep them to yourself.

LADY ANNE. I—I never say anything. Who listens when I speak?

SIR ROBERT. Fat friars listen—and fools. Patter your prayers and look to your household, but—leave to me the guiding of my son.

LADY ANNE. E'en though he be possessed?

SIR ROBERT. Of what? Of the Church lands of Hampsthwaite that lie inside our own lands, the patch of trouble on my estate that our chaplain guards so warily lest some man of ours should take a blade of grass or filch a twig?

LADY ANNE. Possessed of the devil; not of land.

SIR ROBERT (*ignoring her remark*). Ay, would he were so possessed.

LADY ANNE (*horrified*). Of the devil?

SIR ROBERT (*irritably*). No, fool—of lands unbroken by a holy, guarded island in their midst!

(*Curtain.*)

SCENE II.

Fourteen years have passed since the last scene, and Sir Robert now has a beard shot with white. His eldest son, Henry, is a man grown, nearing his twenty-first birthday, a tall, lithe youth, handsome and masterful, who counts his father first with proper respect as head of the family, and then as a friend. Sir Robert has just returned from his annual visit to the Court, and after supper he has retired to his chamber of pleasaunce to learn from his son what has passed at the Hall during his absence. The Lady Anne has been dead for some five years, an event which has left Kettlesing quite untroubled.

Henry is clad in hose of soft russet leather, a plain doublet of dark green with a collar of marten's fur shielding the back of his neck, and at his throat we see his shirt of green silk, clasped at the collar with a brooch of gold. Sir Robert is dressed almost entirely in black, black hose puffed above the knee and black velvet doublet, with a touch of white at his throat where his shirt gleams silkily. Each has a dagger with an elaborately ornamented sheath attached to his belt. The rising curtain reveals Sir Robert reclining comfortably in his chair, and regarding Henry who stands with his back to the big fireplace wherein a wood fire glows.

SIR ROBERT. Taller than ever, Henry. And those shoulders are broadening out, unless my eyes lie.

HENRY (*with a laugh*). The broader the better, Sir, for bearing troubles.

SIR ROBERT. Troubles, boy? Are these light words to break a confession of some mad prank?

HENRY (*smiling*). Nay, father. I've put behind me boyish escapades; but troubles there are and troubles there will be now that so many monks are on the run.

SIR ROBERT. I have been away longer than is my wont, for I had business at the Court touching our welfare here.

HENRY. And in your absence, Sir, I have incurred the grave displeasure of, firstly, Sir Laurence Beckwith, who presumes unduly on his old appointment as my mother's chaplain, and thinks his holy duty still holds him to a course of interference here; and, secondly, the Worshipful Master of the Priory of St Robert's.

SIR ROBERT. Again, Henry! E'er since your arrow, fourteen years gone, sank in the throat of a deer on their Hampsthwaite lands there has been trouble, although you have never lacked correction from me for foolish tricks that seemed to you good jests.

HENRY. True, Sir, you have always paid me full measure for jests that you deemed ill. But touching this matter of the Prior——

SIR ROBERT (*waving his hand to the vacant chair by the fire*). You may sit, son.

HENRY (*sitting*). My thanks, Sir. You left us ten weeks ago, and with the autumn chills many of the vagrant monks from Knaresborough and Bolton have swarmed into Nidderdale. Now all the small monasteries are being uprooted, the chantries suppressed, and the king's orders fulfilled throughout all England, so I learn.

SIR ROBERT (*nodding*). True, Henry, true. I was speaking with Thomas Cromwell but two weeks ago, and have had speech in plenty with the king's commissioners—but of this I will tell when you have done.

HENRY. I would not house these vagrant fellows, monks and beggars by the score each week, eating with appetites grown large in idleness, begging for stomachs swollen with fine living in holy houses of unholy life. I sent them, each and all, unto the Church; to Fountains and to Kirkstall, and with crusts and water helped them on their way. It was the king's will that they should seek refuge in the larger monasteries, and I bore out that will, and sped them on, save when some craftsman cared to work and earn the food and shelter others begged. And for this strict obedience to the king, I am reproved and threatened by the Church. First comes little fat Sir Laurence a-twittering at me, and then he runs off once more tale-bearing to that gaunt fox, the Prior.

SIR ROBERT. Ay, fox he is; and come what may, the hole he digs for himself will be well-lined with gold and most secure. But what is threatened? Some crippling penance?

HENRY. Threats of excommunication.

SIR ROBERT. This is too much! To serve the king and reap reward like this from rats who'll soon be fleeing from the farmer's sling!

HENRY. Wait, Sir. There is grave trouble growing. Here in Yorkshire and farther north, the Church has flamed the passions, killed the wits, of lord and labourer alike. Talk there is of a " pilgrimage," a holy march of nobles, monks, and villeins, to crave the king's wisdom on this matter concerning which the royal will is manifest. Some creeping man of parchment, Robert Aske, lawyer and traitor, is stirring trouble—nay, rebellion!

SIR ROBERT. Son, son! A care for your words! This is a charge too grave for trifling.

HENRY. I know too much concerning it already, and had you tarried but another week, I should have ridden south to join you.

SIR ROBERT (*rising and beginning to pace the room in great agitation*). Can you attest the facts, record them here on parchment so that I can put them into Thomas Cromwell's hands?

HENRY. I have already writ what I have gleaned. (*He takes a sheet of parchment from a secret cupboard in the panelling. Sir Robert reads it slowly.*)

SIR ROBERT. We must be first at Court with this grave news, and must ride south without delay.

HENRY. Nay, Sir. You're weary with one journey; let me be your messenger to King Henry.

SIR ROBERT. I do not see the king on this alone, or even my good friend Thomas Cromwell. I must sow seed, my son; and when I reap—(*he rises*). Rouse all the grooms, and get the horses saddled, Henry.

HENRY. At once, Sir; and we'll ride within an hour. (*He goes, but as he reaches the door his father calls him back.*)

SIR ROBERT. Henry! Let not the threat of excommunication trouble you. The king has that which priests are losing now—power.

(*Curtain.*)

SCENE III.

The Chamber of Pleasaunce at Kettlesing Hall, two years later. The " Pilgrimage of Grace " has come and gone, and the king's vengeance on the rebels has taken its toll of nobles, commoners, and churchmen in Yorkshire in this interval. Sir Robert, trusted by the Court as he is hated by his neighbours and the Church, is entertaining the king's commissioners ; and the three keen-faced men sip spiced, warm wine from silver-gilt cups in company with their white bearded host. Henry de Nidde, now married and already a father, is at Court, with rooms in the Palace at Hampton, where he and his young wife (of the king's choosing) reside in the light of royal approval. The three commissioners are roaring with laughter as the curtain ascends, and Sir Robert smiles indulgently.

SIR ROBERT. Yes, it is a strange fancy for a priest to press.

GEOFFREY MORTON (*the chief commissioner*). By the bones of Becket ! these priests are ever turbulent.

SIR ROBERT. An oath well chosen, my masters ! I hold it shameful that the Canterbury Saint should all these years have marked the memory of a king's weakness.

RICHARD TOFT (*the junior commissioner*). Had our royal master dealt with Saint Thomas à Becket, there would have been no Canterbury pilgrimage to hold the king's justice to scorn.

MORTON. Ay, the king hath a swift way with pilgrimages.

SIR HUGH VANE (*the third commissioner*). We owe our early knowledge of that last trouble to you, Sir Robert.

SIR ROBERT. My family, Sir Hugh, has ever striven to serve the king against all enemies.

SIR HUGH. The de Niddes have held this land here of old time?

SIR ROBERT. Before King William's day. My ancestors were once lords of all Nidderdale. (*He sighs.*) But now—time has buried much of our prosperity; and I must needs listen to the clacking of monks who, though their lands break up those I own, cast envious looks upon my poor estate.

MORTON. The king does not forget a service rendered, Sir Robert; and you are aware of that for which we come; business to which you give your hospitality and help, providing information that we need.

SIR ROBERT. If you assess the value of the lands left to the Church throughout all Nidderdale, does not that mean collection follows fast? That gold and goods are wrung from monks who hoard; that lands are redistributed and lost for ever to the Church's grasping hand?

MORTON. Why ask, Sir Robert? Even the whining priest, Beckwith, of whom you spoke, knows that, else why should he come to you, the lord of Kettlesing, whom he has little cause to love, and implore you to speak favourably to us, and secure the restoration of his lands.

SIR ROBERT (*smiling at the memory of Beckwith's pleading*). From the Church you will never learn the true value of one field or pasturage.

MORTON. And that is where we claim your help, Sir Robert; and you can assess this land that lies within your own.

SIR ROBERT. My help is always given gladly to the king: he does not forget a service rendered.

MORTON. Nor do his commissioners, who are your

N

friends, forget a lightened task or your great good cheer.

SIR ROBERT (*bowing and raising his cup*).   Good sirs, I drink to the lightness of your task.

(*As they all drink the toast a servant knocks and enters.*)

SERVANT.   The late Worshipful Master of the Priory of St Robert desires speech with Sir Robert de Nidde.

MORTON.   Another priest ?   They have a great fondness for you, Sir Robert.

SIR ROBERT.   They know of your presence, good sirs, and I crave your permission to chide this thrusting fox in my own way.

MORTON.   We are all anxiety for this lesson in correction.

SIR ROBERT (*to the servant*).   Tell the Reverend Prior that I am serving my royal master, the king.

SERVANT (*repeating the message in a deep voice*).   Sir Robert de Nidde is serving his royal master, the king.

SIR ROBERT.   Correct.   Offer him the hospitality of the hall, but give no hope of speech with me.

(*Curtain.*)

SCENE IV.

The same as the last, two months after King Henry's death. Sir Robert, thin and worn, wrapped in a great fur-trimmed mantle of silk-lined velvet, sits, or rather crouches, in his chair by the fire.   His son, Henry, sits opposite, a strong, self-reliant man ; dressed with a careless extravagance that matches his easy carriage and confident good manners. A little boy, barely three years old, but richly dressed in velvet and silk so that he is in miniature a fashionable man of the Court, has just been led away by his nurse after kneeling to kiss Sir Robert's hand.

SIR ROBERT.   He will have lands worthy of our family, and you watch our interests with my care, Henry.

HENRY. Fear not that I shall neglect prosperity, Sir.

SIR ROBERT. No, I think you will be wise. And wisdom has guided you in this homecoming; for changes at Court spell misfortunes for many, and with Royal Harry dead there will be a-many nobles crowding to fill their coffers.

HENRY. I made few enemies; but still, self-interest turns all men against each other, and Hampton Court is filled with bitterness and scrambling ambition.

SIR ROBERT (*retrospectively*). I have done well for you and yours, my son. We can stretch our hands out into Nidderdale on all four sides of Kettlesing now. Good friends to me were those commissioners, passing me lands at values that I fixed. (*He rises feebly, Henry helping him to his feet, but as he walks slowly to the window he trips and stumbles over a toy left by his grandson, a little two-wheeled farm-cart painted bright blue, with a crudely carved ox between the shafts.*) Eh! my feet need eyes. Henry, I am an old man, but look (*he points through the window*): where once the Church ruled, there rule I. Ours, Henry—all of it, to Hampsthwaite and half-way to Ripon. The good king's bounty to those who have served him. Land, more precious than gold. Live here in quiet, son, and let these rich lands breed gold for you.

(*A servant enters, after knocking.*)

SERVANT. A monk would speak with Sir Robert de Nidde.

SIR ROBERT. Each day they come and beg this favour or that. It warms my cold age to hear them crave their little favours; and sometimes I grant a once-fat unfrocked monk some little boon—a crust, well water, or a week of labour. There is a great plague of vagrants, Henry, one and all claiming to be holy. (*To the servant*): Admit this monk.

*(The one-time chantry priest of Hampsthwaite, Lawrence
Beckwith, enters, old, thin, and shrunken, dishevelled, and
in a soiled and tattered gown, with sandalled feet stained
with blood and dust.)*

BECKWITH.   Greeting, Sir Robert de Nidde.

SIR ROBERT.   Greeting, Sir Monk.   Greeting and
welcome.

BECKWITH.   Mock not, Sir Robert.   What welcome is
there for me, robbed and outcast ?

SIR ROBERT.   Father, have I ever failed in hospitality ?
Because you have no pension from the king in return
for the surrender of your lands and what wealth
your wit enabled you to hide from that wise fox,
your old master, the Reverend Prior of St Robert's ;
because no royal settlement enables you to ape
this one-time master of yours in his fat retirement,
have you cause to say I mock because I bid you
welcome ?

BECKWITH.   I shall not judge of welcome or of woe
much longer in this England now Mother Church
is dead ; age and beggary kill slowly but with
sureness.

SIR ROBERT.   What would you have with us, apart from
welcome ?

BECKWITH.   Knowing that you hold the Church's lands,
enriched by much of her wealth in Nidderdale, I
come to ask one thing : two yards of land returned
so that I may die and rest in ground still holy though
outraged by greedy hands.

SIR ROBERT.   The matter could be put with greater
courtesy.

HENRY.   Sir Robert, may I speak ?   Throughout my
life, from boyhood, has this holy man tripped me up
with law, seen only in the letter, as cowards must
always look upon the law ; and his greed and that of

all his kind has been a plague on this our England that belongs to us, lords of the soil and masters of its men. Winding his way into my mother's heart, he sought to dominate us all, but was too fearful; and so he stooped to all the coward's shifts, and vented spite on those he could not rule. Did he not intrigue to have me excommunicated for my loyal service to the king's laws?

BECKWITH (*bitterly*). Loyal service to thine own purse, O robber of the poor!

HENRY. What, rob the poor whom we employ from dawn to sundown, working in our fields, whipping them only if they will not work?

SIR ROBERT. We give the poor their living and their bread.

BECKWITH. Living of that kind cannot be named as life.

SIR ROBERT. Yet did the Church work all her labourers as hard, and fought for rights upon them which the lords let lapse. You and your masters took with one hand, and unclosed the other in occasional largesse.

BECKWITH. Our sins discovered us, as will thine.

SIR ROBERT. Come: we'll spend no more words. I grant your yards of earth. Where will you have them turned?

BECKWITH. My thanks are due for this return of that which I possessed. (*He goes to the window and points through it.*) Beyond the meadow that was always thine, there is a pasturage where once a deer was slain unlawfully and certain humble servants of the Holy Church were beaten. It may be seen from here, and I would lie well in the centre there, beneath a mound, raised to remind descendants of your house how your estate was filched from Mother

Church.   Perchance they may be moved to res-
titution.

SIR ROBERT (*smiling pityingly*).   I think not, Father.   The
sword is stronger than the rood !

(*The priest bows his head and leaves the room as the
curtain slowly falls.*)

A half-timbered town house.

CHAPTER XIII

CULTURE AND COMMERCE

KETTLESING HALL during the early days of April, in the year 1580, was the scene of tremendous activity, for the de Nidde family and their neighbours were making preparations to welcome Captain Thomas de Nidde, who was due to return home after his longest voyage. Forgotten were the feuds and hatreds sown by the ambitious and acquisitive Sir Robert. His grandson, Thomas, is very different from the half-mediæval courtier of Henry VIII.'s day. Great changes have come about in the quality of life and manners ; and for the wealthy, long-established families of the country, doors have been thrown open which admit their more progressive members to new worlds of wealth,[1] culture, and adventure ; and for the poor comes a taste of personal responsibility, which as serfdom fades spurs the peasant and the craftsman to work, for poverty is now a crime to be curbed with whips and branding irons, imprisonment, and forced labour. But the land has peace and comparative freedom ; vast freedom in contrast with the rampant militarism that is threatening civilisation in Europe and stalking over the Continent with fire and rapine. Everybody is fully aware of the fact that it is due to the cool courage and superb seamanship of such gentlemen adventurers as Captain Thomas de Nidde that England enjoys her present peace ; and that fact alone would have been enough to rouse half Nidderdale to

---

[1] The Elizabethan period was an age " unparalleled for its money-making activity." *Society in the Elizabethan Age*, by Hubert Hall, p. 58. See Appendix II., Note 11.

greet his return; but Captain Thomas, in addition to having made three voyages to the ends of the earth, sinking the tall ships of the Spaniard when they come his way and interrupting the flow of wealth from the Indies to Spain, is a scheming, courtly gentleman, possessing all the power and vigour of a man of action, clothed with the polish and culture the Elizabethan Court could give to a receptive mind, and imbued with the none too scrupulous money-making ambitions of his time.[1]

Kettlesing Hall has been extended since Sir Robert's day, and the T-shaped plan of the early sixteenth century has grown into an E, with a long central member, that part being the stone " great " hall that has dominated the general form of the manor from pre-Norman times. But the stones which Arkell Scrufa knew are no longer to be seen; and the dirt he and his mediæval descendants knew has vanished. Smoke has been put in its right place, the chimney, during the last few generations, and since the final quarter of the fifteenth century real cleanliness has been possible, for with soot banished, hands can be kept clean, linen remain unsoiled, and hair retain its lustre. The musicians' gallery still spans the upper end of the great hall, supported on columns of turned oak, and the floor of the hall has been paved with smooth stone slabs, and rushes are no longer used, for sometimes the long oak table is moved to one side and the floor is then free for dancing. Carpets are still rare, and are seldom used for floors, being draped on walls or spread on tables. There is a glint of armour on the plastered walls, and above one of the doors a pair of antlers is hung.

There will be dancing to celebrate Sir Thomas de Nidde's return, and for a couple of days the squeak of fiddle, twang of harp, and sound of lutes and pipes marked the rehearsal of the musical programme. The vicar of Hampsthwaite, Master Thomas Dacre, who is also tutor to

[1] See Appendix II., Notes 11 and 12.

Tobacco comes into everyday life.

young master Richard Nidde, has been busily composing treacly lyrics in praise of the sailor-master of Kettlesing. These are being written out with care and patience by Mary Nidde, Richard's youngest sister. There will be a masque the day after the Captain comes home, and there will be feasting for all the poor and lowly as well as for those well favoured in goods up and down the Nidd valley and around the townships within the manor. Nor will Knaresborough be behind in these matters, and the mayor and burgesses, fat, prosperous merchants or Duchy officials, who all appreciate successful ventures to the golden Spanish Main, will accord a civic welcome to the master of Kettlesing, and the mayor will make a rousing speech, for in that age a mayor was a functionary who understood leadership, and civic dignity was dignity indeed, respected and acknowledged.

And then comes the day on which the Captain is expected. His wife, Janet de Nidde, is prepared to give a good account of her stewardship during his absence and to make worthy his welcome. The feast is prepared ; [1] deeds of doom are done in the poultry-yard ; fresh-water fish cooked in a dozen different ways are to tempt the master's appetite ; and of meats there are hams, cured in a way that has made Yorkshire famous ; great rounds of beef, haunches of venison, crisp roasts of eloquent appeal bathed in steaming gravy of ruddy brown as they bask in their oval dishes of shining pewter ; ox-tongues, salted, spiced, and variously flavoured ; mutton seethed and roast, the former served with a sauce of butter, wine, cloves, and parsley. There are salads, apples, pears, walnuts, and—expensive luxury—oranges. Bannocks, oatcake, rye bread, cakes flavoured with cloves and cinnamon, barley loaves ; noble tarts bejewelled with fruit or crammed with game ; sweetmeats innumerable ; and all

[1] For a list of kitchen utensils of the period and the qualities demanded of a master cook, see Appendix II., Notes 13 and 14.

these good things can be enjoyed w
of ale, metheglin, cider, barley win
and the red and white wines of F
attention is paid to these last, ale,
wine being chiefly in demand.

The great hall is set out for the
hidden by the ranks of dishes ; the *d*
against the wall opposite the chim
with silver. Word has been sent th
the Captain's coming, so the prep   well
timed.

There are the usual false alarms of the arrival, and then
there is the deep *boom !* of a small brass cannon, trophy
of an earlier voyage of the Captain's, a dangerous engine,
apt to buck backwards with disconcerting vigour when
fired. The recoil fells the man who fires the charge, but,
bleeding freely from the nose and mouth, he jumps up
again and cheers, as Captain Thomas quiets his horse,
who was not expecting this signal of welcome. The
master of Kettlesing and the four men who have accompanied him dismount. He wears a suit of half-armour,
gilded and engraved, and the breastplate, backplate,
laminated taces covering his thighs, and combed morion
on his head, throw back the afternoon sun, and turn him
momentarily into a figure of flashing gold. There are
greetings, and then a service of thanksgiving in the
church. Follows the feast, at which good fellowship
goes hand in hand with drunkenness.[1]

Conversation has been enriched enormously in a couple
of generations, for imagination, instead of being confined
to the songs or sagas properly considered in the light of
entertainment and generally provided by professional
people, bards, minstrels, or jesters, now flows into the
general talk of any company forgathered at table or
fireside. Ideas have also been wonderfully stimulated

[1] See Appendix II., Notes 15 and 16, for actual meals in England and Scotland.

...scoveries of the age ; and travel and the growing
... of reading have broadened minds and loosened
...ngues. It is a larger world, teeming with golden
possibilities in which Captain Thomas lives, and just now
he is the magnetic pole to which all imaginations are
pointed. For has he not come from the Indies, the golden
Spanish Main, and has he not fought and captured two of
His Spanish Majesty's great ships, releasing from one a
dozen English slaves, doomed to the galley oars, and
taking untold treasure from the other, a homing plate
ship ? Also he has trodden that wonderful piece of
earth, South America, land of the lost Incas, land of
legend, of Children of the Sun and the Golden City of
Manoas ; land of endless romance, calling the adventurous from all the nooks and corners of the earth ; land
where the Spaniard proves his rottenness and the Englishman whets the blade of his enterprise, learning for the
ultimate enrichment of his race that he can open new
markets with his sword and keep them by his word. And
of all this adventuring, looting, trading, war-making
against the colonies of mighty Spain, Captain Thomas
tells his family in the simple, well selected words of a
man who has learnt the music of his language at a Court
where scholars, soldiers, poets, sailors, and statesmen
before they are specialists are one and all cultured
gentlemen.

Captain Thomas sits by the window of the winter
parlour, looking across the green meads to Holy Mound
(as the villagers name a certain lonely grave) in the
meadow beyond, where he raised a church, Kettlesing
Church, in thanksgiving for his safe return after his first
voyage some years before with Drake. He is a big man
with fair curling hair and a silky golden beard trimmed to
a point, softly triangular above his immense, starched
and snowy ruff. He has taken off the velvet cloak which
he kept on his shoulders during the feast, for as he

explains, he feels the cold in England after three years of the torrid tropics. Directly after he had arrived he had washed, and changed his armour and travelling clothes for the rich garments affected by the Elizabethan gentleman who knows something of Court fashions. First there is the great ruff that makes his head look as though it is set on a charger. Then a brown brocade " peascod-bellied " doublet stuffed and quilted to give it its shape, coming to a sharp point at the front below the waist. The sleeves are puffed and a long slit extends down the front of each from shoulder to wrist revealing the lining of scarlet satin. One side of these openings is bordered by a row of big gold buttons, the size of draughtsmen. Both sleeves and body are piped with gold thread and covered with small diagonal slashes through which the scarlet satin peeps. His Venetian hose or breeches are of the same material ornamented in the same way. On his legs, reaching just above the knees, are black yarn stockings tied with ribbon garters. His shoes are of scarlet leather.

His wife, whose hair is dyed the fashionable red-gold colour, carefully curled, and gathered into an elaborate caul of strings of pearls and silver beads, wears a vast stiff white linen ruff edged with silver lace. Her clothes are before all other things, decorative. A quilted green silk low-cut damask doublet with a pearl-sewn stomacher fits closely to her figure, ending in a point in front. For a necklace she has a long string of alternate pearls and cameos reaching to her knees. The vast farthingale billowing out over her hips supports a voluminous skirt of the same material as the doublet, only of a darker shade. Many rings adorn her fingers. The two children are miniatures of their parents, save that the boy does not wear the " peascod " form of doublet nor the girl the farthingale, and naturally their clothes are of cheaper materials and less ornamented ; but the stiff absurdity

of their garments is a serious check to the energetic dis-
position of childhood.[1]

The master of Kettlesing has talked and been talked to
unwearyingly since he set foot on his lands, and as he
looks out upon the peaceful countryside, he falls silent.
Presently he fumbles in a leather pouch strapped to his
belt, draws therefrom a short clay pipe, stuffs the small
bowl with some brown fibre-like stuff, and going to the
fire that warms the room on this chill April evening,
kindles with a twig one end of the packed bowl. He
puts the pipe stem between his lips, and walking back to
the window horrifies his family by puffing smoke from
his mouth and letting it trickle through his nostrils.[2]
This fresh wonder feeds the talk for full another hour, and
then come the inevitable questions concerning London,
the glittering city of growing wealth and elaborate
fashions that Janet de Nidde has never seen. Captain
Thomas describes, as he has often described before, the
full and brilliant life of the place ; the plays, the great
shops of King Street, the palaces, the noble houses of the
Strand with their gardens going down to the Thames,
that crowning beauty of London, with its swans, salmon,
and abundant craft—with skilful phrases he makes the
sights and sounds of the city live for the lady of Kettlesing. She is eager with questions concerning the way
the wealthy merchants live, particularly one, Richard
Crane, who is the Captain's good friend, having invested
heavily in the venture from which he has just returned
and which was marked with such agreeable financial
success. Richard Crane has a fine house, is indeed a
merchant prince, devoted to trade, but by no means
without culture. He speaks Spanish and Italian as

[1] See Appendix II., Note 17.
[2] Taylor, the Water Poet, says : " Tobacco was first brought into England in
1565 by Sir John Hawkins." Queen Elizabeth issued an edict against the abuse
of tobacco in 1584, so that by that time smoking must have been popular among
those who could afford it.

fluently as Captain Thomas ; he has a small library of a hundred volumes or so, and in this he is greatly in advance of Kettlesing Hall, which boasts only half a dozen books apart from copies of the Bible ; his house in the city is well appointed, rich with fine fabrics from Italy and the East, furnished with oak chests inlaid with marqueterie and parqueterie of various woods, imported from Holland, beds wonderfully carved by Flemish craftsmen, chairs of Venetian pattern, with seats of embroidered velvet, great tables with carpets of Turkey work spread thereon ; in all ways a home of wealth and lavish comfort, with every room oak panelled, and every window glazed.   This merchant prince gives fine dinners, and the company thereat lacks neither wit nor noble blood ; manners are polished at that abundant board, and silver forks [1] are used, while silver tongues make conversation pleasant.   Captain Thomas tells of his entertainment by Richard Crane, and speaks of the important part played by his host in the civic life of London.   What royal hospitality that wealthy citizen could dispense, and how excellent the programme he arranged for each day : the wonderful dinner at eleven in the morning, always enriched by strange foreign fruits, preserves, and spices, followed in the early afternoon by a couple of hours at the theatre, in the stage boxes of the Curtain at Shoreditch, or Burbage's theatre at Blackfriars, or perhaps on a warm, sunny day a voyage on the sleek waters of the Thames in his private barge with its silken awning, its comfortable cushions, and well trained crew.   A fine tale could Thomas make from such fine materials ; and when he has done with the sights of London town, he is questioned about the Court and the doings of Her Gracious Majesty.   Those questions had come earlier, but he had parried them because he had a great surprise which he wished to hold back as long

[1] See Appendix II., Note 18.

as possible, but at last he replied to his wife's urgent query :

" And how were you received, dear husband ? "

" With favour, my Lady Janet," he answers, " so great indeed is the privilege of serving such a queen that no reward is needed save her smile."

Janet, despite her doubts of this, agrees.

Cottage homes of the late sixteenth century.

" Still, it has pleased Her Gracious Majesty to reward my services," he continues ; " just now, my dear, I addressed you as my Lady Janet. You have ever been Dear Lady to me, but you may now in very truth claim the title that I gave you, for the queen hath made me a knight."

That is indeed an honour, marking out Sir Thomas as a man exceptional in his time, both for deeds and personal charm, for not lightly did Elizabeth confer the order of knighthood, which was often regarded as the highest reward in her gift. Courtier and adventurer, he settles down at Kettlesing after this third and most successful voyage, when his frail little vessel has returned to England loaded low with Spanish gold and spices ; and he has placed the fortunes of his family on an even firmer base than his grandsire, Sir Robert, achieved by a lifelong devotion to the cause of acquisition. His wealth is greater, for he has gained it in the service of a new power that is stirring in the land and melting the fetters that bound it in the past—the power of commerce. With the breaking of Spanish strength—in which Sir Thomas took part, fitting out two stout ships at York and harrying the straggling galleons of the Armada as they flew north before the great gale—progress took wing, and change became a swifter process than men on British soil had ever known before.

CHAPTER XIV

The Puritan Reaction

DURING the seventeenth century the comfort of home life generally increased. There were more wealthy people in the world, not because there had been any dramatic redistribution of wealth, but because wealth was being created on a scale unknown since the collapse of the financial fabric of Imperial Rome. It is a favourite assumption of some writers that all the increases in wealth for which the sixteenth and seventeenth centuries were notable are directly attributable to the looting of the monasteries. This suggests a complete disregard of certain elementary economic facts concerning the creation of wealth, and also an imperfect idea of the character of Henry VIII. and the nobles by whom he was surrounded. The Tudor land-thieves did not devote their loot to developing commerce or backing trade enterprises of any sort. It is in the highest degree improbable that any trader ever gained an extra penny from the dissolution of the monasteries. It was the imagination, initiative, and energy of English traders, often in close alliance with the courage of gentlemen adventurers, that created such a greater volume of wealth in post-Tudor England. The trader in mediæval times had to contend with the periodic anarchy of private warfare, in a country of brigand-haunted roads, and had moreover to conduct his business under the eyes of people who were ignorantly suspicious of finance, who were incapable of understanding that capital when loaned either as gold or goods deserved to earn interest or rent, and who dismissed any dealings with money that were beyond their limited comprehension as " usury," a crime in the view of orthodox Christianity and one severely punished by the secular arm. And the trader too often had his market wrecked by the action of some blundering autocrat with a military, romantic, or grasping mind whose ideas of wealth were bounded by land, loot, and ransoms. For example, that lascivious spendthrift, Henry VIII., utterly ruined much of England's flourishing trade by debasing the coinage, so that for years English money was discredited in the eyes of European merchants, causing a great set-back to the creation of wealth, although the king's coffers were temporarily replenished.

But the " scientific commercial age " began with the American voyages, and the calm success of the gentlemen adventurers, who set at naught Papal decrees and laughed at the threats of the greatest military and naval power in Europe, marked the end of mediæval times. In 1601 the ageing Queen Elizabeth withdrew and made illegal an established piece of royal interference in trade, namely the granting of " monopolies " under the royal seal to favoured individuals, permitting them to be the sole vendors or makers of certain articles of commerce.

Side by side with the landed proprietors, who farmed their estates and provided the " ruling class " throughout the country and populated the Court, were the merchants. These wealthy, capable people were essentially towns-men, and their increasing wealth was reflected by the increasing importance of towns and cities. In the houses of both classes there are more luxurious things, and there is a nearer approach to the well appointed homes of Romano-British times, although the early seventeenth century home despite its well-made carved oak furniture, rich embroideries, glazed windows, and panelled rooms, is still inferior to the home of thirteen hundred years earlier, for it is heated clumsily and wastefully by great open fireplaces and is without a bathroom.

Extreme comfort and extravagant luxury are no longer royal and noble privileges ; but power is still narrowly restricted, and although the trader has won the right to carry on his business undisturbed, law can be overridden by the " divine right " of kings ; a matter that is presently explored jointly by landholders, merchants —and a king. John Nidde, who is master of Kettlesing in the first half of the seventeenth century, is content enough with things as they are, and is a healthy, unthinking country squire, utterly lacking the adventurous roving spirit of his grandfather, Sir Thomas. He is a little soured by an unhappy marriage, although his wife, Mercy, had most of the unhappiness to bear ; for she was a quiet, serious girl, of a Puritan cast of mind, who contracted through her parents a purely mercenary marriage with this hard-drinking member of the dominant Nidde family. John Nidde, always attracted by a pretty woman, though by no means to be satisfied by devotion to one alone, was too passionate to be repelled by the cold purity of mind and unaccommodating censure of all earthly pleasure that characterised his wife. Kettlesing Hall felt for the first time the chill breath of Puritanism ; and until his son was born three years after his marriage and his wife had died a month later, all the concentrated joyousness of John's drinking and hunting parties was insufficient to dispel the gloom engendered by a silent, solemn woman, always clad in dark, sober hues with a touch of white at throat and wrist ; a sombre figure in the background, hovering on the border of his pleasures like a dark cloud in the corner of a sunlit sky.

Unfortunately his only son, Jonathan, as he was named by his dying mother's especial desire, has marked Puritanical tendencies. But he can find no fault with the boy's courage, for he rides well and boldly, and has a straighter eye than his father for shooting wild fowl. Jonathan is capable, too, and relieves his father of the management of the estate to a considerable extent ; but he is a silent, thoughtful youth, drinking only in moderation and never causing his father a moment of anxiety.

Early in the February of 1649, John Nidde, now a man of sixty-five, and marked by his hard and roystering life, a prey to gout and other complaints, has a party of loyalist friends to dine with him at Kettlesing. An outspoken but inactive supporter of the king, he had been too impressed by the nearness of civil war to risk his lands by openly taking sides, and making infirmity his excuse, he lived peaceably enough at Kettlesing, forbidding his son to engage in the war. The smashing up of the castle at Knaresborough by the orders of Parliament was a salutary object-lesson of the power wielded by the central government, and although John Nidde might give tongue in his cups concerning his rulers, he was never injudiciously critical when sober.

However, on this particular February evening he is reminiscently discursive. It is not difficult to picture the scene in the great chamber at Kettlesing. The walls are warmly panelled in oak for two-thirds of their height, and the chimneypiece has been embellished with decorative plaster work, a carved oak mantel borders the fireplace opening with rather clumsy female figures supporting the narrow shelf, above which in painted and gilded plaster surrounded by an ornate ornamental frame the arms of the de Niddes are bright with heraldic colours. Above the panelling is a decorative frieze of plaster painted with hunting scenes in flat colours, a spirited piece of work executed with complete disregard for perspective by a local craftsman whose father, grandfather, and great-grandfather all worked plaster and decorated it, passing on their knowledge generation

by generation, and thereby unconsciously preserving
mediæval traditions. Over all is a plaster ceiling with
complex strapwork ornamentation. There is a long,
six-legged table of oak, the legs swelling out with elaborately carved melon bulbs, and linked to each other by
a stretcher, on which the feet of those seated at the table
may rest. Chairs with backs and seats of oak, with
carved cresting and sturdy arms and underframing, are
at the head of the table, but joined stools form the
majority of seats. The common life of the hall has
vanished ; the master and his guests are exclusive in the
great chamber ; the servants have their own quarters
and their own hall. The *dressoir* with its silver and pewter
still stands opposite the chimneypiece, and there is a
court cupboard of golden oak which provides more
accommodation for cups and vessels. In movable
property and in luxurious and decorative trimmings to
life, Kettlesing Hall is richer than it has ever been, for
craftsmen are following the increasing wealth of the
country by producing in greater abundance articles of
wood, metal, pottery, glass, and fine textiles. Despite
ordinances against luxurious things, we find upon John
Nidde's table, not only spoons of wood, pewter, and
silver, but forks to help the dainty knives dedicated to the
service of diners and to increase the growing elegance
of table manners.

The food that John Nidde and his guests have spent
a pleasant hour or so in despatching has been well served
and agreeably, not to say extravagantly, cooked. A dish
of marrow bones comes by way of introduction, then
follows an ornate succession of dishes. A leg of mutton
stuffed with a forcemeat consisting of bread-crumbs,
suet, yolks of hard boiled eggs, anchovies, onion, thyme,
and winter-savoury, oysters and a little grated nutmeg,
and served with a sauce compounded of the liquor from
the oysters, a little claret, two or three anchovies, a little

nutmeg, and a bit of onion; after this *tour de force* of kitchen craftsmanship comes a loin of veal roast, then a great dish of stewed chickens and larks. There is a lumber pie containing minced veal and marrow, mixed into a forcemeat with suet, candied orange peel, sweet herbs, an apple or two, grated bread, currants, cloves, mace, nutmeg, and two or three eggs. This is put into the crust with slices of candied citron, orange, and lemon, and then baked, served with a sauce of white wine and sugar thickened with butter and eggs. After this elaborate attack on digestion the company tackle a neat's tongue; a dish of anchovies; a dish of prawns and cheese; and finally a tansy compounded of a quart of cold boiled cream flavoured with cinnamon, nutmeg, and mace, mixed with twenty yolks and ten whites of eggs. To these were added grated biscuits, half a pound of butter, a pint of spinage juice, and a little tansy, sack and orange flower water, sugar and salt. The mixture was then baked and eaten cold with sliced orange and sugar.[1] And there is mellow ale, warmed and spiced; red wine from Portugal and France; rum from the Indies; and a generous bowl of punch brewed by the host. A meal well planned to loosen cautious tongues. We may imagine the curtain rising upon John Nidde, plaintively garrulous, but by no means drunk, sitting back in his chair at ease, a largely-made, red-faced man, bearded and with a neatly trimmed moustache. His long hair is curled and scented. Falling over his shoulders is a deep linen " band " or collar edged with lace. He wears a richly embroidered brown satin doublet with puffed sleeves terminating in deep ruffles or " hand-ruffs." The doublet is buttoned down the front to the waist, below which it is cut away to show his white, fine lawn shirt above the top of his breeches. These

---

[1] Based on a dinner, described in Pepys's Diary, *sub. an.* 1659. Recipes from Smith's *Compleat Housewife*.

latter are of the same material as the doublet, baggy and ornamented at the knee with rows of puffed ribbons of several colours, the garters being tied at the sides in a large bow. He wears black silk stockings. His top-boots of soft russet leather are tied about the middle of the calf, the tops, which are decorated with a wide lace frill, being turned down almost to the ankle.

His guests, all dressed with the same careless richness and elaboration, are settled comfortably in their chairs, and they number four : Sir Roger Nain, Sheriff of Knaresborough ; Matthew Metcalfe, a neighbouring squire ; Thomas Overman, a retired naval officer, who has settled in his native county after a hard life at sea ; and Michael Thompson, an ex-Royalist army officer, compelled to peaceful courses by the turn of events and living frugally at Hampsthwaite.

NIDDE. I repeat, sirs, life differs vastly now from the life I knew when I was a lusty lad. Why, our very children are unlike us.

SIR ROGER. True, true. And I recall that my father said the same concerning me when I had reached years enough to sprout hairs on my chin.

NIDDE. My father consigned me to the devil thrice daily for my way of life ; but my way was not my son's way. Burn me ! but there are times when I've a fear that there's no blood in Jonathan.

OVERMAN. Nay, nay, neighbour Nidde ; ye're too hard on the boy.

SIR ROGER. Belike he favours his mother.

NIDDE. He does ; a mother's son in every look and word.

OVERMAN (*heartily, as he sips a glass of steaming rum and water*). No worse for that, I'll vow.

NIDDE (*sourly*). You knew not my wife, lieutenant.

SIR ROGER (*anxious to curb the tide of reminiscence*).   Now why is it that we old men must needs talk about this and that of our young days whene'er we meet, and measure up the youths we know by doings of our own, like as not to be ill remembered ?

NIDDE.   The times have changed, and who will be bold enough or fool enough to say that they have changed for better times ?

THOMPSON.   Not I, by the devil and all his angels !

METCALFE.   I've nought to complain of, save this prying of officials whene'er I want to take some wench into keeping.   Faith, in the olden days the lord of the manor had rights——

SIR ROGER.   And serfs.   That day is over, Matthew Metcalfe.

NIDDE.   And I say, shame that this and that should be ordered by men who are not men and who judge all gentlemen by the conduct of some toss-pot they've seen flung from a tavern.   These rantings against feasts and good cheer in living, because some joyless presbyter deems that good food gives pleasure, and thrives and prays upon some dismal crust like a stinking rat and wants all other men to do the same !   And, damme ! but my son's that way inclined.

SIR ROGER.   Nay, that I'll not believe.

OVERMAN.   No son of thine could not enjoy good living !   (*There is a general laugh at this, in which Nidde joins.*)

NIDDE.   Believe me or not, sirs, it's the truth.   His mouth's the poorest friend to his belly, for scarce a drain of wine will pass his lips, and but a bite of food.

THOMPSON (*who is rather tipsy, and speaks with the slow solemnity of the half-drunk*).   Dost hint that Jonathan Nidde is not at heart a king's man ?   Blood, but

I'd spit the newt an' I thought it—with such a noble father, too! (*He brushes away a crapulous tear.*)

SIR ROGER. We're 'tween stout walls here; still 'tis ill-advised to speak of " king's men."

NIDDE (*striking the table*). Never! Mine is the Royalist cause; and there my son *is* my son. No word of praise for Parliament has ever passed his lips; no sentiment disloyal to Charles our king. (*He staggers to his feet.*) Gentlemen, gent—(hic)—gentlemen, I drink the king's health.

SIR ROGER. Bless and preserve him in his danger!
(*They drink the toast, and send their glasses smashing to the floor when they are empty.*)

METCALFE (*looking about him nervously*). I trust that we have not been overheard.

NIDDE. Small fear of that.

(*As he speaks the door bursts open, and a tall man enters, wrapped in a great cloak and wearing a wide brimmed beaver hat that shields his face. As he comes into the hall, he throws off the hat which is dusted with snow and reveals himself as Jonathan Nidde, booted and spurred and travel-weary. His father and his guests, who have risen in panic at his sudden entry after their injudicious display of loyalty, resume their seats and try to look comfortable and composed, for the most part failing miserably.*)

NIDDE. I—I scarce expected your return to-night, son.

JONATHAN. I rode hot haste from Knaresborough.

SIR ROGER (*quickly*). For what cause, young sir?

JONATHAN. To bear my father news, and you too, Sir Roger and gentlemen, since you are here.

NIDDE. News—whence?

JONATHAN. London. Five days ago the king went to the block!

SIR ROGER (*pale and leaping to his feet*). Dead! Our king!

" And so perish all tyrants ! "

JONATHAN. Beheaded at the window of his palace in Whitehall.

NIDDE. Oh, this is lying folly!

SIR ROGER. Some rumour, surely.

JONATHAN. Proclaimed in Knaresborough three hours since by officers of Parliament. (*He regards the startled company with something near a smile on his pale and serious face, and then adds quietly but with the fire of conviction*) : And so perish all tyrants!

(*Curtain.*)

The Puritan strictures on good living and feasting bewailed by John Nidde were to become law some two years after that vigorous old Royalist's death. Feasts and habits that smacked of Romish custom were put down by those cold, correct Englishmen who tainted the fine austerity of Puritanism with fanaticism. By order of Parliament, 24th December 1652, it was decreed " that no Observation shall be had of the five and twentieth Day of December, commonly called CHRISTMAS DAY; nor any solemnity used or exercised in Churches upon that day in respect thereof." The same order forbade the consumption of mince pies, Christmas pies, plum porridge, and such-like venerated traditional luxuries of the table. In Needham's *History of the Rebellion* (1661) there are some verses which put this restriction in the pillory of ridicule; and it would be hard to find a better conclusion to a glance at home life under Puritan influence:—

> All Plums the Prophet's sons defy,
>   And spice-broths are too hot;
> Treason's in a December-pye,
>   And death within the pot.
>
> Christmas, farewell; thy days I fear,
>   And merry days are done:

So they may keep feasts all the year,
   Our Saviour shall have none.

Gone are those golden days of yore,
   When Christmas was a high day,
Whose sports we now shall see no more,
   'Tis turn'd into Good Friday.

A small, mid-seventeenth century country house.

CHAPTER XV

THE RETURN TO LUXURY

REACTION comes with the restoration of the Stuarts to the throne of England and to the leadership of society; and after the austerities of Puritan rule, the country sinks back comfortably into easy-going ways, agreeable and occasionally dissolute luxury, and general administrative inefficiency. The home life of the prosperous classes becomes divided sharply into country life and town life, a division foreshadowed by the growing wealth and importance of the merchant princes of Elizabethan days, but brought to special prominence now by the increased importance of towns and cities and the serious beginning of wheeled traffic. The stage coach has yet to come; but the country gentleman, his lady, family, and luggage, can journey to the town without the dire discomfort that attended such travelling a century earlier, when vehicles were as rare as they were costly and clumsy. And if the country squire would keep in touch with fashion and polite society, periodic journeys become necessary, and an annual pilgrimage to London suggests itself as a desirable addition to his plan of life.

Naturally this brings into the country home the modes of the town, and the humbler country folk, denied the luxury of travelling, can be astonished and entertained on Sundays when the squire and his lady enliven church-going with a display of town-cut clothes and the finery that makes men and women blossom like exotic flowers in vivid contrast with the severity of dress so recently imposed by Puritan convention. The variety and quantity of personal possessions owned by moderately wealthy people increases in the latter half of the seventeenth century. In his *Epigram de Mons. Maynard*, Charles Cotton describes a room so finely furnished that it had a disastrous effect on the vanity of its owner :—

> Anthony feigns him Sick of late,
>   Only to shew how he at home,
> Lies in a Princely Bed of State,
>   And in a nobly furnish'd Room,
> Adorn'd with Pictures of Vandike's,
>   A pair of Chrystal Candlesticks,
> Rich Carpets, Quilts, the Devil, and all :
>   Then you, his careful Friends, if ever
>   You wish to cure him of his Fever,
>   Go lodge him in the Hospital.

Clocks are ticking now in many homes. A hundred years earlier a clock was a rare and expensive toy, seldom found except in palaces and great houses ; but from the Commonwealth to the days of Queen Anne clock-making develops apace, and from the brass lantern clocks evolves the bracket clock, and presently the dangling weights are provided with a long case, and so the grandfather clock arrives. Then that queer forebear of the piano engages the attention of the daughters of the house, the virginal, a plaintive anticipation of the spinet, well suited to accompany the songs that blended sentimentality and classic allusions, love songs with a faintly pagan flavour, occasionally lapsing into the outspoken coarseness natural to an age in which the first gentleman of the country was so excessively and publicly lecherous. But Charles II. was a humorist, and infinitely more tactful than his father when the condition of his purse suggested the expediency of overriding the law and extracting money from his subjects.

The Commonwealth was the result of successful war waged against the lingering traces of mediævalism. It made the world unsafe for autocracy, but rendered it passably secure for the commoner. And we find Jonathan Nidd comforting himself with that thought upon the Restoration : at least law and order are unassailably established. He is rather different from the serious young devotee of Parliament who shocked his Royalist father so violently when he brought the news of Charles's execution. As the years have passed, the peculiar genius of his family for safeguarding its interests has asserted itself, and as political changes came about he allowed his loyalties to change too ; but he has altered his views quietly and without appearing to take his stand definitely on one side or the other. It is a different matter when Charles II. returns to the country ; common sense demands an expression of loyalty, a reassurance of allegiance to the throne, which is sent to London in company with many similar messages from prudent country gentlemen and civic officials, merchants, and traders in provincial cities.

Jonathan decides to live quietly at Kettlesing, but he cannot fit himself into the sort of life his father led, and although he hunts and shoots game, yet his greatest pleasure is a long clay pipe and a jar of choice leaf from Virginia to bear him company as he sits by an apple-wood fire in the parlour with some book on his knee, and the dark gold of the oak panelling warmly surrounding him. He has become a great reader, and begins to lay the foundations of a library at Kettlesing. He is delighted to find that his son Matthew is studiously inclined, and with the assistance of the vicar of Hampsthwaite, an untidy little man with a worn and greasy cassock, but a fine, scholarly mind—rare in a country parson of that time— he tutors Matthew until the boy shall be ready to study at Oxford. These educational ambitions are not encouraged by his neighbours.

" What does a lad want with all this learning if he be

not cast for a lawyer's or a preacher's life ? " growls old Sir Roger Nain when he visits Kettlesing and criticises everything with the freedom of an old friend of the family.

" Sir, my great-grandfather, Sir Thomas Nidd, never found that learning hindered him, and he was no preacher," Jonathan replies with a sour smile.

" Faith, he preached bloody fear to the Spaniard, as did all our grandfathers under good Queen Bess, God rest her ! " cries Sir Roger ; and then flares into fiery indignation at the way the Dutch are trouncing the English on the sea. " Sweepings, sir, dust and rubbish ; that's what's in our navy. Why, sir, Blake and all those sour Puritans for whom you had a boyish fancy—now happily cured, or I should not be speaking thus—they made our name what it should be on the sea ! " He glowered at Jonathan and his son, and then burst out : " Send the lad to sea, sir, command what interest I have at Court and send him to our navy—he's got brains and courage, and the first is sadly lacking, from what I hear, in His Majesty's ships."

But the idea finds no favour with Jonathan, and when he visits London, as he does occasionally, it is to browse in libraries and inspect the wares of booksellers. When he makes such journeys he takes a groom and a pack-horse for his wardrobe and to accommodate any purchases he may make ; he also takes a bag of gold ; arms himself with a brace of pistols in addition to his long, thin rapier ; and gives his groom pistols, too, and a stout oak club. Off they ride south, striking a road whereon the Legions once marched behind their eagles, where merchants, pilgrims, beggars, robbers, and holy men have tramped or ridden throughout the Dark Ages and the Middle Ages. Coming through St Albans they pass the very piece of ground where Varasius, that very remote ancestor of Jonathan Nidd, employed a Roman architect to build a British home, fifty-five generations back.

P

London they reached at evening, after five long days in the saddle ; London still walled and dominated by a tall Gothic church, perched upon Ludgate Hill, with a roaring market-place upon one side of it ; a city of narrow ways and shouldering houses of timber and plaster and brick, with smiling windows of diamond-shaped panes enclosed in lead, with gardens peeping out here and there unexpectedly, and a great wealth of taverns.   Jonathan Nidd usually lodges at an inn near the New-Gate, and he makes his last stay there in 1665, returning to Nidderdale with the plague incubating in his blood, dying on the way home ; for in that year London became a disease-stricken city, and all England cowered in fear of the pestilence.

Matthew Nidd, who became master of Kettlesing when he was nine years old, grew up to be a quiet-living man and a student all his days, enjoying his country home and his wealth, settling down to the improvement of his estate, taking but little heed of politics.   He can afford luxuries, and like his father collects books.   Marrying in 1682 the granddaughter of Sir Roger Nain of Knaresborough, he enlarges a wing of the Hall, and refurnishes many of the rooms.

The wedding feast is by far the most impressive function the hall has ever seen, touched as it is with a modish elegance of costume, and enlivened by witty conversation. The virginal has been carried into the musicians' gallery in the hall for the occasion, and a presentable orchestra of fiddles and flutes enables the dancing to be very enjoyable. The hall is thronged with gracious figures ; bewigged gentlemen in the new long coats the king favours, and ladies flashing conquering necks and shoulders from a delicate setting of fine fabric in which the coloured dewdrop of some jewel sparkles ; silks, velvets, and brocades abound, and London fashions glow in the yellow candlelight of the big brass chandeliers.   Matthew Nidd himself wears a large and elaborately coloured and powdered periwig, a loose pleated neck scarf with fringed ends hanging down fan-wise some six inches from the neck, and a long skirted coat of blue brocade tight at the waist, falling nearly to the knees, and close buttoned to the chin, having rows of buttons down the front, and being elaborately embroidered down all the seams with gold lace. Around his waist is a wide silk sash with fringed ends. His breeches, moderately wide, are of the same material as his coat, and they are tied at the knee with a bunch of ribbons. White silk stockings are on his legs, and a pair of shoes with high scarlet heels and large jewelled and enamelled buckles give his neat foot a modish importance. For outdoor wear he has a low-crowned, wide-brimmed beaver hat with a large feather curling round the crown, and tall jack-boots with large spurs.

Mistress Nidd wears a blue satin petticoat and a scarlet satin gown secured in a straight line just above the bosom. Her puffed sleeves of elbow-length are turned up with white and fastened by a bow of blue ribbon. Her face is rather clumsily painted, she wears a couple of patches, and also affects carefully trained " heart breakers " or small curls. Both husband and wife use scent. She carries a dainty lace and cambric handkerchief in her hand, and he has a large, snuff-stained handkerchief secured on the breast of his coat by a jewelled brooch.[1]

The country folk have a share in the good things of the feast, and for the villagers there is an abundance of " mum," which was ale brewed with wheat instead of hops. " Buttered ale " is also provided for their entertainment, and this potent drink is warm and enlivened with sugar and cinnamon, containing no hops. The company in the hall can have their choice of Spanish wines, and burgundy, claret, Canary, and sherry are all drawn from the capacious cellars which the Nidds have always stocked with the best wines the merchants of

[1] See Appendix II., Note 19.

York could supply.[1] There is coffee and even tea, despite the relatively enormous expense of the latter luxury. Apart from straight drinks, beers, ales, and wines, there are mixed drinks, punches, possets, " lambs wool," and cordials such as currant wine, mountain wine, and that most curious and unpleasant drink, cock ale, made in the following way :—" Take 10 gallons of ale and a large cock, the older the better, par boil the cock, skin him, and stamp him in the stone mortar until his bones are broken. Put the cock into 2 quarts of sack to which add 3 lbs. of raisons of the sun,[2] stoned, some blades of mace, and a few cloves. Put all this into a canvas bag, and a little before you find that the ale has done working, put the ale and bag together into a vessel. In a week or nine days' time butter it up, and leave for the same time to ripen as other ale." [3]

The meal they discuss is large and somewhat over-powering. Two meals a day was the late seventeenth century rule, although breakfast would probably be represented by draughts of ale or wine with bread and cheese ; but serious eating was delayed until noon, and at twelve o'clock came dinner. In London a visit to a coffee-house would ease the hunger of gentlemen, where they could sip coffee or chocolate, or soothe their appetite with such vigorous drinks as " mum," " red streak," spiced ale or brandy, stimulating their minds with a glance at the newspapers, for the press had come to life though not to freedom.[4] Supper is at eight in the evening, and

---

[1] See Appendix II., Notes 20, beer ; 21, wines ; and 22, sugar.
[2] Sultanas. [3] *The Compleat Housewife*, E. Smith, 1736.
[4] The restrictions imposed on the publication of news even in book form are suggested by Evelyn in an entry in the *Diary*, dated 5th May 1686. " This day was burnt in the old Exchange, by the common hangman, a translation of a booke written by the famous Monsieur Claude, relating onely matters of fact concerning the horrid massacres and barbarous proceedings of the French King against his Protestant subjects, without any refutation of any facts therein ; so mighty a power and ascendant here had the French Ambassador, who was doubtlesse in greate indignation at the pious and truly generous charity of all the Nation, for the reliefe of those miserable sufferers who came over for shelter."

in fashionable circles " rear-suppers " at nine or ten o'clock.[1]

The wedding feast at Kettlesing Hall begins at noon. In addition to the table the sideboard bears a load of dishes. With the exception of hams and tongues and the fish courses of trout and crayfish, there are no plain dishes, all the meats and sweets being prepared from the most extravagant recipes. There is, for example, leg of lamb marinaded, which consists of small pieces of meat strewn with a seasoning mixture of eschalots, anchovies, cloves, mace, and nutmeg, stewed slowly with white wine, then half - fried, then dipped in yolks of eggs and fried brown in butter, and served with a sauce of its own liquor and sweet breads and forcemeat balls fried in eggs, the whole dish being garnished with lemon.

Another dish called "turienier" was made in the following way :—" Take a large china bowl and at the bottom lay some fresh butter, then get three or four beef steaks larded with bacon, then three or four veal steaks dipped in yoke of egg. Over these steaks place a layer of force-meat, then young pigeons, chickens, and rabbits, sweet breads, kidneys and cockscombs, sheeps' tongues and calves' tongues, whole yokes of hard-boiled eggs, pistachio nuts, forcemeat balls, sliced lemon, barbaries, and oysters." This colossal pie is freely seasoned with butter, salt, nutmeg, sweet herbs, and a quart of gravy is added and a thin layer of butter. The whole is then covered with a lid of thick puff paste.[2] Small wonder eight hours were needed to bake it ! A third dish, typical of the rich and highly flavoured food of the period, was potted swan, which consisted of swan minced with bacon, and seasoned with butter, salt, cloves, mace, and nut-

[1] See Appendix II., Note 23.
[2] *The Compleat Housewife*, E. Smith, 1736. The recipes in this book were compiled over a period of forty years.

meg, then put into an earthenware pot with a little claret and water, and spread with two pounds of fresh butter covered with rich paste. The whole was then baked.

Among the sweets there is baked sack pudding, consisting of cream curdled with sack, or cream turned into curd by mixing with sack, to which is added grated Naples biscuit, half a nutmeg grated, the yolks of four eggs and the whites of two beaten up with sugar and sack. Half a pound of fresh butter is added to this mixture, and the whole, sprinkled with sugar, is then put into the oven to bake. There are also countless small cakes and biscuits, Shrewsbury cakes, jumbles, Yorkshire parkin, lemon cheese cakes, almond cheese cakes, wigs, quinces, jellies, and three kinds of cheeses—Queen cheese, Slip-coat cheese, and New Market cheese. The first two are cream cheeses, and the third a ripened cheese of Cheshire type.

All this abundance is accompanied by the good and rich wines and liquors already enumerated, for in those cheerful days of hard drinking no

"... great big black teetotaller was sent to us for a rod."

Spirits were very expensive at this time and were seldom drunk ; but towards the end of the seventeenth century the home manufacture of gin was encouraged, and the habit of drinking spirits spread, hurrying hundreds of people to courses of debauchery from which the simpler beers and wines of their fathers had rendered them cheerfully immune. The excessive use of gin and other spirits launched the temperance movement half a century later, to be followed by the crowning curse of fanatical abstinence, which the nineteenth century was to label teetotalism and extol as a virtue. But fortunately for their peace of mind and the enjoyment of their excellent food and wine, the guests assembled to celebrate the

marriage of the master of Kettlesing Hall could not
foresee the growth of these evils, or even imagine the
fate that was to overtake the North American Colonies
nearly two and a half centuries later.   The ladies withdrew when the drinking had gained a certain expressive
stage, and as the afternoon advanced the cleavage between
the town and country society was clearly marked.
Matthew Nidd was an exceptional country gentleman,
restrained and studious although fond enough of the
sport the countryside could show ; but he was a tem-
perate man.   Not so his neighbours, who were uproarious ; lapsing into their thick Yorkshire dialect ;
spangling their shouted conversation with coarse jokes
and scarlet blasphemies ; embarrassing those guests
who moved in the polite society of London, and who
spoke a very different language from these squires who
seemed as close to the soil as any peasant.[1]   Congreve
has pictured it in *The Way of the World,* when that
all too rough and ready countryman, Sir Wilfull Witwoud,
hiccups his disastrous way through Lady Wishfort's
drawing-room, roaring out his drinking songs, and
saying to his aunt, who is also his hostess, after she has
deplored his condition : " 'Sheart, an you grutch me
your liquor, make a bill—give me more drink, and take
my purse."   Following the demand with a snatch of
song :

> Prithee fill me the glass
> 'Till it laugh in my face,
> With ale that is potent and mellow :
> He that whines for a lass
> Is an ignorant ass,
> For a *bumper* has not its fellow.[2]

But honest though coarse Sir Wilfull presents a telling
indictment of the foppish ways and affected mannerisms
of the town gentleman when he meets his modish snob

[1] See Appendix II., Note 24.   [2] Act IV., Scene 10,

of a brother whom he has not seen for many years. " The fashion's a fool ; and you're a fop, dear brother," says the straightforward Shropshire knight. " 'Sheart, I've suspected this—B'yr Lady I conjectured you were a fop, since you began to change the stile of your letters, and write in a scrap of paper gilt round the edges, no bigger than a subpæna. I might expect this when you left off honoured brother ; and hoping you are in good health, and so forth—to begin with a Rat me, knight, I'm so sick of a last night's debauch—Od's heart, and then a familiar tale of a cock and a bull, and a whore and a bottle, and so conclude—You could write news before you were out of your time, when you lived with honest Pumple-Nose, the attorney of Furnival's Inn—You could intreat to be remembered then to your friends round the Rekin. We could have Gazettes then, and Dawks's Letter, and the Weekly Bill, 'till of late days."

The country gentleman clings, perhaps a little too earnestly, to realities ; the town gentleman pursues affectation and follows fashion. The country house and the town house have different manners and menus. But an older England lives on in the country mansions, while modish society pursues its trivialities and refined debaucheries, and men wear huge and elaborate wigs, carry muffs, and clothe themselves wonderfully. Society moves about the dignified rooms of the town houses amid the walnut furniture that is softened into subtle curves by the mellowing influence of Dutch crafts-men ; and the ornate people who admire the lacquer screens and cabinets and the porcelain that is set out on shelves and behind the glazed doors of china cupboards have more possessions and variety in their homes, a wider command of entertainment, and a far richer setting for life than their grandfathers. The country is becoming in their eyes a quaint and rough place to which they journey for occasional refreshment and for those sports even the town gentleman deems almost indispensable.   And the country squires and their wives look on, their home life changing but little, although they sometimes visit London for a perplexing glimpse of that upsetting, masterful thing called fashion.

Comfort at the close of the seventeenth century.

CHAPTER XVI

An Age of Unreality

WITH the eighteenth century we begin to enjoy a real abundance of records of contemporary life in every class. In 1695 the Commons refused to renew the Licensing Act for presses and printing, thereby removing the legal obstacle to the development of newspapers. Early in the reign of Queen Anne we find a number of papers issued three times a week, and although a daily paper had made its appearance under the title of the *Postboy* the same year the press restrictions were withdrawn, it only survived for four numbers, and it was not until 1702 that the *Daily Courant*, the first successful London daily paper, was published. It consisted of a single sheet, fourteen inches by eight, printed on one side only. In 1704 Defoe began his paper, the *Review*, with Newgate as his editorial office, for he was still imprisoned as a political offender : it was at first a weekly paper, afterwards being issued twice and then three times a week. Richard Steele's *Tatler* appeared in 1709, to be followed by the *Spectator* in 1711. The *London Post*, *English Post*, *Flying Post*, *London Gazette*, *Observator*, and *Postman*, were some of the papers published in the opening decade of the century, and although a temporary check to the increase of newspapers was occasioned by the duty imposed in 1712 of a halfpenny on papers of half a sheet or less, and a penny on those over half a sheet to a single sheet, the press recovered and grew even more rapidly. The newspaper formed new habits of mind, and in the coffee-house and the home greatly influenced conversation, nor did that influence leave the country untouched.

The novel had also been born, fathered by John Bunyan, and throughout the long Georgian period its possibilities were to be explored by many able pens, witty, bitter, earnest, and inspired. From eighteenth century fiction we get glimpses not only of the conditions and morality of the time, but of what people thought in their own minds about life itself. Current ethics were simple enough : praise God according to the Church of England, or if you were a commonplace person with too much religious fervour to be really respectable, shape your Sunday sayings and doings according to some Nonconformist creed ; hope strenuously for a stroke of luck whereby you inherited a fortune if you did not already enjoy one, and look upon work as a calamitous necessity, an affliction appropriately distributed by an acutely class-conscious Providence. Smollett depicts contemporary morality with an almost savage sincerity. The pages of *Roderick Random* are full of the shifts and schemes to win fortunes practised by the idle adventurer class, composed of people who lived in the hope of patronage which would secure an unearned income for them, or who angled for some heiress whose wealth might save them from the indignity of earning money.[1]

In the country it is, of course, the reign of the squire-archy ; that last phase of fading feudalism. The Nidds, in common with other ruling landowners, enrich their estate by enclosures. The century begins its giddy dance of unreality, all Europe capering to the fashionable flutes of Versailles and aping the antics of a Court celebrated for the most dissolute luxuriousness the world had known since the days of Nero. Numbers of country gentlemen seek the town, for they needs must be in the swim of fashion. The coffee-houses, and later the clubs and other

---

[1] Traill (*Social England*, Vol. V., p. 137) refers to " absence of any moral or intellectual progress," and on p. 138 to the " absence of refinement in English manners,"

haunts of London society, claim many of the young men who, a century before, would have followed the simple pleasures afforded by their country homes. A dark hour of bailiffs and agents is experienced by the countryside. A wealthy landlord games in some macaroni club, and his losses prompt instructions to his bailiff to wring more from his estate. Greater incomes are needed; and wealthy society bubbles along, frothing modishly through life and gradually getting farther away from the realities of living. It becomes an age of fashionable tittle-tattle presently to be represented by one of its typical products, Horace Walpole, a dilettante with great literary gifts, who finds in scandal and gossip the most enthralling objects of life; but before the Horace Walpole stage of fashionable decadence was reached, the eighteenth century witnessed great changes in the manners and social conditions of many classes.

Our concern has hitherto been to show the sort of life lived by fairly wealthy people in a number of periods of history; but now society becomes diversified and infinitely more complicated than it has ever been before. Increased wealth and increased population have changed the face of England, and industrialism is beginning. No longer is it possible to take a country family like the Nidds and say that they are representative of the average culture and wealth of their time, for wealth has been created and graded and distributed in a most perplexing fashion. Britain is immensely rich, yet poverty haunts every city and town; and an intense anxiety for the safety of property gives to this age a character of fearful cruelty, difficult to understand, because men and women are carelessly destroyed for the most trivial offences, and crime assumes the most appalling proportions.[1] The gallows

[1] Traill, *opus cit.*, p. 146, says : "The beginnings of a humanitarian movement seen in Anne's time died away, and brutality was restored to its former reign." He also refers to the "utter contempt of all classes for law and order. Theft, shoplifting, footpadding, street assaults, and highway robbery were daily incidents."

of London and other cities give a practically continuous performance all the year round, and so common does the circumstance of shameful death become, that a big trade grows up in printing descriptions of executions and reports of the speeches of condemned criminals who are permitted to address the crowd gathered to witness the hangings. Much of the serious crime that so disfigures the social history of the eighteenth century may be attributed to the excessive drinking of spirits. Spirit bars in London erected signboards whereon customers were invited to be " drunk for one penny," and " dead drunk for two pence," with " straw for nothing " on which to sleep off the effects of the debauch. In the detailed survey of all the streets and houses of London, which was carried out in 1732 by William Maitland, F.R.S., out of a total of 95,968 houses he found 15,288 licensed houses for the retail sale of liquor, of which more than half were spirit bars.[1] Gin drinking was, so far as the poorer classes were concerned, assuming the proportions of a national vice, and for the wealthy excessive indulgence in port wine was threatening health and comfort and storing up for the generations to come the red-hot torments of gout.[2] Spanish wines, Rhenish wines, Maderia and Canary were drunk : Tokay, Hermitage, Florence, " Irish Wine " (claret), and brandy, rum, pale ale, bitter beer, and " entire," a new kind of beer, were also available. All classes drank tea.

It is an age of excesses, coarse and cruel. Country squire and modish gentleman are at least alike in lechery

[1] Article on " Liquor Laws," *Encyclopædia Britannica*.

[2] " The history of the wine trade in England during the eighteenth century is chiefly remarkable for the rapid decline in the consumption of French wines, and the increasing popularity enjoyed by the wines of Portugal. During the reign of Queen Anne, the existing spirit of hostility towards the French was given definite expression in the famous Methuen Treaty of 1703, whereby Portuguese wines were admitted into England at a much lower rate of duty than those of France and Germany, in return for a similar concession to English manufactured goods. . . . Portuguese wines paid £7 per tun, while French wines paid £55 per tun ! " Article on " The Wine Trade " in *The Times*, 8th June 1914.

and drunkenness, however much they may differ in manners and speech and surface culture. Values have been hopelessly upset, and only in the country, and where landlords have not been drawn into the maze of the fashionable world, do we find conditions maintained in which justice and some regard for the amenities of living are preserved for the common people. The fine gentleman, belaced and powdered, his smooth-shaved face framed in a carefully tended wig, a glittering creature of coloured silks, struts and poses with an easy assurance and a graciousness that put his country-bred contemporary somewhat out of countenance ; for the squire is usually a plain man with a liking for ale and punch and fox-hunting, downright in his condemnation of fops and foppishness. Still, a common philosophy of life for both squire and fop is represented by two lines from a drinking song in *The Beggar's Opera* :

> Women and wine should life employ,
> Is there aught else on earth desirous. . . .

Possibly the fashionable gentleman would have desired to add " gossip " to this simple outline of needs, and the squire might have demanded a horse ; but during the first half of the century women and wine were the chief occupations of the abundant leisure enjoyed by gentlefolk.

To be connected with trade was to be smirched by a shameful association in the view of fashionable people : the contempt evinced for hard work, or work of any kind, and the get-rich-quick instinct which was dominant, do much to explain the reckless gambling of the time. But the merchants and traders, at first rigidly excluded from the enjoyment of fashionable society, were building up wealth for the country ; and presently the son of a rich father might buy his way into the worthless world, and achieve discomfort and perhaps eventual poverty.

Surroundings became richer and richer. Really big

changes rendered even the early eighteenth century house very different from the home of fifty years earlier. For example : " By 1720 a house in Britain or the American colonies could command conveniences of furnishing far more satisfying and varied than anything the later Stuart period could offer. The double chest or tallboy had been introduced early in the eighteenth century, the corner cupboard, too, had appeared, and bureaux and writing tables brought comfort and a new dignity to libraries and studies. Fire screens had also come into use, and lighting was carried out more skilfully than in previous periods, the design of sconces and chandeliers having gained a refinement and decorative quality far in advance of the seventeenth century experiments in illumination. Walnut was used extensively, although mahogany was coming to the notice of craftsmen, and the facility with which this richly-hued wood could be carved suggested a number of possibilities to furniture-makers eager to express their taste for ornamental work." [1]   And back and forth amid these settings of beautiful woods and fabrics, reflected by mirrors in richly carved and gilded frames, the fine ladies and equally exquisite gentlemen postured and paraded ; wonderfully decorative people in magnificent clothes ; but a Romano-British lady or gentleman would have regarded their toilet as woefully incomplete, offensively primitive even, for the eighteenth century home was still far behind the well equipped house of the second, third, or fourth century. The bathroom did not exist.[2]   Paint, powder, and perfumes were more important than soap and water.

Even the country gentleman was affected by the taste of the town, save when he lived in almost savage isolation, cut off from the rest of the country by bad roads, lord of

---

[1] *Time, Taste, and Furniture,* by J. Gloag, Part I., Chap. V.
[2] Some experts have even thrown doubt on the existence of the wash-stand until late in the eighteenth century.

an independent community as self-contained as a mediæval manor. But the town fashions usually took years to penetrate to the country mansions. As the century advanced, roads were improved and highwaymen met with increased discouragement in their romantic and lucrative profession, for the guards and the passengers of stage coaches travelled with firearms handy, and assorted slugs from a blunderbuss did much to improve communications and render the roads of England safe.

George Nidd, who was born in 1713, grew up in company with a number of civilised advantages, and when he inherited the Kettlesing estates in 1747, he divided his time between the attractions of London, Bath (and presently Harrogate), and the great horse race meetings. There had been racing at Epsom in the seventeenth century, but after 1730 it became an annual event, although the great races, the Derby and the Oaks had yet to be established, the former in 1779, and the latter in 1780. Newmarket also drew the gamblers and sportsmen of London and the surrounding country. From his boyhood George Nidd, accompanied by his father, had attended the races at Doncaster, which had begun in 1703.

Although in many ways a typical Georgian grandee, the master of Kettlesing was wise enough to preserve the family fortunes. Only a very small proportion of his income passed across the green table in the gaming club which he visited in London. Incidentally the family fortunes were extended greatly by those enclosures to which reference has been made : the estate grew, and George Nidd was not averse to the creation of wealth in other ways, and his dealings with certain adventurous merchants of York, and the shares he took in ships and their cargoes brought gold from the ends of the earth to line his pockets. Although he married some years before his father's death, he always regarded the Hall as his real home, and thought of his London establishment as a temporary affair. He insisted on moderation, which irritated his wife, who had social ambitions of a most extravagant order. It was not until seven years after his father died and he made Kettlesing Hall his headquarters that he consented to have the place redecorated and refurnished. His wife had already taken the grounds in hand, and a gardener imported from London was given command of a staff of countrymen, and soon the surroundings of the Hall exchanged the formal dignities of smooth hedges and geometrical flower-beds and clipped trees for a carefully contrived wildness.

On an October afternoon in 1754 we may discover the master of Kettlesing and his lady in their respective Sedan chairs, bound for number 60 St Martin's Lane, where the showrooms of Thomas Chippendale, cabinet maker, are situated. The chairmen halt at the arched doorway; my lady alights and walks into the shop, her huge hooped skirts swinging; her carefully dressed hair, puffed at the sides and powdered, surmounted by a cap from which a veil trails over her shoulders. Mr Chippendale bows low. Gentry were gentry in those days, and a tradesman, even though he be a golden craftsman to boot, must know his place if he is to do business. George Nidd nods carelessly in response; he has visited Chippendale before in company with other gentlemen of fashion, and has bought a copy of the craftsman's *Director* from Osborne, the bookseller in Gray's Inn. He wanders about the shop while Chippendale and his assistants show his wife drawings and carry chairs, which they place before her for inspection, as she sits enthroned on a big settee which resembles a double chair.

"Odds, Catherine, have done with your drawing-rooms and boudoirs!" Mr Nidd presently exclaims. He pulls a jewelled watch from his fob, and says: "Half an hour of talk and nothing chosen; Gad's life, we'll never reach the dining-room and we keep this pace!"

Q

Customers for Mr Chippendale, cabinet maker.

" Perhaps, sir, while her ladyship is viewing these designs you may condescend to present your wishes to me," Mr Chippendale ventures to suggest.

" Yes, sir, I will, sir," replies Mr Nidd ; and while his wife keeps those two obliging young assistants on the run, the furnishing of the dining-room at Kettlesing is planned.

" Good chairs, Mr Chippendale, that comfort your body without creasing your coat. 'Slife, would you have me rise from table with a garland pressed betwix my shoulders ? " This protest is brought about by Mr Chippendale's latest chair-back designs with interlacing ribbons and flowers entwined with graceful cunning by a master carver. But George Nidd will have none of them ; and he chooses good broad-seated chairs as simple as the great craftsman can bear to make ; and then the sideboard is discussed. For glass there must be good storage space ; nor are the small, secret cupboards in the sides to be forgotten, cupboards which are to house certain vessels for the relief of gentlemen who have passed the third bottle stage. And then comes the dining-table : fine mahogany is needed here.

" As sweet a piece of timber as I can choose, sir, will go into the top," promises Chippendale, " finely marked in the way of this royal wood."

" A fig for your markings ! " cries Mr Nidd ; " the marks a glass makes when the cloth is drawn are all we shall care for." And his business done, he bids Mr Chippendale to start work with all speed, and then to his wife : " Pray, madam, have you done bleeding my purse ? "

After a growl or two at her tardiness, he leaves her with the expressively obliging Mr Chippendale and his long-suffering assistants, and clambers into his chair, cursing as he directs the chairmen to take him home. Gout is beginning to trouble even this fairly moderate gentleman. He feels that the renovations at Kettlesing will be an excellent excuse for staying there, for town life is becoming detestable to him. He needs quiet, and although the conversation at his remote Yorkshire manor is far from sparkling, he is coming to think that even the vicar's endless grumblings and stories about the difficulties of collecting his tithes [1] could be supported. Also at Kettlesing he will be within riding distance of Harrogate, now rapidly becoming fashionable and always comforting to his rheumatic tendencies and incipient gout.

The day as ordered in London is an exhausting affair. Fielding describes it in *Joseph Andrews* through the mouth of a reformed rake, who regales Parson Adams with an account of his abjured dissipations.

" ' In the morning I arose, took my great stick and walked out in my green frock, with my hair in papers (a groan from Adams), and sauntered about till 10. Went to the auction. Told Lady —— she had a dirty face; laughed heartily at something Captain —— said, I can't remember what, for I did not very well hear it; whispered Lord ——; bowed to the Duke of ——; and was going to bid for a snuff-box, but did not, for fear I should have had it.

" ' From 2 to 4, dressed myself.　(A groan.)
　　　4 to 6, dined.　　　　　　(A groan.)
　　　6 to 8, coffee-house.
　　　8 to 9, Drury-lane playhouse.
　　　9 to 10, Lincoln's-inn-fields.
　　　10 to 12, drawing-room.　(A great groan.)
At all which places nothing happened worth remark.' "

[1] Here are some extracts from a Hampsthwaite book of Tithes, dated 1686-1702: " Miles Wardman, look what arrears for hay tithe." " Thomas Skaife owes two shillings, always he saith he hath paid it." " 1698. William Dove has geese, as to numbers I cannot tell. Enquire." " 1700. Thomas Hutchinson has eight geese yet unpaid. He saith they are lost." Such troubles must have coloured the conversation of many clergymen.

Hardly an intelligent programme, and although we must remember that it was recorded by a satirical genius, the manners and habits of the time do not suggest that it is at all exaggerated. But it was not an intelligent period, being almost as devoid of intellectual quality as of moral stability. The pursuit of pleasure along the path of fashion was conducted with all the pomp of elaborate courtesy, with exaggerations of deportment, and with conversation infected by the insincerity of empty compliments and flowing praises. Masquerades, balls, and assemblies claim the attention of society, and all classes play cards—cribbage, basset, ombre, " commerce," and presently whist.

George Nidd, in common with the rest of his circle, usually dined at 5 p.m., and had tea at 8, and supper at 11. Breakfast would be a very light affair of thin bread and butter and toast ; a mere rallying point after the fatigues that sleep had partially dispelled. The middle classes would dine at 3 p.m., and in the towns and cities there were dives where all manner of people ate at various times of the day. Smollett describes a dive in *Roderick Random*, which Roderick and Strap visit when they first take lodgings in London. " About dinner time, our landlord asked us how we proposed to live, to which we answered, that we would be directed by him. ' Well then (says he), there are two ways of eating in this town, for people of your condition ; the one more creditable and expensive than the other : the first is, to dine at an eating house frequented by well-dressed people only, and the other is called diving, practised by those who are either obliged or inclined to live frugally.' I gave him to understand, that provided the last was not infamous, it would suit much better with our circumstances than the other. ' Infamous (cried he), God forbid, there are many creditable people, and rich people, ay and fine people, that dive every day. I have seen many a pretty gentleman bedaubed all over with lace, dine in that manner, very comfortably for three pence half-penny, and go afterwards to the coffee-house, where he made a figure with the best lords in the land.   But your own eyes shall bear witness.   I will go along with you to-day, and introduce you.'   He accordingly carried us to a certain lane, where stopping, he bid us observe him, and do as he did, and walking a few paces, dived into a cellar and disappeared in an instant.   I followed his example, and descended very successfully, where I found myself in the middle of a cook's shop, almost suffocated with the steams of boiled beef, and surrounded by a company consisting chiefly of hackney coachmen, chair-men, dray-men, and a few footmen out of place, or on board wages; who sat eating shin of beef, tripe, cow heel, or sausages, at separate boards, covered with cloths, which turned my stomach."   Ultimately it is recounted that "our land-lord and we sat down at a board, and dined upon shin of beef most deliciously; our reckoning amount-ing to two pence half-penny each, bread and small beer included."   But George Nidd would not be concerned with such coarse simplicities of fare.   His narrow and fatiguing plan of town life was carried out in richly furnished rooms in elegant houses, with occasional glimpses of finely-laid-out gardens, and in London he knew nothing of the life of any class but his own.   But in the country it was different: he knew his land and his tenants.

The redecoration and furnishing of Kettlesing Hall are completed at last; Mr Chippendale has delivered all his goods; his workmen, under instruction from a London architect, have fitted all the windows with new curtains, and the principal rooms of the old house have acquired a more modish air, and in half a century or so will be mellowed to a restful beauty.   At present their clean newness sparkles; there is even a touch of hardness about them; and George Nidd gives his opinion to my lady of Kettlesing that the place has been ruined.

"Despite that, madam, I find it vastly more pleasing than that gilded tavern of a town house," he concludes, and then takes a prodigious quantity of snuff. He does this to appear at ease as well as by habit, for, in common with most gentlemen and ladies of his day, he uses snuff constantly, and then he nerves himself for the task of announcing to his wife that he intends to sell his London house and live permanently at the Hall. He closes his enamelled snuff-box and taps the lid with his long, thin, carefully-kept fingers, while he outlines his plans. My lady is so put about by her husband's firmness in this matter that she cannot bring herself to appear at dinner that evening; so George Nidd enjoys himself very agreeably with a large bachelor party, which celebrates the new dress the Hall has put on, and drinks to the continued residence of its owner.

The dinner is good in a plain country way, consisting of mutton, ham, chickens, ducks, tarts, and cheese, with such embellishments as capers, gherkins, and mushrooms. After the cloth is drawn, the port goes the rounds and the toasts are drunk with fervour. The King, the Prince of Wales, all the Royal Family are honoured in turn. The wine lulls some of the company to sleep, drives some to vomiting, and others, including the host, to uproarious conversation, obscene anecdotes and jests, and snatches of song. Those who can manage to hold pipes, smoke, helping themselves to the fine Virginian leaf from Mr Nidd's inlaid tobacco-box. Presently the survivors make their unsteady way to the deserted drawing-room, where they promptly fall asleep. A servant loosens the neck cloths and shirts of guests who still remain on the dining-room floor under Mr Chippendale's beautifully figured mahogany table; and in due time they are put to bed or

into their coaches, and the party concludes in general
unconsciousness.

This scheme of life is repeated, though in a somewhat
effeminate and consciously eccentric manner, by George
Nidd's only son, Horace, a modish youth, whose sole
ambition was to be a man of fashion and who found
Kettlesing " vastly fatiguing " and the country " insupportable." Horace Nidd becomes a macaroni, and
justifies the character implied by that bitter verse :

> A coxcomb, a fop, a dainty milk-sop ;
> Who, essenc'd and dizen'd from bottom to top,
> Looks just like a doll for a milliner's shop.
> A thing full of prate and pride and conceit ;
> All fashion, no weight ;
> Who shrugs and takes snuff, and carries a muff ;
> A minnikin, finicking, French powder-puff.

The salacious age of unreality draws to its end ;
awakened very abruptly and terribly before that end is
reached by two revolutions—the American and the
French. Horace Nidd, the dandy and rake, dies in 1803.
The changes that are coming into life with such incon-
siderate haste are too much for this exhausted man of the
worthless world of mode and gossip, who deserted his
country home for the pleasures (so-called) of the town.
His son, Augustus, the child of an early and unhappy
marriage, inherited all the acuteness and strength of his
grandfather, George Nidd, by whom he was educated
and trained in the ways of a country gentleman. The
gouty old squire would take the boy afield and show him
the sport that made him an open-air lover of dogs and
horses before he was fifteen. Like his grandfather,
Augustus turned some of his attention to commerce, and
partially repaired the damage done by his father, for
Horace Nidd gamed and spent money royally, inflicting
deep wounds on the fortune of the family, and even
selling nearly two-thirds of the estate in Nidderdale.

What claim could green fields have beside the green table for " a minnikin, finicking, French powder-puff ? " Like all his kind he was true to the spirit of his century, and throughout his idle, useless life he ran from realities.

An eighteenth century country house.

CHAPTER XVII

AN AGE OF MISFITS

PROGRESS of a very material and spectacular order was the keynote of the nineteenth century. Industrialism, vast new creations of wealth, and a rapidly increasing population provided the world with a new rich class and the poor of that world with abundant misery. It was nobody's business to make social adjustments smooth, and the introduction of machinery and the factory system on a large scale probably caused quite as much wretchedness and disease as the introduction of gin.

A new sort of home was coming into existence, and a vile travesty of a home it was : the brick box of the early nineteenth century industrial slum. If we placed side by side the domed hut of an ancient Briton, the wattle and mud hovel of a mediæval cottar, and the dwelling of a factory worker in the early days of mechanical production, there would be but little to choose between them. The factory worker's home had this terrible disadvantage : it was fixed for all time, rooted in some drab street, incapable of expansion, liable to the utmost horrors of overcrowding from which there was no hope of relief. The pre-Roman British village could grow within certain limits ; expansion was allowed for ; and this was true of the mediæval village ; but the first industrial towns were erected by land-greedy people, whose passion for saving space was matched only by their inhumanity.

But the great rushing wind of progress blew most of these early slums away, replacing them by others, wherein the houses conformed with a few elementary principles of ventilation and sanitation, although throughout the century builders were seldom concerned with making a small house comfortable or even mildly agreeable in appearance.

The building activity of nineteenth century Britain is almost unbelievable. Thousands of homes were erected and nearly every big city was ringed about by suburbs and partly rebuilt, and the aspect of the countryside began to change too, and existing houses were altered and enlarged. Dire things were done at Kettlesing Hall by Alice, the wife of Edwin John Nidde (who reintroduced the final e in his name upon the occasion of his marriage in 1845). Alice Nidde was an accomplished young woman, and with the aid of an architect who had read Scott's mediæval romances to his own æsthetic undoing, she removed all traces of Stuart and Georgian decoration, and made one of those pitiful imitations of a Tudor banqueting-hall that nauseate a more enlightened age, and remain as monuments of a period when wealth had outstripped education and taste. Her treatment of the Hall infuriated her father-in-law, Charles Nidd, and that gouty old widower, who went about his possessions damning this and cursing that with a lucid command of ripe oaths, forbade her to meddle with more than her own quarters and " the fool place where she poured tea down her damned simpering guests." He expressed himself quite in the eighteenth century tradition, and Alice, always full of self-conscious womanly solicitude, said :

" Of course, dear papa *must* have his way," and then by the judicious use of tears, hysterics, and an occasional fainting fit, proceeded to get her way in nearly everything.

Once more the fortunes of the family were extending, for old Charles Nidd had inherited very strongly all the trading instincts of his line, and had made a huge fortune from wool, even as his fifteenth century ancestors had prospered by association with this industry. He was a commercial power in one of those Yorkshire towns industrialism had enlarged and befouled with wealth and slums and vast, sprawling factories.   He died in 1858 in his own long bedroom at the Hall, a room with a great four-post bed and panelled walls unchanged since the days of his jovial, hard-drinking Royalist forebear, John Nidde.   Six months after the funeral, Alice had this room " done up," which, at that time when renovation and ruination were synonymous terms, meant " done for." She was a true Victorian, and could spoil a beautiful home as easily as the men who earned money for her and her kind could spoil the beauty of a countryside with slums and untidy factories, or mar the architectural harmonies of some old town with vilely-proportioned buildings in the complex styles that were scarring all Britain.

The manners and habits of the owners of Kettlesing Hall were those of people conscious of their own worth ; and in possessions and family history they had excellent material for pride.   But they could only trace their line back to Elizabethan days : so far as they knew, Sir Thomas de Nidde might have been some common adventurer who had won a title and founded a family.   Although they drew a great income from their interest in the Yorkshire woollen industry, they affected to scoff at trade.   That attitude of mind was a legacy from the eighteenth century, and it must have kept many people from honest and productive work ; for what could a gentleman do, except borrow or sponge on his friends if ill-fortune assailed him or his means were slender ?   The army, the navy, the law, and the church : those were the only professions open to gentlefolk, although presently it was possible for a well-born man to be a doctor without creating much adverse comment.   We may recall the indignant disclaimer of that poor blackguard, Smangle, whom Mr Pickwick en-counters in the Fleet : even he had a hearty and vigorous contempt for trade.   Mr Pickwick had explained that as he refused to pay some damages he was in the Fleet in consequence.

"'Ah,' said Mr Smangle, 'paper has been my ruin.'

"'A stationer, I presume, sir?' said Mr Pickwick, innocently.

"'Stationer! No, no; confound and curse me! Not so low as that. No trade. When I say paper, I mean bills.'"

What better records can there be of life and manners, social conditions, morality, and taste than those provided for us by Dickens and Thackeray? They have pictured the early part of the century so vividly that those strange, hurrying, complex years seem very much alive to a later age. The nineteenth century world changes rapidly; and most of the people in it actively dislike change, and fight as desperately against progress as the Romanised Britons fought against retrogression.

If it was difficult in the eighteenth century to present typical examples of home life, it becomes almost impossible in the nineteenth. There are so many classes; so many variations of etiquette. But all society is presently pervaded by sentimentalism. There is another large-scale evasion of reality; but it is not the gracefully convenient Georgian form of unreality; it has a special character of its own. It does not cynically admit that evils exist and suggest that morality should be moulded to accord with fashion. Victorian ethics enthrone a certain costive virtue which paralyses humour and intelligence, and in alliance with a renascent English Christianity, puts convention before charity and code before common sense. And the Victorian home was an almost perfect reflection of the Victorian mind: romantic, in a quite respectable way, it must be understood, rich and terribly overcrowded. "The architect did the outside of the house (occasionally with regrettable indifference for the convenience of the inside), and the decorator enriched the rooms with wallpapers of sober colour but powerful pattern, and perhaps he was responsible for the ornate plaster-work of the ceiling and the massive mantelpiece. . . ." [1] Incidentally, that mantelpiece would often be embellished with some lines indicative of domestic peace and general homely felicity, such as :

> East, west,
> Home's best.

Then would come the furnisher " with more pattern on the carpet and curtains and the coverings of the chairs, and furniture—such wonderful furniture, the very latest style, heavy and carved, fretted and moulded, with something for every corner and recess in the house—occasional tables in a multiplicity of designs, whatnots, chiffoniers, curio cabinets, china cabinets, overmantel-shelves for glass and pottery." [2]

Clothes both for men and women are elaborately dull, although the women sin less in this direction than the men, for the stern bewhiskered male has abandoned gaiety entirely, and sober materials and cylindrical shapes dominate dress. The Great Exhibition opens to crowds utterly different in appearance from the crowds of half a century earlier. The world grows steadily wealthier, and in that world of wealth we find our family borne on the rising tide of righteousness and respectability ; and Edwin John Nidde dies in 1888, surrounded by the ordered securities of a period which offered limitless opportunities for accumulating riches. His eldest son, Alfred Edgar Nidde, who was born in 1846, died in 1896, respected certainly, but not in quite the same solid degree as his father, for he was unaccountably tainted by a faint interest in art, and had occasionally attended lectures by William Morris, whereby he definitely lost caste. His only son, Arthur Ponsonby Nidde, was knighted in 1910 for certain

[1] *Time, Taste, and Furniture*, by J. Gloag, Part II., Chap. I., p. 199.   [2] *Ibid.*

discreet political services which were never granted the
light of publicity.   Sir Arthur was an excellent man of
business, and was a sound individualist until the 1914-
1918 war upset his sense of security to such an extent
that he never really recovered, dying in 1925 of cancer,
accelerated by the mental instability produced by economic
conditions beyond his understanding.

We have followed the family farther than that strange
age of misfits, the nineteenth century.   To return for a
space to the close of that age, we see that much new wine

The last of the Georgian period : an early nineteenth century house.

has been poured into old bottles, and that the old bottles
have burst after protesting against these progressive
measures.   A whole social system has been remodelled
in the short space of one hundred years, and home life
everywhere has altered and manners have changed, speech
has changed, and clothing has changed beyond belief in
dullness.   The population of Britain is enormous, and
the self-contained community has practically vanished.
Machine-craft has replaced hand-craft very largely ; and
a labourer of the eighteen nineties often has more actual
personal property than a Saxon nobleman.   It has been
a more humane age, for it outgrew its early cruelties, and
shook off the evil influence of the hard, indifferent

Georgian period, reforming or abolishing savage laws and degrading punishments : it has been an age of growing freedoms and wider opportunities for every class, despite its sentimentalism, its lack of art, and its tinsel virtues. When the gigantic strides made during its middle and later years in the conditions of life, and the conveniences and comforts of life are considered, who can deny that it was also a great age ?

CHAPTER XVIII

"Fit for Heroes . . ."

MR DAVID LLOYD GEORGE, with the picturesque phrasing that enabled such attractive newspaper headlines to be culled from his transitory enthusiasms, proclaimed during the general election after the Armistice of 1918, that England should be a land fit for heroes to live in. Mr Lloyd George being of Welsh origin, his statements naturally became enriched with an almost " bardic " note ; the expressively poetical fictions of the Celt often being presented in the forms of emotional predictions and passionate promises. In considering such statements, it is worth remembering the laws imposed by the Saxons regarding the acceptance of evidence and statements from the British natives, who were of the same stock as the Welsh of to-day.[1]

A land fit for heroes to live in—smooth, suggestive phrase, well-arranged, brave-sounding : a fine piece of political wordmanship. . . . It was implied that the returning heroes who had fought in the Great War should also have homes fit to live in. This urgent regard for the peace-time welfare of warriors had never before been expressed on such a big scale ; but the British Army that had swollen to millions was composed largely of men who were not professional soldiers, and most of them were extremely anxious to return to civilian life. Even the humblest home life had acquired an aura of loveliness and luxury in the eyes of men who had for a few years

[1] In the seventh century, if the plaintiff in a suit was Welsh (British) and the defendant English, the latter need only get landowners to the value of 60 hides to swear him innocent ; if defendant was also British, the value of 100 hides had to be represented.

reverted to the filth and discomfort of a mediæval peasant's existence, with the added horror of old weapons made positively diabolical by twentieth century science. The stink bomb and Greek fire had been revived and improved ; the grenade had taken on a new and terrible significance ; cannon had been magnified beyond all knowing ; and the aeroplane had brought an entirely novel branch of war into effective existence, and together with the tank and the motor lorry had ended the horse and cart phase of warfare, even as railways and automobiles had ended that phase in civilised life. Release from these abominations and from the aching stupidity of military rule gave all home life fresh and fine values, which even the reshuffling of wealth and the creation of new rich and new poor classes could not altogether destroy. But with the gradual completion of demobilisation, the difficulty of housing grew in intensity until a period of disillusionment followed the unspoken worship of home life : how to get the home was the problem. And perhaps for the first time in history the ruling power had to concern itself with housing its people ; for it was difficult to let ex-soldiers shift for themselves as they had always shifted for themselves after the French wars of Edward III. and in the days of Marlborough and Wellington.

The business of trying to make England fit for heroes became involved with appalling difficulties, and the Government was reluctantly compelled to accept more and more responsibilities regarding the welfare of citizens. Soon it became quite impossible for any one to starve, unless they deliberately refrained from applying for State assistance. While unemployment generally meant a distinct lowering of standards, it did not spell starvation as it would have done thirty years earlier.

Compared with the eighteenth century, civilisation had become unbelievably complex. The number of different classes and grades of wealth and culture had been faintly foreshadowed in the last great commercial civilisation, that of Rome. But in no phase of social life of which we have historical records had there been such universally high standards of living ; such an abundance of luxuries ; State-planned security from starvation ; and such reading and writing masses as in the first quarter of the twentieth century. There was, nevertheless, a spirit of discontent abroad, which flamed into ugly colours in the immediate post-war years. So many of the people engaged in the operative side of industrial concerns realised that progress was not an orderly process at all, but something extremely haphazard so far as it concerned individual lifetimes. And the picturesque doctrines of romantic reformers, who suffered either from an inferiority complex or an education that had not taught them how to think, and who suggested that Communism, with a little judicious bloodshed, would accelerate progress, very naturally appealed to men and women who were rather tired of waiting for the land to be made fit for heroes to live in. *Hardly anybody glanced at the past to get the true measure of our progress.* One of the greatest leaders of industry in the Atlantic civilisation, Henry Ford, made the statement : " History is bunk ! " This was apparently the unspoken opinion of many men and women engaged in commerce or administration, though some knowledge of social history would have helped all classes to a vastly different view of their own times.

Individually and in the mass, people were better in health and physique, enjoying greater comfort and more leisure than had ever before been the lot of man, not only in Britain, but throughout a large part of the world. The common phrase, " the good old times," has been utterly discredited by the light of history. But romantic writers, especially those who deal in propaganda for the re-establishment of ecclesiastical autocracy in Europe, have been prolific in the production of idealised, misleading pictures of mediæval times, portraying the life of the twelfth, thirteenth, fourteenth, and fifteenth centuries as a constant round of successful farming, feasting, drinking with a Chestertonian relish good old English ale and mead, and cathedral building and the chanting of praises to a generous-minded deity—all carried on against a background of good fellowship and the mutual admiration of churchman, lord, and serf. Nothing is said about the rights of the lord over his serfs and the net of brutal and humiliating conditions in which the common man struggled for his hard living. Seldom do the romantic historians mention the filth and the entire absence of sanitation that made disease a frequent guest at castle, hall, and cottage ; the misery of ill-rewarded toil that crushed the peasant from dawn to sunset ; the savage laws and punishments, tortures and mutilations ; the general insecurity of the country, and the ignorance and lust that trampled beauty and justice underfoot in the lives of nine-tenths of the people and warped and narrowed the lives of those to whom wealth and rank gave greater opportunities. There has been a reference to Mr Chesterton, that artist in words and curio-dealer in ideas, and his name suggests that of Mr Belloc, and together they recall Appendix IV. in Mr G. G. Coulton's book, *The Mediæval Village*, which is entitled " Interested Misstatements." Therein it is pointed out that " When Messrs Chesterton and Belloc discourse on social history, they are generally quoting, consciously or unconsciously, directly or at second or third hand, from Cobbett." William Cobbett's quality as an historian is carefully examined by Mr Coulton, who suggests that " For popularity and inaccuracy combined, it would be difficult to find any book so conspicuous as Cobbett's *History of the Protestant Reformation*." And Cobbett looks at the life of the mediæval peasant through the rosy-paned window of romance.

Although the foregoing chapters have been concerned with the conditions enjoyed by moderately prosperous people at various periods in over two thousand years of British social history, the general conditions of life at each particular time have been presented without the romantic gilding that makes pictures of the past as false as Victorian Gothic buildings. And from a series of clear glances at the home life of Britain through a score of centuries, we realise that in the first quarter of the twentieth century the personal possessions and homes of people who are poor by contemporary standards are more varied and comfortable than the poor have ever previously enjoyed. Attention focussed on these points should not be mistaken for complacent approval of things as they are. Much could be written, and much has been written, concerning the quality of home life and manners in Britain after the 1914-1918 war and the mild revolution of 1926, called the general strike ; and there is a temptation to embark upon predictions. But with the scope of this book in mind we must content ourselves by asking whether the home life of every class to-day is not immeasurably advanced in comfort, health, and the happiness derived from freedom of opportunity ? No land has ever been fit for its heroes to live in. However, for the comfort of those who incline to a pessimistic view of contemporary social conditions a suggestive comparison made by Mr J. B. S. Haldane may be quoted by way of conclusion : " Bad as our urban conditions often are, there is not a slum in the country which has a third of the infantile death rate of the royal family in the middle ages."

Roman stylus and
wax tablet.

Inkhorn, quill, and
parchment.

APPENDICES

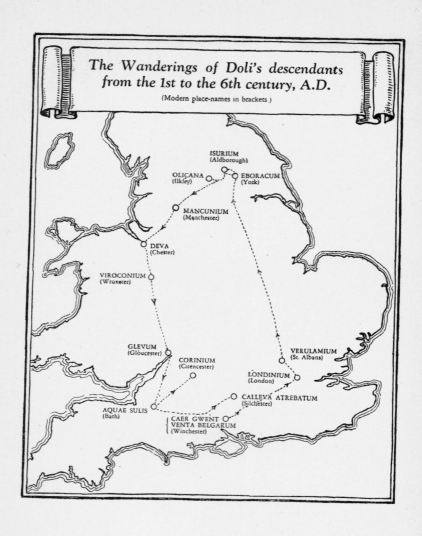

The Wanderings of Doli's descendants from the 1st to the 6th century, A.D.

(Modern place-names in brackets.)

ISURIUM
(Aldborough)

OLICANA
(Ilkley)

EBORACUM
(York)

MANCUNIUM
(Manchester)

DEVA
(Chester)

VIROCONIUM
(Wroxeter)

GLEVUM
(Gloucester)

CORINIUM
(Cirencester)

VERULAMIUM
(St. Albans)

LONDINIUM
(London)

CALLEVA ATREBATUM
(Silchester)

AQUAE SULIS
(Bath)

CAER GWENT
VENTA BELGARUM
(Winchester)

APPENDIX I

GENEALOGICAL TABLE

The genealogy of the hypothetical family whose personal history has threaded its way through the chapters of this book is set out here, showing the descent in the main line of Harold Francis Ponsonby Nidd, Esquire, of the early twentieth century ; tracing the generations back to that ancient Briton, Doli of the Belgic Tribe, who lived in the third century before Christ.

Date of Birth.	Name.	Date of Death.	Locality of Lifetime.
B.C. 246	DOLI	B.C. 200	Cær Gwent.
214	GWELT	161	Do.
185	LLAID	98	Do.
155	PENRY	93	Do.
131	CORIG	81	Do.
101	GRIFF	34	Capital of the Catuvellauni (St Albans).
69	WAN	23	Do. do.
43	GWENT	A.D. 19	Do. do.
12	CASSIVEL	65	Verulamium (St Albans) and Londinium(London).
A.D. 18	UASSI (VARASIUS) . .	102	Do. do.
48	VARASIUS SECUNDUS .	123	Do. do.
77	JULIUS	157	Do. do.
117	JULIUS VARIES . . .	198	Do. do.
145	JULIUS TERTIUS . . .	218	Do. do.
173	VARIES CLAUDIUS . .	259	Eboracum (York).
199	CLAUDIUS TITUS. . .	270	Do. do.
239	TITUS PAULINUS . .	325	Do. do.
268	PAULINUS FLAVIUS . .	348	Do. do.
296	FLAVIUS AURELIANUS .	361	Do. do.
321	AURELIANUS VELVA .	388	Do. do.

Date of Birth.	Name.	Date of Death.	Locality of Lifetime.
A.D. 357	VELVA	A.D. 409	Eboracum (York).
386	VELVA CONSTANTIUS .	458	Do. do.
415	CONSTANTIUS VALENS .	470	Nidderdale.
446	VALENS	501	Calleva Atrebatum (Silchester) and A q u æ S u l i s (Bath).
GERMANUS *b.* 470, *d.* 512.	JULIAN *b.* 472, *d.* 507 (no issue).	CONSTANTIUS *b.* 474	521	Elmet.
VELVA, *b.* 513, *d.* 577.			Corinium (Cirencester).
ŒWULF, *b.* 572, *d.* 640 (no issue).			Wessex.
A.D. 502	BREAC (THE FRECKLED)	568	Elmet.
528	PENRY	584	Do.
553	TAFYN	611	Do.
580	VERTHGER	660	Nidderdale (from now until the twentieth century the family lands and interests are in Nidderdale.)
634	URTFRID	692	
668	BERTFRID	724	
692	EADMUND	729	
719	EADWARD	763	
749	ÆLFRITH	800	
769	ETHELWOLD	823	
809	URTFRITH	868	
850	ETHELFLÆDA = ULFKETIL	888	
868	THORKETIL	909	
893	SWEYN	930	
924	HAROLD	971	
950	HAROLD LODBROK . .	1002	

Date of Birth.	Name.	Date of Death.	Locality of Lifetime.
A.D. 981	GUDRUN	A.D. 1039	
1006	ARKELL SCRUFA (THE CURLY-HEADED) . .	1064	
1033	ERIC	1086	
1050	SIGFERTH	1100	
1079	EDMUND	1128	
1101	ROBERT DE LA NIDDE .	1149	
1133	FRANCIS DE LA NIDDE .	1175	
1161	RANDOLPH DE LA NIDDE	1209	
1194	JOCELYN DE LA NIDDE .	1244	
1224	BRIAN DE LA NIDDE .	1270	
1249	ROGER DE LA NIDDE .	1288	
1282	HENRY DE LA NIDDE .	1333	
1310	STEPHEN DE LA NIDDE .	1367	
1341	NICHOLAS DEL NIDDE .	1390	
1365	WILLIAM DEL NIDDE .	1413	
1395	JOHN DEL NIDDE . .	1445	
1421	HUGO DEL NIDDE . .	1484	
1448	HUBERT DEL NIDDE .	1494	
1480	Sir ROBERT DE NIDDE .	1540	
1512	HENRY DE NIDDE . .	1569	
1538	Sir THOMAS DE NIDDE .	1601	
1563	RICHARD NIDDE . .	1607	
1584	JOHN NIDDE . . .	1650	
1627	JONATHAN NIDD . .	1665	
1656	MATTHEW NIDD . .	1709	
1683	ROGER NIDD . . .	1747	
1713	GEORGE NIDD . . .	1783	
1742	HORACE NIDD . . .	1803	
1768	AUGUSTUS NIDD . .	1819	
1798	CHARLES NIDD . . .	1858	
1823	EDWIN JOHN NIDDE .	1888	
1846	ALFRED EDGAR NIDDE	1896	
1870	Sir ARTHUR PONSONBY NIDDE	1925	
1895	HAROLD FRANCIS PONSONBY NIDDE . .	. .	

APPENDIX II

LIST OF NOTES

1. Arrival of Danish War Band at a Hall.
2. Social Ranks and the Services due from each in the Early Eleventh Century.
3. Trial by Ordeal of Fire.
4. Character of the Normans.
5. Thirteenth Century Etiquette.
6. Payment in Kind.
7. The Black Death.
8. The Statutes of Labourers.
9. The Statutes of Labourers.
10. The Cost of Clothing (1547).
11. The Elizabethan Character.
12. The " Golden " Age.
13. Sixteenth Century Kitchen Utensils.
14. The Qualities Demanded in a Master Cook at the End of Elizabeth's Reign.
15. Some Elizabethan Meals.
16. Scottish Cuisine in 1598.
17. Contemporary Criticism of Fashionable Costume in the Reign of Elizabeth.
18. Forks and Spoons.
19. Cost of Clothes, 1672.
20. Beer.
21. Wines.
22. Sugar.
23. The Daily Round at the End of the Seventeenth Century.
24. " The Compleat Gentleman," 1678.

NOTE No. 1.

ARRIVAL OF DANISH WAR BAND AT A HALL.

Source—*Deeds of Beowulf* (trans. Earle).

The street was stone paven ; the path guided the bondedmen. The war corslet shone hard ; the polished ring-iron sang in its meshes when they in grey harness came marching to the Hall. The sea-weary men set down their broad shields against the terrace of that mansion. They then seated themselves on the bench ; their mail coats rang, harness of warriors ; the spears stood stacked together, ash timber with tip of grey. Then was there for the Gothmen all together in the beer hall, a table cleared. A thane attended to the service, one who bore in his hands a decorated ale-can. At times a minstrel sang . . . there was laughter of mighty men ; music sounded ; the words of song were jovial. . . .

They enjoyed the copious feast, and with fair courtesy quaffed many a mead bowl.

NOTE No. 2.

SOCIAL RANKS AND THE SERVICES DUE FROM EACH IN THE EARLY ELEVENTH CENTURY.

Source—*Rectitudines Singularum Personarum* (*c.* 1030). Translated from the Latin version in Thorpe's *Ancient Laws and Institutes*.

The *Thegn's* [1] law is that he do three things for his estate. Military service, the repair of fortifications, and bridge building. Also on many estates more land-duty is forthcoming at the king's command, for example, deer-hedging at the royal palace . . . and many other things.

The *Geneat's* [2] services are many and various according as they are fixed on the estate. On some he must pay rent and a grass-swine [3] every year, ride, carry, and lead loads, work and support his lord, reap and mow, cut the deer-hedge, and keep it firm . . . and carry messages far and near whenever he may be ordered.

The *Cottar's* [4] duty is what is fixed on the estate. On some estates he must work for his lord every Monday in the year and three days

---

[1] Noble.
[3] Payment for putting swine to pasture.
[2] Retainer.
[4] Cottager.

a week in harvest. On others he must work every day through the whole of August, and must mow an acre of oats in a day. He ought not to pay rent. He should have five acres in his holding, more if it is the custom on the estate, and if it were any less in extent, it is too little because his work is often required. He must pay his hearth penny on Holy Thursday as every free man ought to do.

The *Gebur's* [1] services are manifold, in some places heavy, in others moderate. On some estates he must work at week-work at such work as is required from him every week throughout the year, and at harvest three days for week-work, and from Candlemas [2] to Easter thrice.

If his horse is being employed on behalf of his lord, he need not work whilst his horse is away. On Michaelmas [3] day he must pay ten pence rent and on Martinmas [4] twenty-three, a sester [5] of barley and two hens; at Easter a young sheep and two pence.

As often as it shall fall to his lot, he shall lie from Martinmas to Easter at the lord's fold. From the time when ploughing first begins until Martinmas he shall plough one acre every week and shall himself prepare the seed in his lord's barn. . . . And every gebur shall give six loaves to the swine-herd when he drives his herd to pasture. Wherever this is the custom, it is the rule that the gebur must have for the stocking of his land two oxen, and one cow, six sheep, and seven acres sown on his yardland. But after that year let him do every duty that pertains to him; and let implements be given him for his work and furniture for his house. On his death his lord may claim everything.

This custom exists on some estates, but, as has been said before, in some places the custom presses more heavily, in others more lightly, since all land customs are not alike. On some land the gebur shall pay honey-rent, on some meat-rent, on some ale-rent. It behoves him who holds the office of steward to see that he always knows what are the conditions belonging to a particular estate or what is the custom of the people.

*   *   *   *   *

A *slave woman* is entitled to eight pounds of corn for food, one sheep or three pennies for winter food, one sester of beans for lenten fare, and in summer whey or one penny.

All *slaves* are entitled to a Christmas feast and an Easter feast, and in harvest a handful of corn besides their dues.

---

[1] Tenant farmer.   [2] 2nd February.   [3] 29th September.
[4] The feast of St Martin, 11th November.
[5] Probably about 8 bushels.

NOTE No. 3.

TRIAL BY ORDEAL OF FIRE.

Source—*Ancient Laws and Institutes* (Thorpe).
Laws of King Athelstan.

And concerning the ordeal we enjoin by the command of God, and of the archbishop, and of all bishops ; that no man come within the church after the fire is borne in with which the ordeal shall be heated, except the mass-priest, and him who shall go thereto.   Let there be measured nine feet from the stake to the mark, by the man's feet who goes thereto.   But if it be water, let it be heated till it low to boiling.   And be the kettle of iron or of brass or of lead or of clay.   And if it be a single accusation, let the hand dive after the stone up to the wrist ; and if it be threefold, up to the elbow. And when the ordeal is ready, then let two men go in of either side ; and be they agreed that it is so hot as we before have said.   And let go in an equal number of men of either side and stand on both sides of the ordeal, along the church ; and let these all be fasting on that night ; and let the mass-priest sprinkle holy-water over them all, and let each of them taste of the holy-water, and give them all the book and the image of Christ's rood to kiss ; and let no man mend the fire any longer, when the hallowing is begun ; but let the iron lie upon the hot embers till the last collect ; after that, let it be laid upon the " stapela " (pile of wood), and let there be no other speaking within, except that they earnestly pray to Almighty God that he make manifest what is soothest.   And let him go thereto ; and let his hand be enveloped, and be it postponed till after the third day, whether it be foul or clean within the envelope.   And he who shall break this law, be the ordeal with respect to him void, and let him pay to the king one hundred and twenty shillings as " wite " (fine).

NOTE No. 4.

CHARACTER OF THE NORMANS.

Source—*England under the Normans and Angevins*, by H. W. C. Davis, C.B.E. (Vol. II. of *A History of England* in Seven Volumes), edited by Sir Charles Oman.

It would be easy to exaggerate the degree of Norman originality. Genius of any kind was rare among them ; in the higher kind they were totally deficient. But there are two types of ability each invaluable to a race of pioneers. . . . On the one hand we have the great *soldiers* . . . men who are equally remarkable for foresight in council and for headlong courage in the hour of action, whose wits are sharpened by danger and whose resolution is only stimulated by obstacles ; incapable of peaceful industry, but willing to prepare themselves for war and rapine by the most laborious apprenticeship ; illiterate but shrewd ; violent but cunning ; afraid of nothing and yet instinctively inclined to gain their point by diplomacy rather than by force. On the other hand there are the *politicians* . . . cautious, plausible, deliberate ; with an immense capacity for detail and an innate liking for routine ; conscious in a manner of their moral obligations, but mainly concerned with small economics and gains ; limited in their horizon, but quick to recognise superior powers and to use them for their own objects ; indifferent for their own part to high ideals, and yet respectful to idealists ; altogether a hard-headed, heavy-handed, laborious and tenacious type of men. . . . The soldiers gave her (England) unity, the statesmen gave her peace, and both in a curt, high-handed, and ungracious way served a useful purpose as drill-sergeants. They raised the English to that level of culture which the continental peoples had already reached, and left it to the Plantagenets to make England in a turn a leader among nations. . . . Rufus was typical of the knighthood of the times. Contemptuous of priests and monks, oppressive towards the peaceful and industrious, merciless to those who sinned against the feudal contract. Towards loyal knights, whether they were his friends or enemies, Rufus was courteous, lenient, and exact in the observance of his plighted word. He took a delight in a bold feat of arms even if performed at his expense . . . his ordinary retinue might easily have been mistaken for an army and was almost as destructive. Thieves and robbers of the vulgar kind trembled before the Red King's face. . . . But the knights of the household were privileged offenders. Whenever they accompanied the king they lived at free quarters on the countryside ; on their departure from a homestead they staved the casks of ale and mead and burned or sold the provisions which they had not been able to consume. It was lucky if they did no worse ; for the law was powerless to protect life or limb or female honour against the favourites of the king. At the news of the king's approach his subjects fled for shelter to the woods and hills.

Note No. 5.

Thirteenth Century Etiquette.

Source—*Gleanings After Time*, edited by G. L. Apperson, I.S.O.
Notes from Fra Bonvesin's *Fifty Courtesies of the Table*
(Ambrosian Library at Milan). A set of fifty rhymed
maxims or " courtesies."

Once seated, one is above all warned not to neglect to say grace.
" It is to the extreme gluttonous and vile, and showing great contempt of the Lord, to think of eating before having asked His
blessing." Grace said, one is enjoined to sit decently at table, not
with the legs crossed, nor elbows on the board. " Do not," one is
next recommended, " fill your mouth too full ; the glutton who
fills his mouth will not be able to reply when spoken to." " When
thirsty, swallow your food before drinking." " Do not dirty the
cup in drinking ; take it with both hands firmly, so as not to spill
the wine. If not wishing to drink, and your neighbour has dirtied
the cup, wipe it before passing it on." The sixteenth courtesy is
noteworthy in its recommendation to those taking soup not to
" swallow their spoons," while they are further admonished, if
conscious of this bad habit, to correct themselves as soon as possible,
as also of the breach of good manners in eating noisily. " If you
should sneeze or cough, cover your mouth, and above all turn
away from the table." Good manners, one is told, demands that
one should partake, however little, of whatever is offered ; if,
that is, the proviso is made, one is in good health. Do not mix
together on your plate all sorts of viands, meat, and eggs ; " it may,"
thoughtfully adds the writer, " disgust your neighbour." " Do
not soak your bread in your wine," for, remarks Fra Bonvesin, for
the first time asserting his own personality, " if any one should
dine with me, and thus fish up his victuals, I should not like it."
The twenty-fourth " courtesy " is a recommendation to avoid
placing either one's knife or spoon between your own plate and that
of your neighbour. If with ladies, one is told to carve first for
them ; " to them the men should do honour." " Always remember
if a friend be dining with one, to help him to the choicest parts."
" Do not, however, press your friend too warmly to eat or drink,
but receive him well, and give him good cheer." " When dining
with great men, cease eating while he is drinking, and do not drink
at the same time as he." " Let those who serve be clean, and," adds

S

the careful monk, apparently foreshadowing Leech's comic sketch of the scented stable-boy waiting at table, " let the servants be free from any smell which might give a nausea to those eating." Capital advice is further given not to wipe the fingers on the table-cloth, a sentiment in which all thrifty housewives will concur. " Let the hands be clean, and above all do not at table scratch your head, nor indeed any portion of your body." " Do not, while eating, fondle dogs or cats or other pets ; it is not right to touch animals with hands which touch the food." " When eating " (with *homini cognoscenti*, adds the writer), " do not pick your teeth with the fingers," Fra Bonvesin once again coming forward to express his personal disgust at this habit. " When at table avoid wrangling and noisy disputes ; but if any one should transgress in this manner, pass it over till later—do not make a disturbance." " If you feel unwell at table, repress any expression of pain, and do not show any suffering which would inconvenience those at table." " If you happen to see anything in the food which is disagreeable, do not refer to it ; if it is a fly or other matter " (presumably included in this would come the familiar hair), " say nothing about it." " In handling your bowl or plate at table, place your thumb only on the edge." " Do not bring with you to table too many knives and spoons, there is a mean "—in other words, Horace's *Est modus in rebus*.[1] " If your bowl or plate is taken away to be refilled, do not send up your spoon with it." " If your friend is with you at table, be cheerful and continue to eat while he eats, even if you have had enough before he has finished ; he might otherwise, out of shame, stop before his hunger was satisfied." Closely connected with this admirable piece of advice, applicable to all time, the succeeding admonition is not uninteresting, as illustrative of the customs of a period before electro-plate was to be found in every house, when each guest, it must be remembered, carried at his girdle his own serving-knife, an indispensable piece of finery, generally as highly decorated as the owner's taste and means could afford. " When eating with others," remarks Fra Bonvesin, who has now reached his forty-eighth " courtesy," " do not sheath your knife before every one else at table has done the same."

---

[1] In the past, it will be remembered, each guest was supposed to carry with him his own knife and spoon ; forks, though known from a very early time, not being generally used till comparatively recently.

NOTE NO. 6.

PAYMENT IN KIND.

Source—*Mediæval England,* edited by H. W. C. Davis.
Section IX., *Country Life,* by George Townsend Warner,
M.A.

At first we may picture the manor going on almost entirely without
interchange of money. Payments are made " in kind " or in labour.
It is, as economists say, under a natural economy. By degrees, as
money becomes more plentiful, the use of it creeps into country
districts. Then begins the practice of *commutation of service.* Villeins offer to pay money instead of their services ; the lord agrees
to take the money. How fast this process spread is difficult to say.
We know that while in Henry I.'s day the exchequer took much of
its payments in kind, by Henry II.'s time money was usually paid ;
but the king, though the greatest of manorial lords, cannot be taken
as a type. He was in advance of the rest. But by the time of the
Black Death (1348), it appears as if commutation of service had
become fairly common, and after that time it went on with increasing
rapidity.[1]

This practice of commutation of service is of very great consequence. It is the first step in the gradual substitution of the free
labourer for the servile tenant. We may note three things : (1)
commutation was a matter of agreement between lord and villein ;
(2) a new period begins in rural history when a money economy
takes the place of the old natural economy, when money has become
common enough to take the place of payments in service or in kind,
since as soon as payments are made in money a man enjoys a larger
measure of freedom : he may be no better off in material comfort,
but he is to a far greater extent master of his own time ; and (3) the
fact that lords were willing to accept money instead of services shows
that there was in existence a considerable number of labourers who
could be hired. Had it not been so, the lords would have found
labourers to cultivate their demesne land, and the money paid to
them would not have been an acceptable substitute for the commuted
services. The practice of commutation led to the growth of a class
of *copyholders,* or enfranchised villeins, who were so called because
their title-deed was a copy of the entry in the manor court-roll which
recorded their bargain with the lord.

[1] The extent to which commutation had gone in 1348 is discussed by T. W.
Page, *The End of Villeinage in England* (New York, 1900), on a statistical basis.

Note No. 7.

The Black Death.

Source—*Mediæval England,* edited by H. W. C. Davis.
   Section IX., *Country Life,* by George Townsend Warner,
   M.A.

The quiet annals of the country-side were rudely broken into by the Black Death.   This appalling pestilence destroyed near one half of the population, and it was no whit less fatal in the country than in the towns.   We can easily understand that agriculture would be paralysed when half the workers lay stricken ; we shall be prepared for the scarcity of food that followed ; we can well believe that the harvest lay rotting in the fields with none to gather it.   Scarcity, nay even famine, had indeed been no unknown thing in English rural life ; rather it had been all too common ; but the Black Death brought with it a chain of results peculiarly its own.

The first consequence was a sharp rise in prices ; then, since the former " living wage " no longer afforded a living, there followed a rise in wages.   This placed the landowners in a difficult position. Those who had accepted commutation of service, who had agreed to take money instead of work from their villeins, found that the money they received no longer represented the work they had lost. They had commuted when the wage of the hired labourer was low ; now that it was high their money would not go so far ; and they could not pay for enough hired work to replace the villein services which they had lost.   The first remedy which occurred to the landowners, and therefore to the Crown and Parliament, who represented mainly the landowning class, was to return to the old state of things, to " put back the clock by legislation."   The successive Statutes of Labourers ordered that men were not to ask or take higher prices or higher wages.   If prices did not rise, there would be no need for higher wages. . . . Merchant and craft guilds regulated prices of commodities in the towns ; why should not Parliament do the same in the country ?   However, Parliament's action, in spite of the ferocious penalties imposed and rigorous inquisitions by the Justices appointed under the Statutes of Labourers, came to nothing ; the rise in prices went on, and with it the rise in wages.   The landowners were left confronted with a diminished revenue, a scarcity of labour, and the problem which is familiar in English agriculture, of how to make two ends meet.

Various attempts were made to solve it. The first was to cast the burden of finding labour on an intermediary. Landowners began to let land at a rent, and as the tenants, in many cases the old villeins, had no money to find stock, the landowner himself provided stock and seed, for which the tenant had to return an equivalent at the end of his term. These *stock and land leases* give us the beginning of the modern farmer. Hitherto, there has been but two persons on the land, lord and labourer. Henceforward a go-between becomes more common, till we get the familiar triple division of landlord, farmer, and labourer.

This was a sensible plan, but it could not prove a complete remedy. All labourers, whether free or servile, were anxious to profit by the higher wages which were offered by many, in defiance of the Statutes of Labourers. It was easy to run away from a lord who offered only the legal rate, or who desired to maintain the old plan of taking services instead of commutation, and though the law provided plenty of penalties, certainly in no way wanting in ferocity, yet to put men in prison did not mend matters. " Men in prison reap no fields." Where serfs did not escape singly, they became mutinous collectively. The discontent of those to whom freedom seemed over-slow in coming culminated in the Peasant Revolt of 1381. When order was again restored, after an outburst of burnings, robberies, murders, and executions, the legal position of the villeins remained as it had been. Practically, however, they had won an almost complete victory. Serfdom fell rapidly into desuetude ; wages remained at their higher level ; labour continued to be more expensive. Hence a new policy was urgently called for. . . .

The problem was how to do with less labour. Sheep-farming instead of arable farming offered a solution ; and as the woollen manufacture was growing rapidly in England in the end of the fourteenth century and throughout the fifteenth, while there was also a ready market for wool in Flanders, this was a very profitable solution for the lords. Yet this sheep-farming brought hardships on the labourers. To keep sheep it was necessary to throw together large tracts of ground and to enclose them with hedges. Hence the lords began first to enclose the common land that had hitherto pastured alike the cattle of both lord and villager ; and the villager soon found himself pinched for pasture land for his few beasts. Further, the lords wished to enclose their demesne lands. Where these lay separate from the land held in villeinage no hardship followed. But the demesne often lay intermixed with the villeins' land. Under the two or three field systems, land was not held in a block. Each tenant held a number of scattered acre or half-acre strips. This curious plan was the outcome of necessity and equity. When one of the two or three great fields lay fallow, it was plain that if a tenant held all his land in that field he would be poorly off for food during the year of fallowing. Of necessity he must hold some land in each field. But, further, these great fields differed in fertility, one part from another. Hence, in common fairness, the land was split into smaller strips, so that all might share alike ; and the acre or half-acre was a convenient day or half-day's ploughing. Thus the arable land of England was mostly " open-field," a mass of strips, scattered among various holders, each strip separated off by nothing but a balk of unploughed ground. Where the demesne land lay scattered among the land held in villeinage in open field, it was clear that to enclose it was necessary either to re-allot or to drive off the villein tenant altogether. This last plan was too tempting to be resisted. Consequently the lords set themselves to get rid of what villeins remained, and to use all the land of the manor for sheep. This process of depopulation went on vigorously. The Tudors legislated against it, but even in Elizabeth's day it was not entirely stopped.

Note No. 8.

The Statutes of Labourers.

Source—*Statutes of the Realm.*

Whereas lately against the malice of servants which were idle, and not willing to serve after the Pestilence, without taking excessive wages, it was ordained that such manner of servants, as well men as women, should be bound to serve, receiving salary and wages accustomed in the places where they ought to serve, as in the twentieth year of the King that now is, or five or six years before : and that the same servants refusing to serve in such a manner should be punished by imprisonment of their bodies ; and now, forasmuch as the King is given to understand in this present Parliament by the Petition of the Commonalty that the said servants having no regard to the said ordinance, but to their ease and singular covetousness, do decline to serve great men and other, unless they have wages to double or treble of that they were wont to take, to the great damage of the great men and impoverishing of all the Commonalty : Wherefore, in the same Parliament, by the assent of the prelates, earls, barons, and other great men of the said Commonalty there assembled, to refrain the malice of the said servants, be ordained and established the things underwritten :—

First, that carters, ploughmen, drivers of the plough, shepherds, swineherds, dairymen, and all other servants, shall take wages accustomed the said twentieth year or four years before, so that in the country where wheat was wont to be given, they shall take for the bushell ten pence, or wheat at the will of the giver, till it be otherwise ordained. And they shall be hired to serve for a whole year, or by other usual terms, and not by the day; and none shall pay in the time of hay-making but a penny the day; and a mower of meadows for the acre five pence, or by the day five pence; and reapers of corn in the first week of August two pence, and in the second, three pence, and so till the end of August, and less in the country where less was wont to be given, without meat or drink; and that all workmen bring openly in their hands to the market towns their instruments, and there shall be hired in a common place and not privily.

Also, that none take for the threshing of a quarter of wheat, or of rye over two pence, and the quarter of barley, beans, pease and oats one penny, if so much were wont to be given . . . and that the same servants be sworn two times in a year before lords, stewards, bailiffs, and constables of every town, to hold and do these ordinances; and none of them shall go out of the town where he dwelleth in the winter to serve the summer, if he may serve in the same town . . . and that those which refuse to take such oath or to perform that they be sworn to shall be put in the stocks by the said lords by three days or more or sent to the next gaol there to remain till they justify themselves.

Also, that carpenters, masons, and tilers, and other workmen of houses shall not take by the day for their work but in the manner as they were wont, that is to say: a master carpenter three pence and another two pence, a master mason four pence and other masons three pence, and their servants one penny, tilers three pence and their knaves one penny, plasterers and other workers of mud walls and their knaves by the same manner without meat or drink, one shilling from Easter to Michaelmas. . . .

Also, that cordwainers and shoemakers shall not sell boots nor shoes nor none other thing touching their mystery, in any other manner than they were wont the said twentieth year; also, that goldsmiths, saddlers, horsesmiths, spurriers, tanners, curriers, tanners of leather, tailors, and other workmen, artificers and labourers, and all other servants not here specified shall be sworn before the justices to do and use their crafts and offices in the manner as they were wont to do. . .

Note No. 9

The Statutes of Labourers.

Source—*Statutes of the Realm.*

Because a great part of the people, and especially of workmen and servants, lately died of the Pestilence, many seeing the necessity of the masters of great scarcity of servants, will not serve unless they receive excessive wages, and some are rather willing to beg in idleness than by labour to get their living. We considering the grievous incommodities, which of the lack, especially of ploughmen and such labourers may hereafter come, have upon deliberation and treaty with the prelates and nobles, and the learned men assisting us, ordained that every man and woman in England of whatever condition they may be, bond or free, able in body, and under sixty years of age, not living by merchandise, or being an artificer, and not having property whereby they may live, shall serve the master requiring him or her.

Note No. 10.

The Cost of Clothing (1547).

Source—*Costume in England*, by F. W. Fairholt, F.S.A.,Vol. I., p. 239.

The prices of wearing apparel in England at this period may be gathered from the bill of expenses of the famous Peter Martyr and Barnardus Ochin, in 1547, who were invited to this country by Archbishop Cranmer. The original bill is in the Ashmolean Museum ; it has been printed in the *Archæologia*, Vol. XXI., from whence the following few extracts have been obtained :—

	s.	d.
Payd for two payer of hose for Bernardinus and Petrus Martyr	11	4
Pd. for a payer of nether stocks for their servant	2	0
Pd. for three payer of shooe for them and their servant	2	4
Pd. for two nyght cappes of vellvet for them	8	0
Pd. for two round cappes for them	6	0
Pd. for two payer of tunbrydg' knyves for them	2	8
Pd. for two payer garters of sylke ryband	2	6
For ryband for a gyrdyll for Petrus Martyr	1	2
For two payer of glovys for them	1	0

Note No. 11.

The Elizabethan Character.

Source—*Society in the Elizabethan Age*, by Hubert Hall.

When we find the land changing hands on all sides, granted by the Crown to needy courtiers, laid out to advantage by able specu-lators, and cultivated with untiring diligence by the highly-rented tenant farmer or husbandman, we might have given credit to the age for some apparent improvement.   As it was, the position of the tenant, of whatever degree, was indeed immensely improved by the competition of the age.   Land was no longer regarded as a military or labour fee, but as a serious industry and profitable investment. For half a century a violent land-fever raged in town and country. The Crown was a ready seller, and found still more eager buyers. These new men, officials, merchants, lawyers, usurers, jostled the ancient owners, impoverished by mismanagement and extravagance, and each other.   Both alike joined in an attempt to wrest from the sub-tenant his vested interest or fixity of tenure in the land. . . .

Then a new class of society was formed, courtiers who plundered the people, landlords who evicted their tenants, officials who cheated the Government, merchants, usurers, and pandars, who preyed upon the vices of the great, and the woes of the unfortunate. All reserve, all decorum had gone out from the life of the people. They observed no fast day, neither did they enjoy any holiday as of old.   They gorged themselves with unwholesome food till they were decimated by loathsome diseases.   The towns were flooded with tippling-houses, bowling-alleys, tabling-dens, and each haunt of vicious dissipation.   Murder, rapine, and every form of lawless violence were practised with comparative impunity.   The state of society was the worst that had ever before been in the land.   And where, all this time, was the influence of the Church at work ? There was no pretence even of such influence.   The bishops were mostly starveling pedants, creatures of a court faction, whose fingers itched after filthy lucre ; or else good, plodding, domesti-cated men, with quiverfuls to provide for ; graziers or land-jobbers who had mistaken their vocation.   Narrow, harsh, grasping, servile, unjust, they were despised as much by their masters as they were hated by their flocks.   The inferior clergy, the typical parson or parish priest, scarcely existed at all.   Half the parishes in the many dioceses had no proper cure. Many more were provided for with a trembling conformist, or a lewd and insolent bigot. In the best cases the curate was at the mercy either of the Crown or the amateur theologians, his parishioners.

Note 12.
The "Golden" Age.

Source—*Society in the Elizabethan Age*, by Hubert Hall.

It jars upon our sensibilities to find our heroes of the field or flood, leaders in the Council or in the camp, lying and plotting to outwit each other in the struggle for power and place, snarling and fighting over the fatness of the land. We shudder to think that during the perils of the Armada the finances of the navy were administered by a pack of ravening wolves, according to the testimony of its official chief ; that the armies of Elizabeth abroad were allowed to shiver and starve at the mercy of governors and patentees who embezzled the grants which should have clothed and fed them ; and that courtiers and wits flourished upon odious monopolies, and that judges grew fat upon extortionate bribes. With good reason we may call the Elizabethan a "golden" age, for gold was the national divinity, and God and Mammon were by both high and lowly served with a zeal for which many of their descendants have cause to be grateful.

We little think, when we peruse the melancholy tale of disease, starvation, and shame, so needlessly undergone by the heroic champions of England's liberty against the invading might of Spain with her invincible Armada, from what obscure and insignificant causes the difficulties and hardships of the Island seamen may have chiefly arisen. It is certain, however, that the sight of the Spanish sails in the offing spread less dismay amongst the English crews than the appearance of their own empty magazines and lockers ; and that the enemy's shot caused far fewer casualties in their list than the mouldering rations of the Government.

Note No. 13.

Sixteenth Century Kitchen Utensils.

Source—*The Fairfax Inventories.*

A nobleman's kitchen at the end of the sixteenth century and commencement of the seventeenth century contained the following utensils :—

The furnace pan for beef.
The beef kettle.
Great and small kettles.
Brass kettles, holding from sixteen to twenty gallons each.
Copper pans with ears.
Little kettle with bowed or carved handles.
Boards.
An iron range.
A tin pot.
Pot hooks.
A galley bawk to suspend the kettle or pot over the fire.

Dripping-pans.
An iron peel or baking shovel.
A brazen mortar and a pestle.
Gridirons.
Iron ladles.
A laten scummer.
A grater.
A pepper mill.
A mustard quern.
A salt-box.
Iron racks.
Spits, square and round, and various sizes.
Bearers.
Crooks.

In the larders (wet and dry) and pantry were :—

Moulding boards for pastry.
A boulting tub for meal.
A little table.
A spice cupboard.

A chest for oatmeal.
A trough.
Hanging and other shelves.

Here follows the return of pewter, brass, and other vessels belonging to the kitchen :—

Pewter dishes of nine sizes (from Newcastle).
Long dishes for rabbits.
Saucers.
Chargers.
Pie plates.
Voider.

} Silver-fashioned.

A beef-prick.
Fire shovels and tongs.
A brig (a sort of brandreth).
A cullender.
A pewter baking pan.
Kettles of brass.
A skillet.
A brandreth.

A shredding knife.	A brass pot-lid.	
A chopping knife.	Beef-axes and	⎫
An apple cradle.	knives.	⎬ For
A pair of irons to make wafers with.	Slaughter ropes.	⎭ Slaughtering.
	Beef stangs.	

In the beef-house was an assortment of tubs, casks, and hogsheads. Table knives, spoons, and drinking-vessels presumably belonged to another department.

NOTE NO. 14.

THE QUALITIES DEMANDED IN A MASTER COOK AT THE END OF ELIZABETH'S REIGN.

Source—*Old Cookery Books and Ancient Cuisine*, by W. Carew Hazlitt.

Braithwaite, writing *c.* 1617, says : " The master cook should be a man of years ; well experienced, whereby the younger cooks will be drawn the better to obey his directions. In ancient times noblemen contented themselves to be served with such as had been bred in their own houses, but of late times none could please some but Italians and Frenchmen, or at best brought up in the Court, or under London cooks ; nor would the old manner of baking, boiling, and roasting please them, but the boiled meats must be after the French fashion, the dishes garnished about with sugar and preserved plums, the meat covered over with orangeade, preserved lemons, and with divers other preserved and conserved stuff fetched from the confectioner's : more lemons and sugar spent in boiling fish to serve at one meal than might well serve the whole expense of the house in a day." He goes on to describe and ridicule the new fashion of placing arms and crests on the dishes. It seems that all the refuse was the perquisite of the cook and his subordinates in a regulated proportion, and the same in the bakery and other branches ; but, as may be supposed, in these matters gross abuses were committed.

NOTE No. 15.

SOME ELIZABETHAN MEALS.

Extracts from Wild Darrell's Diet at Warwick Lane from
16th April to 14th July 1589.

Source—*Society in the Elizabethan Age*, by Hubert Hall.

Wednesday dyner, April 16 (1589).

A pece of bief	xviij^d
A legg of mutton	xx^d
ij chickens and bacon.	xx^d
ij chickens and ij pigions rost	xviij^d
For dressinge all	vij^d
For parsly, cloves, and sawse for the mutton . . .	vj^d
Bread and beare	xvj^d

o 8 9

Supper, eodem.

A shoulder of mutton	xx^d
iij pigions	viij^d
For roastinge the mutton, pigions, ij chickens and ij rabbettes	xj^d
For sawse, soppes, and parsly	v^d
Bread and beare	xiiij^d

o 4 10

Fryday dyner, Maij 2.

A side of habdyn and another of grene fishe . . .	xiiij^d
Foure playses	xij^d
ij whitinges	viij^d
Conger	viij^d
Butter	iiij^d
Lettise for sallett.	ij^d
A pynt of white wyne and another of clarett. . . .	vj^d
Suger	ij^d
A pound of butter	v^d
For dressinge the fishe	viij^d
Oyle and suger for sallett	ij^d
More for butter	ij^d
A pound of candles	iiij^d

o 7 3

Extracts from Diet.

For rostinge a side of venison and sawse	xvj^d
A neck of veale	xiiij^d
A brest of mutton and radishes	xix^d
A pece of linge	viij^d
Mackrell	vj^d
ij grene geese	ij^s viij^d
Orenges	ij^d
A leman	j^d
Cheese	ij^d
Cockles	iiij^d
Strawberies, 3 pyntes	xij^d
A quart of creame	vj^d
Egges	iiij^d
Pease	ij^d
Pescods	ij^d
A yonge capon	xviij^d
A pound of cheries	iij^d

Note No. 16.

Scottish Cuisine in 1598.

Source—*Old Cookery Books and Ancient Cuisine*, by W. Carew Hazlitt.

An edifying insight into the old Scottish *cuisine* among people of the better sort is afforded by Fynes Morison, in his description of a stay at a knight's house in North Britain in 1598.

" Myself," he says, " was at a knight's house, who had many servants to attend him, that brought in his meat with their heads covered with blue caps, the table being more than half furnished with great platters of porridge, each having a little piece of sodden meat ; and when the tables were served, the servants did sit down with us ; but the upper mess, instead of porridge, had a pullet with some prunes in the broth. And I observed no art of cookery, or furniture of household stuff, but rather rude neglect of both, though myself and my companion, sent by the Governor of Berwick upon bordering affairs, were entertained in the best manner. The Scots . . . vulgarly eat hearth-cakes of oats, but in cities have also wheaten bread, which, for the most part, was brought by courtiers, gentlemen, and the best sort of citizens.   When I lived at Berwick, the Scots weekly upon the market day *obtained leave in writing of the governor* to buy peas and beans, whereof, as also of wheat, their merchants to this day (1617) send great quantities from London into Scotland.   They drink pure wine, not with sugar, as the English, yet at feasts they put comfits in the wine, after the French manner : but they had not our vintner's fraud to mix their wines."

NOTE NO. 17.

CONTEMPORARY CRITICISM OF FASHIONABLE COSTUME IN THE REIGN OF ELIZABETH.

Source—*Costume in England*, by F. W. Fairholt, F.S.A.

The most notorious of the satirists of the day was Philip Stubbes, who published his *Anatomie of Abuses* in 1583, and gave therein a luminous account of the excesses reigning in England at that time ; not, however, without highly colouring the picture with his own Puritanical feeling.   Thus, he declares, " No people in the world is so curious in new fangles as they of England bee " ; and laments, according to the fashion of all grumblers at apparel, time out of mind, that it is impossible to know " who is noble, who is worshipful, who is a gentleman, who is not," because all persons dress indiscriminately in " silks, velvets, satens, damaskes, taffeties, and suche like, notwithstanding that they be both base by birthe, meane by estate, and servile by calling ; and this," he adds, with due solemnity, " I count a greate confusion, and a general disorder : God be merciful unto us."

But let us listen while he descends into particulars.   He is justly indignant at the painting of ladies' faces that now became usual ; and, after some pages of argument, he speaks of their hair, " which of force must be curled, frisled, and crisped, laid out in wreathes and borders, from one ear to another.   And, lest it should fall down, it is under-propped with forks, wires, and I cannot tell what, rather like grim, stern monsters than chaste Christian matrons.   At their haire, thus wreathed and crested, are hanged bugles, ouches, rings, gold, silver, glasses, and such other childish gewgawes."   Bad as all this is declared to be, he expresses his utter horror at the still worse custom of wearing false hair, and dyeing it " of what colour they list." [1]   Then comes a tirade against French hoods, hats, caps, and kerchiefs, " and suche like " ; of silk, velvet, and taffety, which even merchants' wives " will not sticke to goe in every day," with close caps beneath of gold and silver tissue ; and, worse than all, " they are so far bewitched as they are not ashamed to make holes in their ears, whereat they hang rings, and other jewels of gold and precious stones " ; but this, he says, " is not so much frequented amongst women as men."

But the zeal of Master Philip absolutely boils over when he speaks of the great ruffs worn by the ladies ; and " the devil's liquor, I mean *starche*," with which they strengthen these " pillars of pride." His rage increases when he considers, that " beyond all this they have a further fetche, nothyng inferiour to the rest, as, namely, three or four degrees of minor ruffes, placed *gradatim* one beneath another, and all under *the maister devil ruffe !!* " each of them, " every way pleated and crested full curiously, God wot.   Then, last of all, they are either clogged with gold, silver, or lace of stately price, wrought all over with needle worke, speckeled and sparkeled here and there with the sunne, moone, and starres, and many other antiques strange to behold.   Some are wrought with open work downe to the midst of the ruffe and further ; some with purled lace so closed, and other gewgawes so fastened, as the ruffe is the least part of itself."   In those days when umbrellas were unused, much did it delight these saints to see the ladies caught in a shower ; for " then their great ruffes strike sayle and flutter like dishecloutes " about the necks of the wearers, the poor " drowned rattes " they so religiously detested. This accident was sometimes prevented by the use of " supportasses or under-props of wire, covered with gold thread, silver, or silk," which held out the pleats of the ruff.   The ladies' high head-dress, with a bow and feather, just peeps above its grand circumference. Stubbes goes on to say, they also wore " doublettes and jerkins, as men have here, buttoned up the breast, and made with wings, welts, and pinions on the shoulder pointes, as mannes apparell is for all the world.   Their gownes be no lesse famous then the reste ; for some are of silk, some of velvet, some of grograme, some of taffatie, some of scarlet, and some of fine cloth, of x, xx, or xl shillynges a yard."   To add to the extravagance, they are overlaid

---

[1] It was the fashion to dye it yellow at this time in compliment to the Queen, whose hair was of that colour. Her Majesty, as well as her great rival, Mary, Queen of Scots, patronised wigs.   Elizabeth had eighty attires of false hair at a time.   Mary had many sent to her while in captivity at Lochleven, and after her retreat to Carlisle she received " ung paque de perruques de cheveux."   It is recorded that her attendant, Mary Seton, was particularly ingenious in displaying them to advantage, and that Her Majesty changed them every other day.

with lace two or three fingers broad, or else edged with velvet six fingers broad, with sleeves hanging to the ground, or " cast over their shoulders like cowe tailes." Then they have equally costly gown and kirtles, " so that when they have all these goodly robes upon them, women seem to be the smallest part of themselves, not naturall women, but artificial women; not women of fleshe and blood, but rather puppits or mawmets, consisting of rags and clouts compact together."

Not having the space that Stubbes allowed himself, I [Fairholt] cannot do more than allude to the gaily-coloured silk, worsted, or cloth stockings he descants upon. The corked shoes, pantoffles, and slippers, black, white, green, and yellow, covered with gold and silver embroidery ; the scarfs, the velvet masks, the scented gloves, with " the devil's spectacles," their looking-glasses, carried with them at the girdle wherever they go.[1]

NOTE No. 18.

FORKS AND SPOONS.

Source—*Old Cookery Books and Ancient Cuisine*, by W. Carew Hazlitt.

The prejudice against the fork in England remained very steadfast actual centuries after its first introduction ; forks are particularised among the treasures of kings, as if they had been Crown jewels, in the same manner as the *iron* spits, pots, and frying pans of His

[1] Mr G. L. Gomme, F.S.A., communicated the following list of draperies, etc., sold at Norwich in 44 and 45 Elizabeth, to *Notes and Queries*. " It will be seen that it includes most of the woollen fabrics mentioned in this history and glossary :—Cloth of arras, bayes, bewpers, boulters, boratoes, buffins, bustyans, bombacyes, blanketts, callimancoes, carrells, carpettings, coverlettes, chambletts, cruell, dorincks, dornix, duraunce or damaske, frisadoes, fringe, fustyans of Naples, felts, flannells, grograines, garterings, girdelings, knitt hose, knitt petty-cots, knitt sleeves, knitt gloves, knitt cappes, knitt hatts, knitt coifes, knitt sockes, linsey woolseyes, mockadoes, minikins, mountaines, makerells, oliotts, Paris clothes, pomettes, plumettes, perpetuanas, perpicuanas, rashes, rugges, russells, russells sattins, sattins reverses, sattins of Cipres, Spanish sattins, serges, syettes, sayes, saylace, grograine lace, and lace of all sorts, stamells, stanimes, scallops, tapessary or tapestry, tukes, tamettes, tobines, thrummes, valures, woadmolles, worstedds, worstedd yarn, woollen yarn." See *Appendix to the Thirty-eighth Report of the Deputy Keeper of the Public Records*, p. 444.

Among the many varieties of dresses in Elizabeth's reign, the following, a few from her new year's gifts, may be worth noting :—" Loose gownes, trayne gownes, strayte boddyed gownes, jupes, kirtells, waste robes, night rayles, round kirtells, cloaks, shoulder cloaks, inner sleeves."

T

Majesty Edward III. ; and even so late as the seventeenth century, Coryat, who employed one after his visit to Italy, was nicknamed " Furcifer." The two-pronged implement long outlived Coryat; and it is to be seen in cutlers' signs even down to our day. The old dessert set, curiously enough, instead of consisting of knives and forks in equal proportions, contained eleven knives and one fork for *ginger*. Both the fork and spoon were frequently made with handles of glass or crystal, like those of mother-of-pearl at present in vogue.

In a tract coeval with Coryat, the fork-bearer, Breton's " Court and Country," in 1618, there is a passage very relevant to this part of the theme : " For us in the country," says he, " when we have washed our hands after no foul work, nor handling any unwhole-some thing, we need no little forks to make hay with our mouths, to throw our meat into them."

Forks, though not employed by the community, became part of the effects of royal and great personages, and in the inventory of Charles V. of France appear the spoon, knife, and fork. In another of the Duke of Burgundy, sixty years later (1420), knives and other implements occur, but no fork. The cutlery is described here as of German make. Brathwaite, in his " Rules for the Government of the House of an Earl," probably written about 1617, mentions knives and spoons, but not forks.

NOTE No. 19.

COST OF CLOTHES, 1672.

Source—*Costume in England*, by F. W. Fairholt, F.S.A.

The expense of a gentlewoman's dress at this time was consider-able, as may be seen by the following bill for a suit made for Louise de Querouaille, Duchess of Portsmouth, to appear in a masque at Whitehall in 1672 :—

" For making a dove-color'd and silk brocade coat, Rhingrave breeches and cannons, the coat lined with white lutestring, and interlined with camblett ; the breeches lined with lutestring, and lutestring drawers, seamed all over with a scarlet and silver lace ; sleeves and cannons whipt and laced with a scarlet and silver lace and a point lace ; trimmed with scarlet figured, and plain sattin ribbon, and scarlet and silver twist .

£ s. d.

2 0 0

	£	s.	d.
Canvas, buckram, silk, thread, galloon, and shamey pockets	o	11	6
For fine camblet to interline the coat	o	6	o
For silver thread for button holes	o	3	o
For 6 dozen of scarlet and silver vellam buttons .	1	1	o
For ½ dozen of breast buttons	o	o	6
For 10 yards of rich brocade at 28s. per yard . .	14	o	o
For 8 yards of lutestring to line the coat, breeches, and drawers, at 8s. per yard	3	4	o
For a pair of silk stockings	o	12	o
For an embroidered belt and garters	3	15	o
For 36 yards of scarlet figured ribbon, at 18d. per yard	2	14	o
For 36 yards of second sattin, at 5d. per yard . .	o	15	o
For 75 yards of scarlet and silver twist . . .	o	15	o
For 22 yards of scarlet and silver vellam lace, for coat and cannons, at 18s. per yard	19	16	o
For 4 yards ½ of narrow lace for button holes . .	o	12	9
For 1 piece of scarlet	1	12	o
For a black beaver hat	2	10	o
For a scarlet and silver edging to the hat . . .	1	10	o
For 36 yards of scarlet taffaty ribbon	o	18	o
Totall is	£56	15	9 "

NOTE No. 20.

BEER.

Source—*Old Cookery Books and Ancient Cuisine*, by W. Carew Hazlitt.

The English beer of bygone times underwent many vicissitudes, and it was long before our ancestors conquered their dislike to the bitter hop, after having been accustomed to a thick, sweet liquor of which the modern Kentish ale is in some measure a survival. Beer was made from a variety of grain; oats were most commonly employed. In France they resorted even to vetches, lentils, rye, and darnel. But, as a rule, it was a poor, thin drink which resulted from the operation, and the monks of Glastonbury deemed themselves fortunate in being allowed by their abbot to put a load of oats into the vat to improve the quality of the beverage; which may account for Peter of Blois characterising the ale in use at Court in his day (he died about the end of the twelfth century) as potent—it was by contrast so.   The first assize of ale seems not to have been enacted till the reign of Henry III.

NOTE No. 21.

WINES.

Source—*Old Cookery Books and Ancient Cuisine*, by W. Carew Hazlitt.

In *Colin Blobol's Testament*, a whimsical production of the fifteenth century, Tent and Valencia wines are mentioned, with wine of Languedoc and Orleans.   But perhaps it will be best to cite the passage :—

" I trow there shall be an honest fellowship, save first shall they of ale have new backbones.   With strong ale brewed in vats and in tuns ; Ping, Drangollie, and the Draget fine, Mead, Mattebru, and the Metheling.   Red wine, and claret, and the white, with Tent and Alicant, in whom I delight.   Wine of Languedoc and of Orleans thereto : Single beer, and other that is double : Spruce beer, and the beer of Hamburgh : Malmsey, Tires, and Romany."

But some of the varieties are hidden under obscure names.   We recognise Muscadel, Rhine wine, Bastard, Hippocras, however. On the 10th of December 1497, Piers Barber received six shillings and eight pence, according to the " Privy Purse Expences of Henry VII.," " for spice for ypocras."

NOTE No. 22.

SUGAR.

Source—*Old Cookery Books and Ancient Cuisine*, by W. Carew Hazlitt.

The exact date of the first introduction of sugar into England continues to be a matter of uncertainty.   It was clearly very scarce, and doubtless equally dear, when, in 1226, Henry III. asked the Mayor of Winchester to procure him three pounds of Alexandria sugar, if so much could be got, and also some rose and violet-coloured sugar ; nor had it apparently grown much more plentiful when the same prince ordered the sheriffs of London to send him four loaves of sugar to Woodstock.   But it soon made its way into the English homes, and before the end of the thirteenth century it could be procured even in remote provincial towns. It was sold either by the loaf or the pound. It was still exorbitantly high in price, varying from eighteen pence to three shillings a pound of coeval currency ; and it was retailed by the spice-dealers.

In Russell's *Book of Nurture*, composed about 1450, it occurs as an ingredient in hippocras ; and one collects from a letter sent by Sir Edward Wotton to Lord Cobham from Calais in 1546, that at that time the quantities imported were larger, and the price reduced ; for Wotton advises his correspondent of a consignment of five-and-twenty loaves at six shillings the loaf. One loaf was equal to ten pounds ; this brought the commodity down to eightpence a pound of fifteenth century money.

Note No. 23.

The Daily Round at the End of the Seventeenth Century.

Source—*London Life of Yesterday*, A. Compton-Rickett, M.D., LL.D., page 289.

We rise at nine, and those that frequent great men's levees found entertainment at them till eleven ; or, as in Holland go to tea tables. About twelve the *beau monde* assembles in several coffee or chocolate houses, " St James'," the " Smyrna " . . . Coffee Houses, and all these so near one another that in less than an hour you see the company of them all. We are carried to these places in chairs, which are here very cheap, a guinea a week or one shilling per hour, and your chairman serves you as a porter to run on errands. . . . If it is fine weather we take a turn in the park till two, when we go to dinner. . . . The general way is to make a party at the Coffee-house to go to dine at the Tavern, where we sit till six, when we go to the play, unless you are invited to the table of some great man. After the play, the best company generally go to " Tom's " and " Will's " Coffee-houses near adjoining, where there is playing at picquet and the best of conversation till midnight.

Note No. 24.

" The Compleat Gentleman," 1678.

Source—*The Compleat Gentleman*, by J. Gailhard, 1678.

When he walks, if he meets with any magistrate, or other to whom respect is due, let him put off his hat and give them the hand ; when he is in conversation let him not play with his hair, bite his nails, scratch his head, blow his nose without turning aside his head, or pick it or his ears with his fingers, or spit often.

His clothes must be suitable to his age and quality, neat and clean, yet not proud at it if they be rich. Let him keep his face, nose, teeth, and hands from being dirty and foul and those parts covered which modesty forbids to be shown. At table, he must not sit down till grace be said by him or some other ; the like is to be observed when he rises ; as to washing before or after meals let him follow the custom of the country ; keep his mouth and fingers clean ; cut his morsels whether bread or meat, nor hold it in his hand, nor lean his elbow on the table. Avoid being greedy in eating or making too much noise with his mouth, which ought to be empty when he speaks, or licking his fingers or knawing of bones.

APPENDIX III

A LIST OF BOOKS

This list does not comprise a complete range of authorities consulted in the preparation of the book or referred to in the chapters. It is merely concerned with indicating a few works that are easily accessible and which enlarge upon various aspects of the different periods of history we have touched on.

ARCHITECTURE—

Romano - British Buildings and Earthworks. John Ward, F.S.A.
Londinium (Architecture and the Crafts). Professor W. R. Lethaby. (1923.)
The Growth of the English House. J. Alfred Gotch, F.S.A., F.R.I.B.A.
The Evolution of the English House. S. O. Addy. (1910.)
Early Renaissance Architecture in England. J. Alfred Gotch, F.S.A., F.R.I.B.A.
Architecture of the Renaissance in England. J. Alfred Gotch, F.S.A., F.R.I.B.A.
The English Home from Charles I. to George IV. J. Alfred Gotch, F.S.A., F.R.I.B.A.
The English Fireplace and its Accessories. L. A. Shuffrey.
Domestic Architecture in England. Turner and Parker. (Four volumes, 1877.)

COSTUME—

History of British Costume. J. R. Planché.
Costume in England. F. W. Fairholt, F.S.A. (Two volumes, 1896.)
English Costume. George Clinch.
Costume and Fashion. (The evolution of European dress throughout the earlier ages.) Herbert Norris. (1924.)

FOOD—

Old Cookery Books and Ancient Cuisine. W. Carew Hazlitt.

FURNITURE—

The Encyclopædia of Furniture. Compiled by D. Hermann
. Schmitz (Schloss Museum, Berlin), with an Introduction
by H. P. Shapland. (1926.)
The Dictionary of English Furniture. Edited by Percy
MacQuoid and Ralph Edwards. (Vol. I., 1924 ; Vol. II.,
1926.)
Early English Furniture and Woodwork. Herbert Cescinsky
and Ernest Gribble. (Two volumes, 1922.)
Time, Taste, and Furniture. John Gloag. (1925.)

SOCIAL AND GENERAL HISTORY—

A History of England. Seven volumes. Edited by Sir
Charles Oman.
Social England. Six volumes. H. D. Traill. (1894-97.)
Constitutional History of England. Stubbs.
Sports and Pastimes. Strutt. Edited by Cox. (1903.)
The Roman Occupation of Britain. Haverfield and Mac-
donald.
Roman Britain. R. G. Collingwood, F.S.A. (1923.)
The Roman Era in Britain. John Ward, F.S.A.
Last Days of Roman Britain. Edward Foord.
Roman York. Gordon Home. (1924.)
Roman London. Gordon Home. . (1926.)
Note : An excellent though cautious Map of Roman Britain,
scale 16 miles to 1 inch, is published by the Ordnance
Survey. (1924.)
Ancient Laws and Institutes of England. Edited by B. Thorpe.
The Anglo-Saxon Chronicle. (Everyman Library.)
Bede's Ecclesiastical History. (Everyman Library.)
The Saxons in England. Kemble. (1849.)
Scandinavian Britain W. G. Collingwood, F.S.A.
Domesday Book and Beyond. F. W. Maitland. (1897.)
Feudal England. Round. (1895.)
Villeinage in England. Vinogradoff. (1892.)
The Village Community. Seebohm. (1890.)
The Mediæval Village. G. G. Coulton.
Chaucer's Canterbury Tales. (Ed. Skeat.)
Chaucer and his England. G. G. Coulton.
The Manor and Manorial Records. N. Hone.
English Wayfaring Life in the Middle Ages. Jusserand.
Parish Life in Mediæval England. Cardinal Gasquet.

SOCIAL AND GENERAL HISTORY—*continued.*

Froissart's Chronicles.   (Everyman Library.)
The Paston Letters.   Edited by James Gairdner.   (Three
  volumes, 1895.)
England in the Age of Wycliffe.   G. M. Trevelyan.   (1899.)
Society in the Elizabethan Age.   Hubert Hall.
A Survey of London.   John Stow.   (Everyman Library.)
The London Life of Yesterday.   A. Compton-Rickett.   (1909.)
Hogarth's London.   H. B. Wheatley.   (1909.)

The following would naturally be included in any course of
reading that was concerned with the late seventeenth and eighteenth
centuries :—

The Diaries of Evelyn and Pepys.   Bishop Burnet's *History of
  My Own Times.*   Horace Walpole's Letters.

Sketch Map of
NIDDERDALE
and District

Moors and Mountains

Great Whernside 2310

Masham

Greenhow Hill

Skipton

Pateley Bridge

R. Ure

Darley

Fountains Abbey

Ripon

Ilkley

Kettlesing

Birstwith

Hampsthwaite

Tang Beck

Ripley

R. Nidd

Boroughbridge

Aldborough

Otley

Harrogate

KNARESBOROUGH

K N A R E S B O R O U G H   F O R E S T

R. Aire

R. Wharfe

R. Nidd

Kirkstall Abbey

Wetherby

R. Ouse

LEEDS

Roman road from Ilkley (*Olicana*)
to Aldborough (*Isurium*) — — — —

Tadcaster

YORK

INDEX FOR THE CHAPTERS

Where the page numbers are shown in italics, thus, *77*, a reference
to a footnote is indicated.

THE END